The Lord of the Economic and Financial Apocalypse: The Dark Reality of Inflation and It's True Causes

Giuseppe Ruffini B

Published by Giuseppe Ruffini B, 2024.

While every precaution has been taken in the preparation of this book, the publisher assumes no responsibility for errors or omissions, or for damages resulting from the use of the information contained herein.

THE LORD OF THE ECONOMIC AND FINANCIAL APOCALYPSE: THE DARK REALITY OF INFLATION AND IT'S TRUE CAUSES

First edition. January 18, 2024.

Copyright © 2024 Giuseppe Ruffini B.

ISBN: 979-8224989607

Written by Giuseppe Ruffini B.

Giuseppe Ruffini B.

The lord of the economic and financial apocalypse

The dark reality of inflation and its true causes

332.41
R923s Ruffini, Giuseppe
          The lord of the economic and financial apocalypse: The dark reality of inflation and its true causes (online resource) / Giuseppe Ruffini. – 1 ed – San José, C.R.: Ruffini B., 2023
          Book (299 págs) : book : pdf; 5.7 Mb.

          ISBN: 978-9968-0-591-0

          1. Economic. 2. Inflation. 3. Economic policy 4. Employment in public services. I. Title

Acknowledgments

Special thanks to my wife, Laura, who has accompanied me in the creation of this work, and for her research work. Thank you for our daily walks of inspiration and creative discussions.

A special recognition to my great Panamanian friend Jaime Moreno, for his help and deep revision of the book, investing a lot of time in this process. Thank you, Jaime.

Thanks to Miguel Angel Quesada, for his valuable contributions in the correction of the work.

I thank my friends Luis Manuel Castro and Oscar Villa for their point of view and for the time they have dedicated to the work.

Thanks for the faithful collaboration of Andrea Soto in the layout of the work and the execution of the graphics.

Preface

Preface

In a society where information and news circulate at a speed that the human eye can barely comprehend, everything is communicated almost instantaneously. Many times, we have predictions of events even before they occur. It could be said that it is a reality where transparency predominates; citizens are spectators of a narrative that provides them with certain answers for almost everything that involves them and induces in them an evening-time acritical numbness. All the questions and the consequent answers are already given, there is no need to think critically, reflect, or develop elaborate logical theories, except for those defined as conspiracy theories, which are only outlandish ideas to deal with the boredom of the day.

Do the information we receive and the interpretation of the facts correspond to the truth or something remotely resembling it? Or are we able to see the reflection of a different reality?

The current situation is dominated by an excess of information. What we don't need is precisely more news. Much of the news we are bombarded with comes from various sources, such as television, newspapers and online platforms. It comes delivered with different types of sauces during the day and at night. Social platforms are the new megaphones through which we gather information, stay informed on various topics, and believe we have the answer to everything.

This oversupply of news and stimuli produced by the super technological society in which we live generates a lot of noise and modifies our perception of our environment. In the end, it distances us from understanding what is important, leaving us dazed by so many impulses to which we are constantly exposed. In addition to the excess of information and news, globalization puts within our reach a plethora of consumer products, which provides a sense of satiety within a life that has become alienating and empty.

In perspective, a new global virus has marked the beginning of a significant change in the way we live on Earth. Young people now prefer to stay at home, work in telework mode or play video games in a virtual and fantastical reality that is safer and disconnects them from their real lives and personal interrelationships.

Our world is gradually moving towards self-extinction where the demographic evolution of the global population (See: Chap. 3 Fig. 3) is reaching disturbingly low proportions. The major Western economies are replacing baby diapers with adult diapers for the elderly through an involution into senile societies.

How many economic news are truly incisive? How many filters are applied in order to present a different and better reality? In this complex environment we encounter great economic theories that cannot give clear and conclusive answers to the events that occur since they are the fruit of the era in which they were conceived. Similar to these ancient economic theories, there are others that are considered modern[1] that, in many cases, offer nothing new except for the adjective that defines their name, being only a mere justification of the status quo.

Government interventionism in Western economies seems to be an instrument to feed a bureaucratic machine incapable of truly dealing with the economic and social problems of that society. The real needs of citizens are far from the areas of public intervention, resulting in a continuous decline in their living standards and a victimization by a system that generates an inverse redistribution of wealth. Some few are fortunate and will become increasingly richer, while millions of others will have less every day. The middle class is the victim of this dystonic system, which evolves in an irrational and uncontrolled manner resulting in a continuous reduction of its purchasing power. This is the result of an aging of the political-administrative systems and their interference in the economic and monetary spheres, which have become incapable of meeting the present-day challenges.

This book analyzes the phenomenon of inflation and how it has been destroying the purchasing power of families over the years in a non-traditional way, trying to find the real reasons that constitute and cause the problem. The palliatives to this loss of wealth of the middle class will be analyzed, from the true nature of inflation, how it is generated, and the way in which it destroys patrimonies. The impotence and inability of institutions to control these events, being in many cases the origin of the same problems.

The inflationary phenomenon is described by economic institutions as a fairy tale. The analysis focuses primarily on measuring it, with limited understanding of its causes and solutions. However, there is a lack of understanding of the causes and potential solutions to address the impact on society, and most of the population suffers from its effects.

A new theory of inflation is needed to understand the current moment and the societal challenges we face in comprehending and addressing its significant impact on the society.

1 The lord of the apocalypse

1.1 Boss of bosses

If we were to try to group the personalities of the villains of the crime world into categories, we would finally find three typologies of characters with well-defined characteristics and a common denominator. This common denominator is that all of them are nefarious beings, some with attributes that render them truly harmful and some with particularly malevolent tendencies.

The first group are the enforcers, the soldiers of the criminal organizations, people without feelings who carry out orders regardless of the inhumanity involved.

The second group are mid-level bosses similar to the managers of large companies, characters in search of notoriety to advance their careers within the organization. Like the enforcers, they are not guided by principles of humanity. However, the key difference is that these are smarter and much more manipulative.

In the third group we are in front of the truly dangerous characters of the story. They are radically different from the other two groups, being the puppeteers of criminal organizations. Their appearance is different from the others, these are fine-looking individuals, and their manners are also refined. They have sophisticated intellects, may appreciate art, know how to navigate high society environments, may even collaborate in charitable causes, and sometimes communicate with bureaucrats and politicians of the state. But let us not be fooled, they are much worse than the others. These puppeteers are the ones who give orders, issue sentences, and build and structure criminal activity. Sadly, I have more bad news for you. The story is not likely to have an idyllic, Disney-like ending. It will more likely end dramatically, perhaps closer to true fairy tales than to their positively revisited fables.

There has always been an underlying question in the justice and police spheres: whether there is someone higher - someone not named, seen, or known. This ultimate boss, the maximum puppeteer, is the one who activates and outlines the strategy of the bosses and their organizations. Sometimes this character could be just a myth, a shadow of reality. And I have more bad news for you here: this character indeed exists in history. I am referring to the Lord of the apocalypse, the great chief of the four Horsemen that will lead us to chaos and destruction. I would like to clarify that this writing has nothing to do with the sacred scriptures, even though I just mentioned the concepts of the apocalypse and its horsemen, because strangely, they explain very well the current picture in which we live. Perhaps it is just a coincidence or a literary license on my part. I hope you will excuse me. When we talk about the lord of the apocalypse, we are referring to inflation, the havoc it wreaks in workers' lives and its capacity for destruction. Inflation cannot be seen or felt, it is asymptomatic, but it is among us and by the time we begin to notice it, it has already inexorably and violently destroyed the fruits of our labor.

1.2 From the symbolism of the 4 horsemen to the realism of their images

Strangely and unfortunately, the examples of the Apocalypses in recent years, beyond religious symbolism, have concrete and realistic representations in the daily lives of most citizens of the planet. The world and its human inhabitants, since their historical and conscious presence on the planet, have always had to struggle with the four apocalyptic calamities. If we want to analyze the past, these phenomena have accompanied the development, evolution and, at times, involution over thousands of years of human history.

1.2.1 The plague as the pandemic

The plague, as the pandemic of 2020 has been in this bleak picture an unusual event. In the past, human beings have survived countless epidemics, ranging from the Black Death to Ebola and other influenza-like viruses. However, the reaction to these contagious diseases had never materialized as a global event, so widespread in the aggressiveness of the response by the health authorities of the wealthiest states. This disastrous and calamitous event in terms of human lives and economic destruction, has been or could be compared to the horseman of the apocalypse in terms of deaths and government response actions. For the first time humanity had to aggressively confront catastrophic events related to a contagious disease. Many countries across the globe have implemented these responses with the closure of cities and confining people to their homes for several months. Only the poorest countries were unable to react in this manner, and the effectiveness and necessity of these measures still remain unknown.

1.2.2 The war

The war, like the plague, has also been an element, a conductive thread of humanity throughout its history. Once a war ends, the circumstances are fostered for the beginning of a new one and thus, history repeats itself endlessly. However, the war that is developing in Eastern Europe between Russia and Ukraine is a little more worrying than the war conflicts of the last decades, for a simple reason that is easy to understand. First, we have on one side a nuclear power fighting with a former country in its sphere of influence. On the other side we have other nuclear powers supporting the second country at war. As you may understand, this situation poses a significant threat to mankind. I consider this second horseman to be a real element and its impact on global affairs current and unprecedented.

1.2.3 Hunger and death

Although they have accompanied mankind throughout history, these other horsemen of the apocalypse have not yet had such a clear and perceptible manifestation as the first two. However, considering the possibility of a full-scale war accompanied by some other type of pandemic, these last two horsemen would finally come to visit us in a much more violent way than we have seen from them so far. But let's recall one important detail: Russia and Ukraine are the world's largest producers of grains, so please make your own considerations.

What makes the global outlook and the future perspective worrisome, in this somewhat catastrophic logic, is the arrival of the lord of the apocalypse, inflation. This endemic evil, when out of control, can become the fuel for highly unbalancing events that have a much greater impact on society than could be expected under conditions of apparent normal stability.

1.3 Limits of the theories

This monetary phenomenon and its economic implications have grounded many economists, making it a subject of extreme interest for this category of scholars. Throughout the centuries, as I mentioned, there has been an abundance of writings on inflation, one of the most intriguing topics of modern society.

We find a large number of pages, theories and mathematical formulas that support a wide variety of considerations, and suddenly something new emerges that invalidates much of the basic doctrine, presenting new scenarios and new paradigms that need to be understood.

What are the limits that prevent us from developing a sufficiently comprehensive theory to describe this phenomenon?

The limits lie in the complexity of the environments under analysis, their interrelationships, and contaminations. In an aseptic laboratory, it is easy to isolate the elements in order to test and document a series of events. Things change as soon as we apply the models under analysis to the complex reality of the environment they are meant to explain. Here the variables at play increase hyperbolically, as do their interrelationships. Finally, there is a background inertia in transmitting impulses that do not exist in a laboratory, therefore, the results vary, which generates the need for more explanations and theories to describe the initial phenomena.

If we were to regroup the theories on inflation, we could find some analytical foundations in the different background explanations they give us. This indicates that the different paths to explaining the phenomenon demonstrate a common feeble ground of viability and consistency within the most common theories.

The limits we face when studying and explaining inflation with any theory on which to base our analysis lie in the specifics. "The devil is in the details" and they confuse us. The inflationary phenomenon is analyzed with models that are too closed, making it impossible to explain and understand beyond the obviousness that it represents. This leads us from the observation of small details to the loss of vision on the totality of the problem and of our ability to explain and understand it. Based on that crucial consideration, to explain inflation coherently, we must abstract from the smallest details and achieve a real global vision of analysis.

1.4 Keynesians[2] versus monetarists[3]

Two apparently antagonistic economic philosophical theories, both in their basis and historical development, have guided the reflections and possible explanations of inflation in the last century. On one side we find the Keynesians, and on the other, with a relatively "opposite" vision, we find the monetarists. Milton Friedman[4] was the father of the school of economic thought that developed the monetary theory. This theory states that governments, through central banks, are the entities that control the amount of money in circulation and the money supply in a given economy; therefore, its expansion or reduction translates into an increase or decrease in aggregate demand. However, according to this theory, the effects on Gross Domestic Product or employment are short-term and are not permanent. The monetary theory of inflation relates this phenomenon to the amount of money in circulation. An increase or decrease in money in an ideal laboratory context where all other economic variables remain unchanged would cause increases or decreases in inflation. This school of thought, often associated with neoliberalism, also relates to the monetary theory of inflation.

According to neoliberalist thinking, in short, state interventions in the economy through a more aggressive monetary policy lead to an increase in inflation. Simplifying the concept to a maximum, we could affirm that the market would be better off left alone with minimal government intervention; therefore, the forces of demand and supply, which in extreme synthesis constitute the market, would be able to more effectively adjust and balance the different economic variables such as production, employment levels and inflation.

The Keynesian theory conceived by John Maynard Keynes[5], on the contrary, considers the state's activity in the market to be a fundamental instrument to increase the production of a country, reduce its unemployment and finally control inflation. As you can see, we are in front of two profoundly different schools of thought. Now, the objective of this work is not to analyze which of the two basic philosophies is the most correct or the most current; what we ultimately need to understand is how these theories are incorporated into government actions or, in other words, how the political system incorporates them into its economy-controlling activities. Upon analyzing these two theories in depth, we, however, discover that, although they are considered philosophically antagonistic, they in fact have many similarities, and therefore they have common elements and grounds.

1.5 Chaos theory

All plain and simple, right?

Well, not so much. The great limit we face when applying theory to practice is to discover that reality is somewhat more complex than theory. Theoretical models therefore work very well on paper and laboratory experiments are successful in the aseptic environments they delimit. In an environment as complex as today's globalized world, the number of variables and their interrelationships are almost infinite (if you will allow me the poetic license) and practically uncontrollable. This reflection is not intended to highlight inconsistencies or possible errors in the theories, but simply their limits when applied in the real world. These limits, when we put theory into practice, to calculate the phenomenon of inflation and to implement strategies for its correction are particularly dangerous because they can divert countries and ultimately investors toward realities far removed from the truth. We can therefore affirm that, although economics is based on mathematical formulas, it is not an exact science because it is not capable of giving exact numerical explanations. In my opinion, here lies the great limitation of the economic sciences.

We could, however, ask for help from chaos theory, which, in terms of theoretical analysis, could be perfectly applicable in its essence to economic theory. After all, if a butterfly fluttering in Brazil could cause a tornado in the United States, imagine what a delay in a government debt payment could produce in the same country. The consequences could be intriguing and it would certainly be challenging to apply this effect within an economic model. However, we must reflect on the word chaos and its most common misinterpretation. If we think of chaos as the infinite complexity of the universe, we can never confuse it with disorder (yes, you heard me right, disorder.) The chaos theory is finally not applicable to the calculation of inflation and its mathematical models, because the environment in which inflation is born, measured and conceptualized is a very disorderly one with diverse types of contamination. On the contrary, the chaos of the universe can be a representation of the purest perfection, the divine vision of infinite complexity could be affirmed.

1.6 Pollution factor

One of the most difficult elements to decipher is undoubtedly the pollution factor. To describe it correctly, consider the multitude of economists who want to explain this phenomenon. But if we look at this environment correctly, we can categorize these professionals into two different groups: those who work with the government of their countries directly as its employees or indirectly as employees of "autonomous" institutions, and those who do not work for the government and are totally independent.

One could observe that individuals working for government institutions may have different considerations compared to those who do not work for the government.

In the end, inflation does not look good, and this simple consideration makes the problem clear: High inflation is not in the interest of governments. High inflation can affect gross domestic product readings, and the well-being of its citizens.

Another element to analyze is the point of view of foreign investors and the attraction of foreign capital for investment and job creation. High inflation coupled with a low gross domestic product, known as stagflation, makes a country a less attractive investment location.

Recognizing a high level of inflation can be a negative factor for the governing party and its re-election. Let's not forget that inflation ultimately destroys wealth and impoverishes particularly the middle class and segments of the population with lower incomes, which happen to represent in many cases the majority of the voting population.

We should therefore first ask ourselves whether the numbers provided by the statistical institutes represent the phenomenon and describe it correctly, or are rather not so representative. What are the factors that influence the results of inflation analyses?

Finally, contaminating factors depend on erroneous interpretations of the phenomenon by those who should be analyzing it more correctly and accurately. These erroneous interpretations give us wrong or highly erroneous data. It is quite evident to understand how in an environment with so many interests involved and with so many usable variables, the final results can be contaminated and, therefore, there is no chaos theory that can adequately explain that complexity, which cannot be included as a quantifiable variable in any functional mathematical model.

1.7 Different polluting elements, "to pivot or not to pivot – this is the dilemma"

To fully understand the contaminating factors, an important consideration arises to which we must provide an answer. I refer to the question: Could the numbers representing inflation be adjusted by requirements other than the mere academic exercise? Or could they simply be improved to make them look different? I will give you some additional examples in this regard. We have seen that inflation does not look good, but let's imagine an inflation that is several percentage points higher than the nominal one. What would be its effect on the state's balance sheet? How much would it cost in terms of interest that the state must pay in full? This is not to mention inflation-indexed bonds, which are also affected by high inflation rates.

"To pivot[6] or not to pivot—this is the dilemma[7]. When will the dilemma of pivoting in restrictive monetary policy arise? *Let Hamlet rest in peace*, after all, life has been much harder for him than for us. To aid in understanding the reflections that follow, this famous Shakespearian phrase may prove helpful. Many decades of very soft monetary policies have resulted in an abrupt increase in the monetary base and the consequent increase in nominal inflation. To contrast the new reality of high nominal inflation, monetary authorities around the globe have been forced to take monetary restrictions through the injection of securities into the banking system, known as "Quantitative Tightenings[8], and through a hike in interest rates. These policies have a direct effect on financial market indices. For a state, therefore, dealing with high inflation implies taking robust actions to control the phenomenon. These actions are transmitted to the results of stock prices. Therefore, in this view, the consequences of these actions can be devastating for investors. This generates a lot of pressure on the monetary authorities to keep interest rates low through the high finance lobbies. It is enough to recall all the discussions in 2022 and 2023 surrounding the Pivoting concept. Pivoting is nothing more than the beginning of the change in the Federal Reserve's monetary policy. Financial investors and analysts were focusing their discussions on the potential occurrence of the pivot moment in 2022 and 2023, speculating on the potential onset or less of this pivot moment. It is funny to think about how dangerous and damaging inflation is, so much so that it should be the main concern of the financial sector. Analysts as well as politicians have shown a preference for holiday periods and times of easy money with low interest rates near zero over controlling inflation.

This example will make it easier to understand that there are many different types of contributing factors that affect how inflation is calculated and conceptualized.

The primary influential factors are whether the weights assigned to goods and services for calculating inflation represent the spending pattern of a country, or instead, do not correspond exactly to reality.

A second typology of factors is the conceptualization of inflation and how it is measured over time.

A third typology for complex and multi-country realities such as the European Union or the United States is the difficulty of aggregating data that is sometimes very different from each other.

It is also important to consider the pressures that different interest groups exerted on the government and monetary authorities, to prevent both a dramatic increase in the inflation rate and the draconian measures necessary to control it.

If we carefully reflect on all the contributing factors and the forces in the field, we should be able to come to an eye-opening conclusion: The inflation values we have been reported are perhaps not an accurate representation of reality and are possibly partly functional in offering a different image of reality.

2 Inflation

2.1 Inflation

To visualize inflation correctly, we should think of it as an asymptomatic, chronically degenerative disease that robs us of our lifetime.

Beyond any other philosophical considerations about money and the different symbolisms it can assume in our lives, there is a much simpler and intuitive concept to understand. To earn money, you need to invest one of the scarcest assets a human being possesses, that is time. You invest your time, and finally, the sum of these temporary spaces in which you work represent moments of your life. Inflation stealthily and sometimes inconspicuously steals your time, or, in other words, steals a little bit of your life.

When asked for the definition of inflation, we could find many, but in my opinion, the most accurate one is the following:

The average cost difference between my current purchases and purchases of identical items made in the past.

If we extend this same definition to an economy, it would be: **The average cost difference that households pay today for exactly the same items (goods and services) that they acquired in the past.**

If we analyze the definition, we observe three components:

1. Cost, which represents the loss of value of money through time.
2. Time, the time span over which it is measured.
3. The goods, products and services under analysis that make up a ''basket of goods'', as a representation of the expenditure of the typical family and, at an aggregate level, the basket of goods that represent this phenomenon at the level of a country or a nation. The concept refers not to a single product or good but to the average value of a set of products, goods and services.

The concept of inflation must be well understood, since it is always composed of these three elements and varying them would constitute manipulating the information.

Although its visualization is not so difficult to conceptualize, calculating it becomes more challenging due to the inclusion of fundamental variables that must be taken into consideration.

The quantities of goods and services traded in a country undoubtedly represent the main challenge when synthesizing their price evolution. At the same time, inflation is affected by geographical characteristics. Therefore, this aspect is a further complication, representing possible different behavior and price evolutions for different geographical areas. In the United States, inflation in one state does not necessarily coincide with inflation in another. At the same time, if we consider the US dollar, there are also other countries that adopt it as their national currency (e.g., Ecuador, Panama and El Salvador in Latin America). Inflation within these countries, even if they adopt the same currency, will most likely not coincide with inflation in the United States.

The calculation of inflation is based, therefore, on the data produced by the statistical institutes of the different countries or states, and after this first analysis, in order to arrive at a single data to synthesize it, it will be necessary to find a fair compromise of weights.

In the particular case of the Eurozone, we as a result have different inflation rates, depending on whether we are referring to individual countries or to the overall inflation rate of the entire area.

Therefore, we can speak of inflation as representing the loss of value of money over time. When a basket of goods becomes more expensive over time, my purchasing power decreases, resulting in a reduced ability to acquire the same number of products and services with the initial amount of money.

The essential elements that characterize inflation are the cost levels of products and services, the time, and the goods under analysis. Cost levels of goods and services within a time frame are, therefore, the key variables that describe this monetary economic phenomenon. Any manipulation of these elements can significantly alter the outcome of the calculation.

2.2 Other monetary and economic phenomena related to inflation

Economic recessions: Economic recessions are normal times when an economy stops growing and for various reasons begins to decline, registering a decrease in both the Gross Domestic Product (GDP) and in its employment level. This phenomenon can be described as normal within the economic cycle of an economy. In simplified terms, nothing goes up infinitely and corrections are in fact normal and healthy for any economy.

Stagflation: On the contrary, in stagflation, there is an increase in the costs of goods and services, but not in the quantity of goods and services traded. In this scenario everything becomes more expensive, but the economy in real terms does not grow, but rather decreases.

This phenomenon is simply an economic recession with inflation.

If we classify them according to their degree of threat, stagflation is much more sinister than inflation, because stagflation gives an apparent idea of economic growth, which is not the case.

In other words, there will be an increase in the cost of living without an increase in the production and consumption of goods and services in real terms. As a result, over the long term, there is a significant devaluation of the purchasing power of families, leading to increased poverty.

Deflation: Deflation is the opposite phenomenon to inflation; in this case, there is a decrease in prices. It is not as normal and common an economic event as inflation, and when it has occurred it has typically been limited to short periods of time, unlike inflation, which is a continuous and constant endemic evil for all economies.

Economic depression: Economic depression is related to recessions, but it is a completely different phenomenon. In an economic depression, we have a decline in the major indicators of an economy, including gross domestic product and employment over an extended period of time.

The difference between a recession and a depression is that in a recession, the economy declines for a few months (two quarters) to a maximum of two or three years, while in a depression the economy declines for more than three years.

Now we understand that an economic depression is much more serious than a recession.

The characteristics of a depression are similar to those of a recession but with a manifestation of phenomena that are more prolonged in time and of greater incidence. High levels of unemployment and a decrease in available credit represent these phenomena, causing a prolonged drop in productivity and the country's declining Gross Domestic Product.

The economic results of a depression include bankruptcy of companies, default on government debt, and a prolonged bear market[9] for stock indexes. Moreover, there is a high likelihood of economic deflation exacerbating the situation.

If we compare recession and depression, recession is a normal state of the economic cycle, while depression is something extraordinary that occurs very rarely; when it does occur, it is a very serious moment in the economy signaling that it will be affected for many years to come. A typical case is the great depression of the 30's, where it took almost 30 years for stock indexes to return to the values prior to the economic collapse.

2.3 Inflation and its relative normality levels

When we talk about inflation, it does not necessarily have a negative connotation. We could ask ourselves: at what moderate levels could it represent the state of a healthy economy? What would constitute moderate levels of inflation to define it as a normal state of the economy?

Inflation levels that can be registered in an economy[10] :

- Moderate, up to a maximum of 5%.

- High, occurs between 5% and 10%.

- Very high or galloping, ranging from double digits to 100%.

- Hyperinflation, when inflation is higher than 100% (Argentina, Venezuela, etc.).

We can understand, therefore, that inflation within a range between 0 and 5% can be considered moderate; however, the monetary authorities of the main industrialized countries ideally consider that it should be around 2%.

The reasons that have allowed for the relative control of inflation levels over so many decades are basically of three types.

Globalization is a strongly deflationary element, reducing the price of many products because goods produced in markets where labor and energy costs are lower are traded. Therefore, the ease of international trade and the integration of markets have been the main elements determining this "**apparent**" control of inflation for many decades.

Productivity is another element that allows an economy to control its price evolution. To thoroughly understand how productivity works we must think of a very simple concept which is: do more with less. It means, therefore, to produce more with lower cost—producing the same goods at a lower cost is a deflationary factor.

However, should we ask ourselves if we can be satisfied with these two basic explanations? Not so, unfortunately. To understand the enormous damage that inflation has caused we have to contextualize it within a few more parameters that describe its real evolution over the years.

The fundamental element is to understand the formula and how inflation is calculated and the consequential implications on the results obtained through these calculations. Another fundamental element we must ask is: What does the increase in value of financial assets represent in relation to the exorbitant flood of money in the economy? The increases in the value of these assets are not incorporated into the inflation calculation.

2.4 Beyond the definition

There is an abundance of literature on this phenomenon. There are, however, few relatively clear answers to the possible repercussions that this endemic evil is causing to society. If we want to study inflation, we have the possibility of studying clear definitions of the phenomenon. But I have the impression that things become more complex the more we want to delve further into the underlying reasons and causes that generate them, to finally reach concrete and real solutions that allow us to cure it.

We easily come across answers that seem to be the result of paraphrasing the same definitions; in other words, when reading and studying the phenomenon many times the answers are nothing more than the same definition worded in different terms. Therefore, one of the great dilemmas surrounding inflation is caused by the interests that revolve around it. We should reflect on the interests of the different powers and economic groups surrounding inflation, hence the difficulty in finding clear answers to an apparently incurable evil. Solving hazards like potential floods in a village becomes easier when the population agrees to work together to save their homes and belongings. With inflation, the reality is different and much more convoluted.

Inflation is undoubtedly a destructive and devastating phenomenon for the middle-class and lower-income groups, but it is not necessarily the same for those who have more or for those who have power; in some cases, the readjustments caused by inflation can even be beneficial for some. In the case of public debt, if the State's revenues increase as a result of inflation, or of the change in the tax brackets of taxpayers and companies, this means more money coming in and, therefore, a greater control of the debt itself. In all these situations we are facing an important dichotomy: on the one hand we have the interests of the people who are significantly and negatively impacted by inflation; on the other hand, politics and the government, which can benefit from a certain degree of inflation. Here things get complicated in facts, but not in manners, no government will recognize that it will wait for inflation for a rebalancing of public finances, rather the discourse will be absolutely in line with popular common sense. Whether things will be done correctly is another story. At the end of the day, politicians in all latitudes of the world have accustomed us in the best of hypotheses to see them fail to fulfill exactly what they promised or in the worst of cases to do exactly the opposite. The problem becomes more complicated when we add the interests of corporations and large groups to the chess game of the State, where even in some cases a little inflation may not be so harmful.

2.5 Is the inflation calculated by the statistical institutes a correct representation of the phenomenon?

To answer this question, one must carry out a complex analysis of different factors that come into play when calculating inflation. Factors that go beyond the simple number which can represent or synthesize inflation in a temporal arc, factors that contribute to build inflation as we know it.

Numbers, in their essence, represent an abstract concept of purity. However, when we consider numbers and their usefulness to explain complex phenomena with qualitative interrelationships, purity becomes lost.

Purity is lost when numbers are used to reach predefined conclusions or to construct a priori conclusions that are not the simple representation of a phenomenon, but a representation of a reality constructed with the intention of giving a better picture of the situation. Numbers, depending on how they are used, can therefore yield different data. It may, however, be a bit difficult to understand the point I am referring to. It is the construction of data according to a predefined narrative, rather than the use of numbers as an instrument of pure observation and analysis. Then the numbers can be or become functional, to modify the reality they are meant to describe and create a perceived and instrumental reality aligned with the objectives of the person manipulating the numbers.

Are the data provided by the statistical institutes regarding inflation correct or are they instrumental to explain and mitigate the aspect of this phenomenon?

We will try, throughout the first chapters, to give an answer to this question; obviously, we will not provide a conclusive answer, they are simply ideas around complex concepts that, nevertheless, can have a devastating and destructive power within your life.

3 Where inflation comes from

3.1 Causes that determine the inflation phenomenon

If we were to ask ourselves what are the causes that trigger inflation, the traditional answer would lead us to factors related to demand and consumption, or to an increase in company costs, wage increases, expectations about inflation itself, and many other logical elements that could describe the problem analytically. The limitation of this methodology of analysis is that it can describe the phenomenon without giving us a true diagnosis of the triggering reasons. We will try to arrive at the construction of the problem starting from a traditional perspective until we discover the real reasons behind it, moving from the obvious to the less obvious.

Demand or consumption: According to the traditional limited view, the first cause of inflation is an increase in the demand for goods or services. Since goods and services are scarce, obviously, as demand increases, those who offer goods and services increase their prices.

Cost: Continuing with this simplified perspective, another factor that generates inflation is the increase in the production costs of goods and services. When companies transfer these price increases to the products or services they provide, the increase in costs ends up causing inflation.

Wages and expectations: Finally, wage increases due to inflation expectations or for other reasons such as contract renewals or personnel shortages force companies to pay more. Consequently, a sustained rise in wages within an economy becomes an inflationary factor. The same inflation expectations can lead companies to increase their prices and raise their workers' wages, both of which are inflationary.

3.2 The new inflationary spiral and an ailing system

In order to analyze current inflation, the phenomenon must be divided into two perspectives: the first one explains how inflation has manifested in the last post-pandemic years, and the other one analyzes the phenomenon more critically and objectively describes why we are experiencing a context of tendentially inflationary society and its underlying reasons.

The more we analyze the events of the 2020 pandemic, the more we realize that the combination of these events has generated the perfect storm. In response to COVID-19, most governments quarantined their countries.

The result of this global measure to deprive people of mobility was that we were forced to stay at home. Non-essential companies were closed, and many jobs were replaced by remote work or teleworking. These actions had a radical impact on the global way of living.

Once the majority of the planet's inhabitants had been vaccinated -in some cases, forcibly - and after many sales by pharmaceutical companies, the world finally reopened. Now, let's visualize the moment when a return to normality finally came. At that point society was not prepared logistically to return to the pre-pandemic routine.

These events caused an indescribable impact on the global supply chain, which added to the increase in energy costs. After thousands of years of human existence on the planet, we discovered that humanity needs energy, gas, oil, coal, etc. to function. We also discovered that the new energy sources did not produce enough energy for the consumption required by the world economy, and that the increases in energy production resulting from renewable sources have so far not reduced the consumption of fossil fuels. Global society proved to be more energy-guzzling than previously thought. Perhaps by considering regions, such as India and Africa, that are in the process of transformation through the rapid economic development phase, this would be quite easy to explain. In the end, this discovery was so interesting that coal was dusted off again in countries known for their strong environmental consciousness, such as Germany.

3.3 From an oversupply to a scarcity of energy sources

But let's take a step back to the pandemic period. On April 20, 2020, oil futures traded in negative values. Let's try to understand why this happened. First, let's examine how futures contracts work: a price for a specific good is agreed between two parties in the future, where one of the parties agrees to pay a certain price to the other, which in turn agrees to deliver the product at this contract price at a predetermined date. Normally, before maturity, many operators of this market close their contracts before expiration by means of monetary settlement between the price of the futures contract and the current value. This activity is known as "cash settled"[11]; otherwise, the contract would be executed through the exchange of money for the commodity that is the object of said contract.

In case there are price differences between the value at which the future was purchased and the value at the time of maturity, this is settled with a cash payment. If the futures contracts are not closed in cash, there is what is called physical delivery[12]. As these exotic words say, it means that the raw material that is the object of the contract of the future is delivered in exchange for the agreed amount. It can be compared to pre-purchasing a pack of cigarettes at a set price, in agreement with the store owner, for the weekend.

In April 2020, the price of a barrel of oil became worth minus forty (-$40) dollars, a totally unprecedented event. This happened because all the oil reserves were full, as well as their deposits. There were tankers loaded with oil that had to be unloaded, but there was no place to store the barrels. One day the price went negative, which was unbelievable, considering from a theoretical perspective that you were paid to receive the raw material. Imagine now the little house of a futures trader[13] in New Jersey, and his yard full of a few thousand barrels of oil. It's an interesting urban lease, isn't it? Beyond a new form of urban decor, this would have been impractical for all parties.

The above example clearly explains the contraction in demand during that disastrous period for mankind. Like with oil trade, although without reaching negative values, something similar happened to all raw materials and many products used in the world's industrial manufacturing. Businesses were closed, the travel and tourism industry collapsed, offices had been shut down, while people were locked in their homes.

What the pandemic ultimately caused were the unique conditions for what we could define as a perfect inflationary storm once the world would reopen. So far everything is apparently clear and therefore many mistakenly claim that we have understood the phenomenon in a correct and articulate way.

3.4 Impact on the global supply chain

The sharp increase in demand due to the reopenings, as many economists have pointed out, could have been the trigger and origin of the current inflation. Most economists consider this process the natural outcome to explain the post-pandemic inflationary spiral. To me it would be like telling a patient with a high fever that they are hot and may even be sick. The basic and simple processes that cause this limited view of the post-pandemic inflationary spiral can be reviewed as follows:

1. The world reopens, and people can now go out and spend more.
2. The increase in demand from families and individuals generates pressure on the market.
3. This pressure causes inventories of goods and services to decrease, generating more buying pressure.
4. Prices, on the other hand, are increasing due to supply shortages and demand pressure.
5. Increases in prices are the plain cause of inflation.

3.5 What they don't tell us well

What many government-related economists fail to describe correctly is the flood of monetary base that occurred in the pandemic period, which, added to the events that impacted the supply chain, arrives at a more articulate explanation of the inflation that has hit us in recent years. (Fig. 1.2) During the pandemic period, the governments of developed countries began providing monetary stimulus to the economy. These stimuli created new money out of thin air. The process was the result of an unlimited expansion of the monetary base. Up to this point, we find some logical explanations of the phenomenon, but it is necessary to dive deeper into other elements that describe the problem in more depth to be able to analyze the problem more completely and exhaustively.

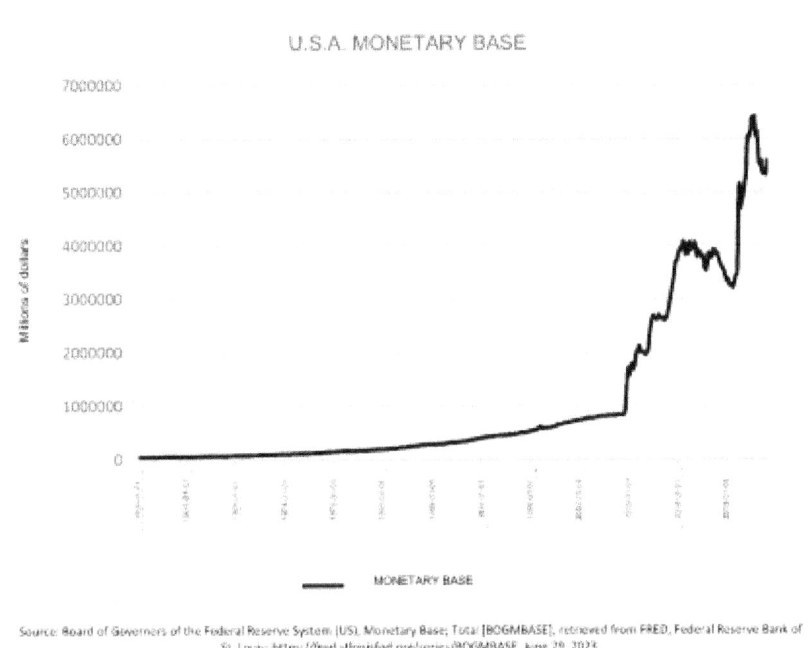

Source: Board of Governors of the Federal Reserve System (US), Monetary Base; Total [BOGMBASE], retrieved from FRED, Federal Reserve Bank of St. Louis; https://fred.stlouisfed.org/series/BOGMBASE, June 29, 2023.

Fig. 1: This Graph shows the evolution of the monetary base in the United States. We can observe how it has increased steadily over time. What is striking, however, is the exponential acceleration since the financial crisis at the end of the first decade of the 2000s (2007-2010), which stands out significantly from the evolution of previous decades in a completely different and unprecedented pace.

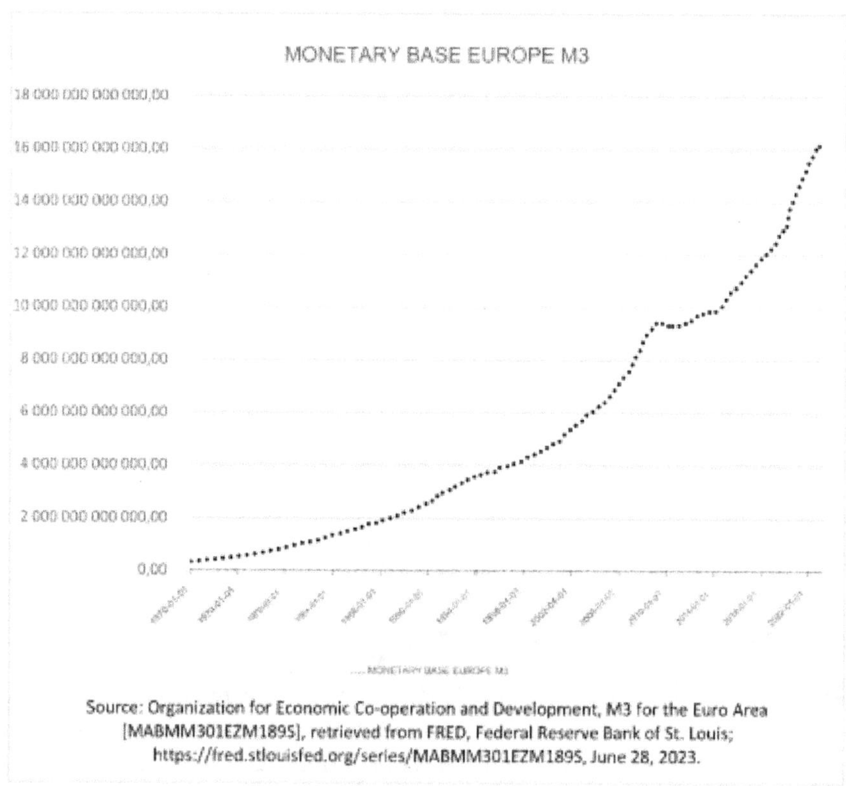

Source: Organization for Economic Co-operation and Development, M3 for the Euro Area [MABMM301EZM189S], retrieved from FRED, Federal Reserve Bank of St. Louis; https://fred.stlouisfed.org/series/MABMM301EZM189S, June 28, 2023.

Fig. 2: Graph of the evolution of the European monetary base aggregate M3. We can see how, like the monetary base in the United States, it grows at a rapid pace, especially from the 2000s onwards. The injection of money into the economic system has a similar behavior throughout the major economies of the planet.

3.6 Demographic factor

The demographic structure of a country or geographic region, such as Europe or the United States, determines the type of goods and products marketed within its territories. A country with many children will need many nurseries, while a country with many elderly people will need many nursing homes. The purchasing or investment desires of a 27-year-old professional or her 75-year-old grandmother are not the same.

The aging of the population alters the labor force of the labor market, as well as the state's balance sheets.

The aging population of a country leads to a reduction in tax collection:

- A reduction in the labor force.

- A reduction in industrial production.

These are just some of the factors in the relationship between economics and demographics.

To maintain a stable population structure, demographers agree that a fertility rate[14] of at least 2.1 kids per women is needed. If we analyze the fertility rates of Western or developed countries, we find as a common characteristic that their fertility rates are significantly below the 2.1 kids per women limit. Industrialized countries have been aging dangerously and at a steady pace for many decades (Fig. 3). We can observe that as a society becomes richer, young people tend to prioritize other aspects of life and exhibit curious behaviors such as replacing the experience of parenthood with the care of pets. It is important to note that this is not a criticism of pets, as I personally appreciate them greatly, but I find it curious how the value of sexuality has been lost over time among couples as well as at a biological level[15] considering how testosterone levels in human males are declining.

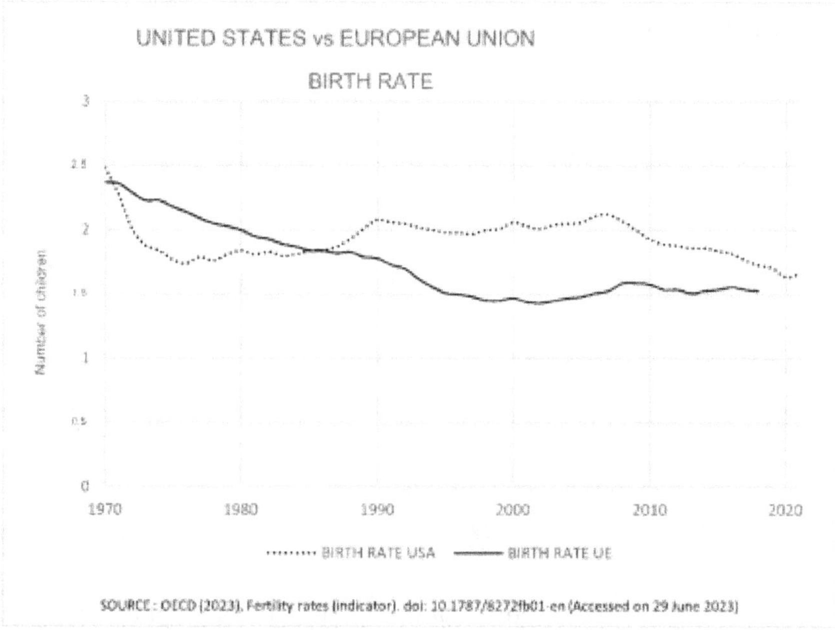

Fig. 3: Graph of birth rates in the European Union and the United States, from 1970 to the present. As seen in the initial observations of the data, the birth rates in both continents are declining. A fertility rate below 2.1 kids per women affects the country's population structure; in the first period it causes the aging of the population, which in the medium term translates into a decrease in the population.

Another highly worrisome element related to demographics is the development of virtual reality. Human beings, by nature, do not cope well with frustrations; the simple fact of interacting with others can be a source of frustration, rejection, and misunderstanding. The development of the metaverse and virtual reality has made life easier for many, who no longer need direct physical interaction with others. It is safer to create an ideal life for yourself from the comfort of your own home, rather than going out, meeting new people, and eventually finding the ideal partner and having your own offspring. For many young people, the traditional path of finding a partner and starting a family is no longer part of their plans. Instead, virtual reality, which is becoming more advanced every day, offers them opportunities for safe recreation. This trend can have an even stronger negative influence on the demographic development of countries. It is safer to meet your own virtual partner than to meet them in a ballroom or at the entrance of a movie theater. If you ask me, I consider this new way of life extremely cold, but it is part of today's reality, and we cannot ignore it. We must then, without a doubt, ask ourselves this serious question: Are we predestined to extinction?

Honestly, I hope not!

An aging population entails major structural changes in the economy. The western developed world is affected by a serious demographic change throughout its countries. As a result, these changes have a significant unwanted impact on their economies. Europe, the United States, but also the most industrialized countries in Asia such as China, Japan (Fig. 4) and Korea are aging. Therefore, this phenomenon has a direct correlation with the economic development of these countries.

The age pyramid gives us a graphic illustration of the population structure of a nation. If we analyze it over the years in these countries, we can see how the population has aged, and we can predict the evolution of consumption and Gross Domestic Product. If we compare the age pyramids of developed countries over the last 50 years, we can see how the population has been aging; in other words, the young are decreasing and the old are increasing. This goes hand in hand with the population growth rate which, on the contrary, has been steadily decreasing over the last decade. Another interesting element to consider is comparing the age pyramid of the main industrialized countries with some of the developing economies of Africa, Asia, or Latin America. From this analysis, it is clear how, on the one hand, we have an increasingly aging population, while, on the other hand, the different age segments are dominated by the young. However, looking at the world birth rate, we see a somewhat frightening picture of its decline over time, which also indicates a global trend towards an aging population.

The steps leading to these demographic changes always reflect the same pattern: the abandonment of rural areas, an improvement in income and a sharp reduction in the birth rate.

3.7 Reflections on the demographic evolution in the world

ASIA

When discussing Asia, the analysis becomes complex due to the varying stages of development across the different countries. For instance, Japan shares similarities with Europe and other Western economies, while China, India, and other Asian countries are still in the early stages of their potential development.

China's birth control policy is changing its age pyramid to resemble that of Western economies, a development that deserves an important reflection. In fact, in response to this factor, once the administration of this great country realized the problem, it changed this rule[16]. India, which, on the contrary, has not implemented birth control policies, is seen to have a more robust population growth rate than China (Fig. 5).

When comparing the demographic pyramids of China and India, we see that India's (Fig. 6) demographic structure is projected to evolve in a longer and more sustainable manner over time.

China, however, still has a very large working population; therefore, for a long period of time, it will remain the engine of the world. India might be expected to eventually replace China. As we have seen, the age pyramid in India still denotes a prospect of strong population growth. Additionally, there are also other areas in Asia where there is still significant population growth, such as Vietnam and Cambodia.

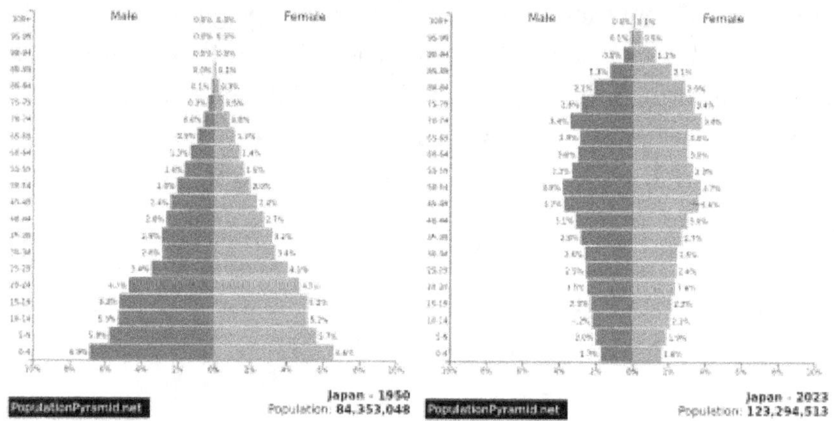

https://www.populationpyramid.net/: Sources[17]

Fig. 4: Comparative population pyramid between 1950 and 2023 for Japan. The case of Japan is particularly emblematic, as it is the first of the Asian powers to enter a process of strong industrialization. If you look at its age pyramid, you can see how from 1950 to 2023, the age structure of this country evolves with a significant aging of its population. For those interested in analyzing Japan's demographic projections for the next 50 years, you might see a significant decline in the country's population. If we were to hypothesize a significant increase (which is quite unlikely) in birth rates, we would find ourselves in a situation where the percentage of the population of reproductive age has decreased so significantly that even under this hypothesis it would be very difficult to recover the lost population.

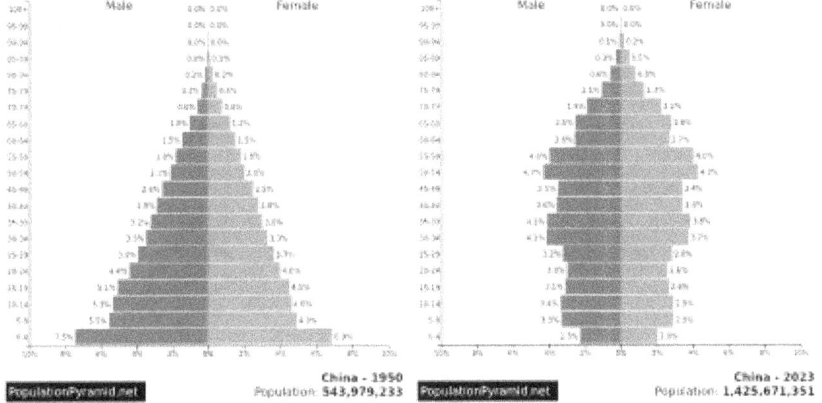

https://www.populationpyramid.net/: Sources see note 6

Fig. 5: Comparative population pyramid between 1950 and 2023 for China. Another emblematic case is China's population evolution. The Chinese planning authorities introduced the one-child-per-family policy because they were concerned about an abrupt demographic growth of its population. However, China is today, together with India, on the podium of the most populated countries on the planet. Observing the evolution of its age pyramid, one can see how it is gradually evolving towards an aging population, which is becoming more and more like Japan's demographic structure. The authorities have modified the one-child-per-family rule. Despite this policy change, it is not known whether the new regulations will allow China to maintain a stable population structure over time. Contrary to the wishes of its planners, it is likely to enter a demographic cycle similar to that of Japan.

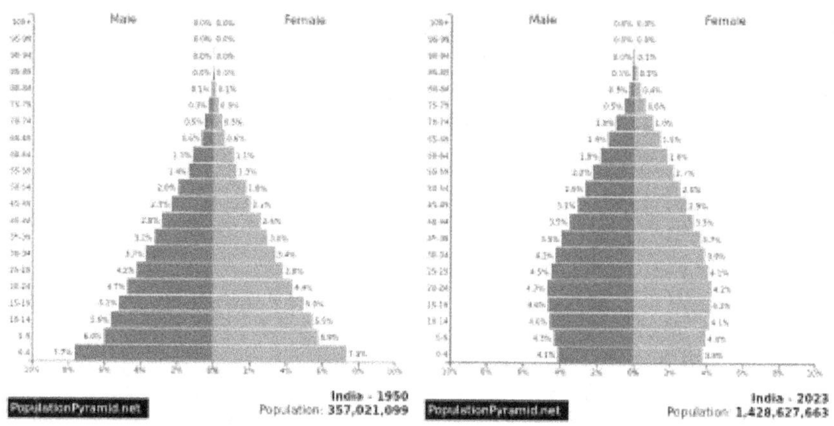

https://www.populationpyramid.net/: Sources see note 6

Fig. 6: Comparative population pyramid between 1950 and 2023 for India. India competes with China for the position of the most populous country in the world. Looking at its age pyramid, it is possible to state that it will almost certainly occupy the top seat in the coming years. Unlike its counterpart, this country did not implement birth control through government policies, which explains a different age pyramid structure compared to a situation where population planning objectives dominated for many years.

3.8 Latin America and Africa

If we analyze its evolution over time, we see that Latin America increasingly resembles Western and developed economies. We can affirm, then, that according to the better economic conditions of a region, there is a decrease in the birth rate which has significant economic consequences, as we have already seen.

Latin America is dangerously approaching the demographic decline of the most developed economies. However, in my opinion, its demographic pyramids still present a situation that is not as concerning as that of the so-called first-world economies.

Undoubtedly, Africa is the youngest continent (Fig. 7) and we can expect significant population growth from it. Many African countries lack sufficient infrastructure. As a result, Africa is also likely to experience an important economic growth in the coming decades.

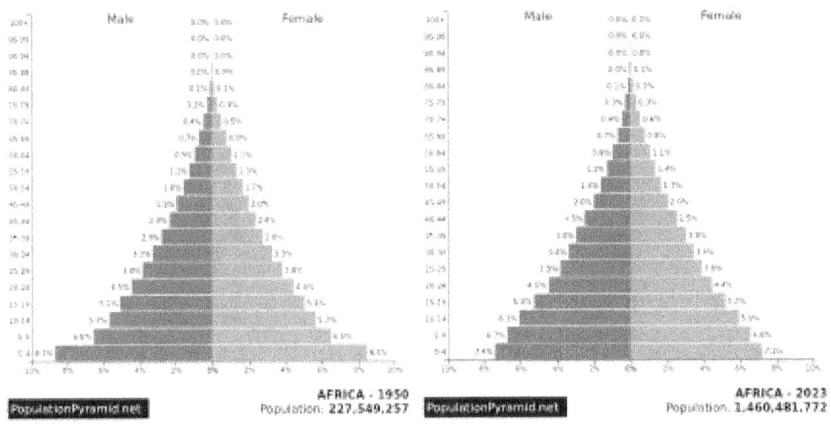

https://www.populationpyramid.net/: Sources see note 6

Fig. 7: Comparative population pyramid between 1970 and 2023 for Africa. Africa undoubtedly represents the continent that can supply the world with new young people. It is important to analyze the reasons for this population exuberance. Unlike the other continents, it does not have as much economic and industrial development, the rural areas are demographically and population-wise stable. The process that leads to a decrease in the birth rate usually occurs due to migration from small towns to the cities, accompanied by the industrialization of the country and improvements in the economic conditions of families. However, the basic question is whether these economic improvements are real or apparent, since they lead to a decrease in population, an aging of the demographic structure of a country and in the medium term will have very serious economic consequences on the nations suffering from this phenomenon.

3.9 Western developed countries and Japan

From the economic standpoint of the Gross Domestic Product growth, over the last decades these countries have experienced the negative effects of aging populations and low birth rates[18] (Fig. 8,9,10). Mainly to address these negative effects of the birth rate problem, expansionary unjustified monetary policies have been implemented. However, all artificial and forced actions made at the monetary policy level end up causing more problems than benefits. Adding water to ready-made soup does not mean that we will have more food, because at the nutritional level the amount of nutrients will be the same; we simply create an illusion of abundance which in reality is nothing but a meal without salt, without flavor, and without nutrients.

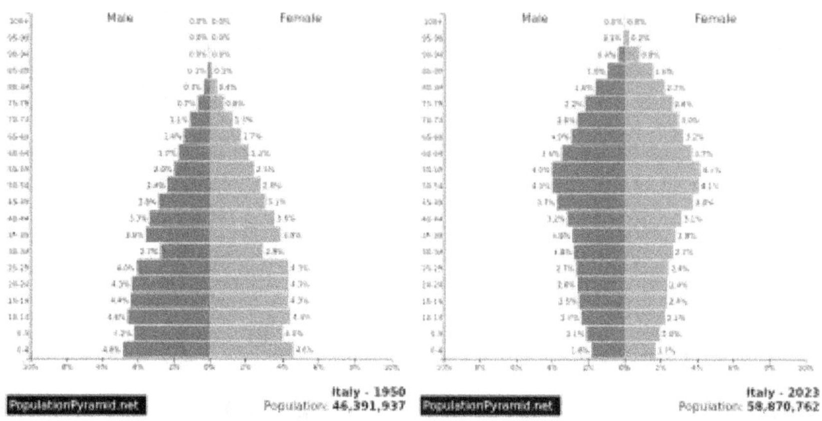

https://www.populationpyramid.net/: Sources see note 6

Fig. 8: Comparative population pyramid between 1950 and 2023 for Italy. The case of Italy, like that of Japan, is significant in demonstrating how a society can in a few decades move towards "quasi" self-extinction. When analyzing the age pyramid of Italy, we can see that the majority of the population is of pensionable age, which indicates that it is difficult for them to reproduce in the coming years, the biological clock can sometimes be very unforgiving, this is an undeniable fact. This beautiful country famous for its food, its "design" and the joviality of its population, is another interesting case that shows how strong state interventions in the economic life of a nation, rather than fostering the basis for a stable economic and social growth, comprise the empty example of the irrationality of public spending that accompanies the senility of its people with a high level of unemployment and the lowest wages among developed countries. In other words, Italy is the demonstration of many of the theories that will be presented in this book, including the irrationality of public spending, the reverse redistribution of wealth, and the destructive power of inflation. Rejected!

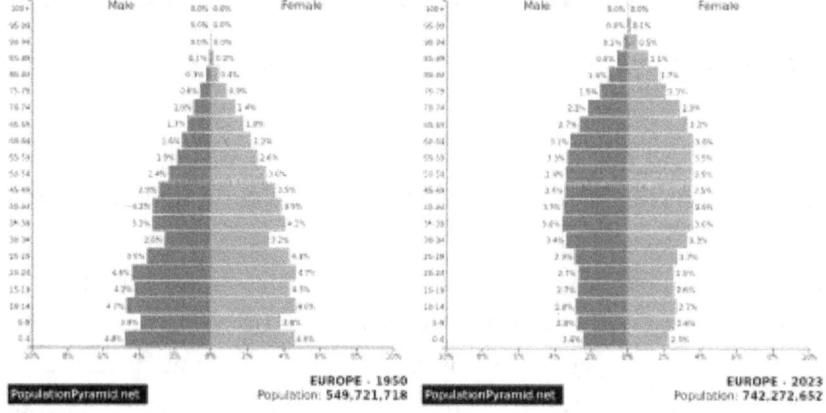

https://www.populationpyramid.net/: Sources see note 6

Fig. 9: Comparative population pyramid between 1970 and 2023 for Europe. Europe is also known as the Old World; its age pyramid confirms this definition. Although its demographic structure is not particularly critical like Italy's, it is with some years of difference quite similar. Now, in such a situation it becomes incomprehensible how these largely ex-colonialist countries can be averse to migration – an action that can serve to repopulate them. In fact, we could say that in the coming years, the social and cultural structure of the Old World will change radically to a large extent due to migration from Africa. **Even if these nations were to oppose it, that would be short-sighted.** *This natural phenomenon of history will change Europe. If Europeans no longer want to have children, others will arrive from Africa in search of a better destiny for their children. In this respect, European governments should integrate the new migrants in a decent and efficient way.*

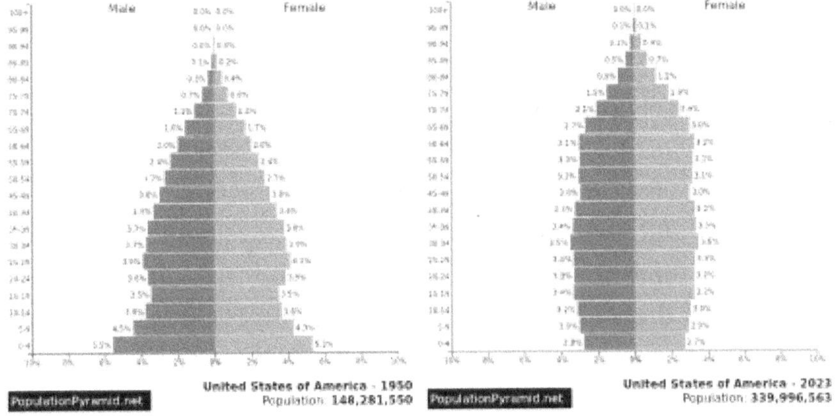

https://www.populationpyramid.net/: Sources see note 6

Fig. 10: Comparative population pyramid between 1950 and 2023 for the United States. The demographic structure of the United States, although not as marked, has an evolution like that of Europe and other industrialized countries. In the United States, unlike Europe, there are strong migrations from Latin America, which are more difficult to control since there are thousands of kilometers of border. For those who regularly travel to the United States and Canada, these two countries are the perfect example of multi-ethnic societies with an increasingly important Latin American population. I personally believe that thanks to the strong migration from Central and South America, North American countries will manage to maintain a more stable population over the years than European countries, since it seems to me that, unlike European countries, in this case there is a greater capacity for integration.

3.10 What would happen under normal conditions in our economies?

We have seen that all the monetary measures implemented by governments are aimed at sustaining the economy up to incomprehensible levels of expansion, when under normal conditions, what should have happened was a reduction in economic activity accompanied by periods of economic recession. In my opinion, we are currently witnessing, therefore, the result of a series of preposterous policies, which are the main causes of the current inflation and of the discouraging prospect of what will come. Historically, any upward movement is followed by a downward movement, especially if it is exponential. A few years of strong economic recession might be in store for us. It would be logical to expect some readjustments in stock market values and, consequently, a reduction in what I define as stock market inflation, but this is an unlikely possibility. Perhaps the most likely scenario will involve becoming aware of the loss of value of most of the fiat currencies, realizing that the high stock market values do not represent a financial bubble but the reality of the money that has lost much of its value. The system should somehow at some point achieve a more sustainable equilibrium; however, bear in mind that no one has a crystal ball. This book aims to encourage critical thinking and analysis of the current situation and possible solutions from a different perspective.

I repeat, in economics, there are many theories, but there are many more variables that can sometimes invalidate those same theories.

3.11 Public expenditure and debt: The gallows of modern societies

It is strange that when talking about inflation no one mentions its main cause, which is public spending and debt. We hear economists and politicians involved in government activities talk about the patient being sick with a high fever, but no one addresses the underlying issue, which should be: What is the cause of the disease? Truisms upon truisms and nothing concrete, no conclusive reasoning of substance.

If we analyze public spending and debt (Fig. 11), there are some important characteristics to highlight:

Steady increase over time.

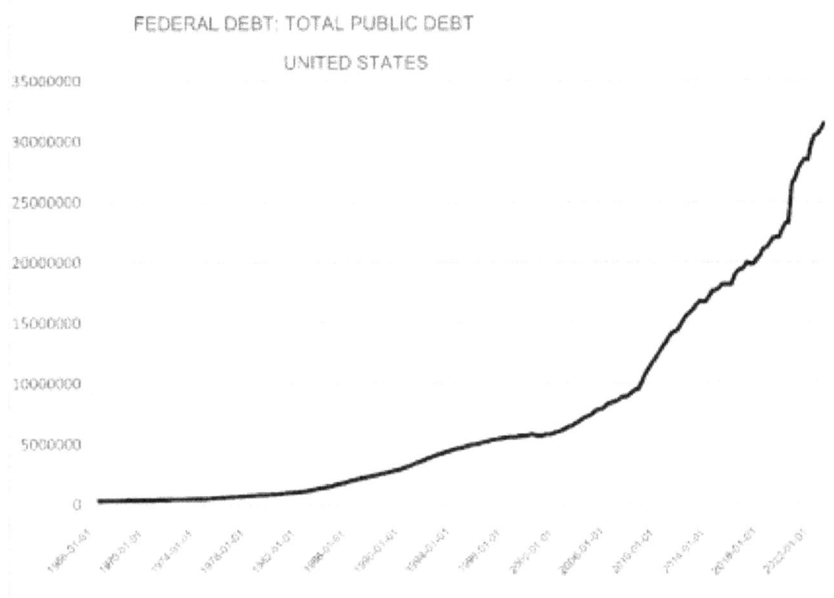

SOURCE: U.S. Department of the Treasury. Fiscal Service, Federal Debt: Total Public Debt [GFDEBTN], retrieved from FRED, Federal Reserve Bank of St. Louis; https://fred.stlouisfed.org/series/GFDEBTN, June 29, 2023.

Fig. 11: This graph illustrates how public debt has evolved in an uncontrolled growth over time. As shown, the public debt of the United States since the beginning of the year 2000 has increased about 6 times in only two decades.

- Inability of governments to reduce them or, in other words, spending cuts.

- Strong incidence of interest on the balance sheets of each State.

We have witnessed a steady and continuous increase in spending and public debt in synchrony with a downward trend in interest rates over time.

A question arises: how has an expansion of debt, and at the same time reductions in interest rates (Fig. 12,13) been possible in a controlled inflationary environment? In the last forty years we have experienced events that have kept inflation **relatively and apparently** under control despite a sharp reduction in interest rates.

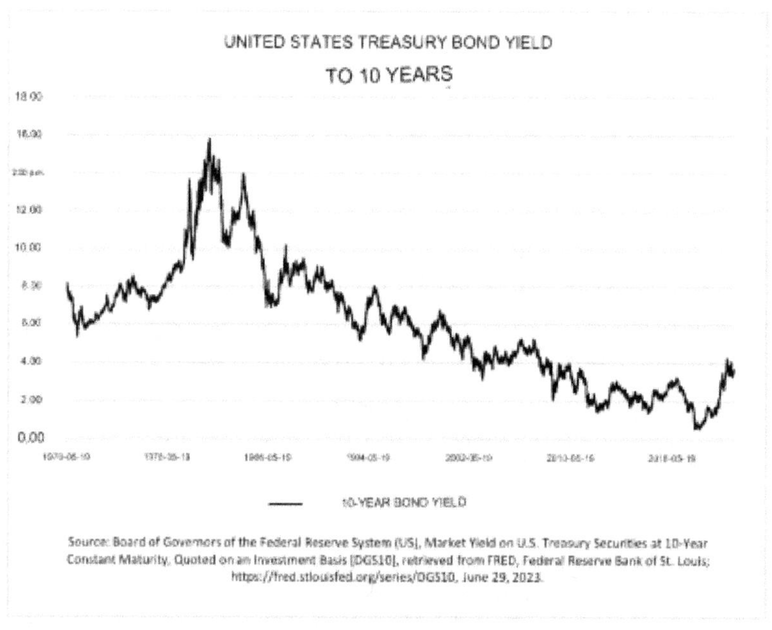

Fig. 12: 10-year bond yield graph. If we analyze the interest rates of 10-year bonds issued by the U.S. government, we see that they steadily decrease until they reach a value near zero at the end of the second decade of the 2000s. On the one hand we have a steady and continuous increase in public spending and public debt, but on the other hand we have the expression of the loss of value of money represented by a sharp decline in its profitability. Although there is a small upturn in the yield of these 10-year bonds, it is the result of the restrictive monetary measures taken by the central banks over the course of 2022. However, it could be considered that this is not a trend that can be maintained in the long term, being more likely that the trend of the last decades will continue, with a decrease in the yields of these securities near the zero value.

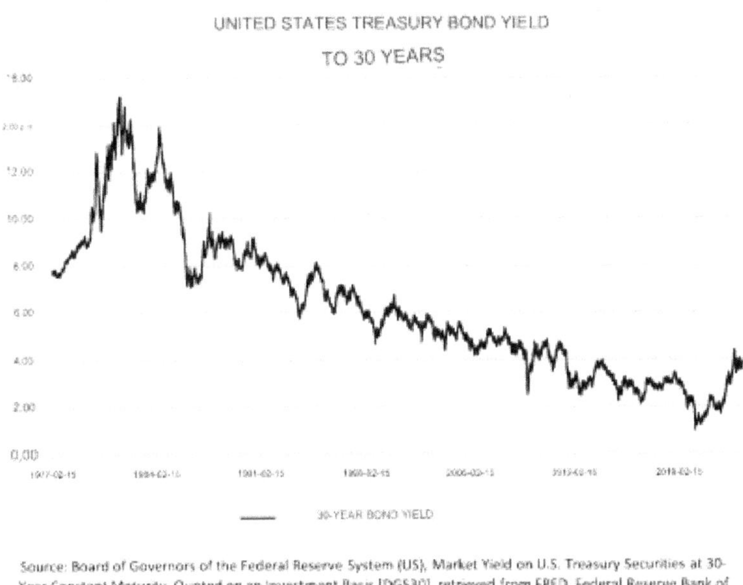

Source: Board of Governors of the Federal Reserve System (US), Market Yield on U.S. Treasury Securities at 30-Year Constant Maturity, Quoted on an Investment Basis [DGS30], retrieved from FRED, Federal Reserve Bank of St. Louis; https://fred.stlouisfed.org/series/DGS30, June 29, 2023.

Fig. 13: Yield plot of 30-year U.S. Treasury bonds. The same considerations made for 10-year bonds also apply to bonds with a 30-year maturity date. In this regard, please note that in the twelve years between 2010 and 2022, the interest rates paid for this type of bond have been between 2% and 4%, touching the minimum point close to zero. This trend is particularly emblematic if we consider that a 30-year bond implies that this money is committed for three decades and due to such a long term, it should normally "theoretically" pay much more.

- Productivity generated by new technologies has reduced the cost of finished products.

- Globalization has been another factor that has contributed to the apparent control of inflation.

- Decrease in the quality of goods and services offered in the market.

Finally, the crucial question is whether the inflation figures given to us in recent years by the statistical institutes are correctly measured or whether their measurements underestimate the factual reality. Obviously, from a situation with near-zero interest rates to an increase in interest rates, the balance sheets of the states will be under enormous pressure. Most of the countries face a complicated predicament, on the one hand, inflation lowers the value of total debt; on the other hand, rising rates greatly increase the cost of this debt.

At the corporate level, the same occurs. The very low cost of money has generated the proliferation of what are known as "Zombie companies"[19]. The indiscriminate use of debt instruments by healthy companies through share buybacks has been unbalancing the balance sheets of many healthy companies towards high debt overexposure. This is another common consequence of a near-to-zero cost of money.

3.12 Who is responsible for inflation?

3.12.1 Policy and the public administrative system

Politics and public administration are mainly responsible for inflation, although nobody recognizes it; let's remember that this problem is not well received by voters. Analyzing politics in the economic structure of a country would visually be like the condemned man digging his own grave with a shovel. That is what happens when we go to the urns, or when we do not, something that in my opinion is even worse, because we leave it to others to make decisions and refrain from having a say in the matter. The fundamental problem to acknowledge is that politics have strayed far from the ideal vision with which it was originally conceived.

3.12.2 How do politicians affect inflation?

Ideally, political work should be a noble profession for the common good. It has practically become an end for itself, where a fortunate few receive unjustified salaries and benefits to complicate the lives of the people they serve. Public spending should be recognized as one of the main contributing factors to inflation, as it directly affects aggregate demand by increasing it.

This is a highly inflationary component of the economy.

This process creates a vicious circle, as increased spending leads to higher taxes, increasing public debt, and the expansion of the monetary base, ultimately resulting in inflation and harming the economy as a whole.

3.12.3 Essential areas of government activity

Recently, due to work-related obligations, I had the opportunity to visit several major cities in the industrialized western hemisphere, and was stunned by the number of homeless people, many of them with obvious mental problems on the sidewalks and in sub-zero temperatures. I asked myself, shouldn't a country take care of the marginalized, giving them a minimum of hygienic living conditions, a roof to sleep under, and medical care? Well, I think so, they should as a rule of law take care of the weakest and help them! Now, make no mistake, this is not a socialist proclamation, the countries that define themselves as such have the same problems. This is, on the contrary, a liberal proclamation, which considers the state overextended in areas that do not concern it and that finally lead it to spend or rather to squander the taxpayers' money shamefully. I wonder if, by reducing 10% the defense budget, or the same 10% of the benefits paid to the politicians, would it not be possible to take better care of these human beings? It would be good for you to ask yourselves this question before casting your votes.

The essential areas of a government's activity should be limited:

- Health
- Education
- Security
- Justice
- Defense
- Regulations

But what are the ultimate goals of politicians? The basic problem to be answered is whether politicians and their main objectives coincide with the main needs of their constituents or whether, on the contrary, the objectives are divergent.

- To remain at the position with its noblest part sitting in warm and comfortable chairs.

- To be reelected.

- To have more power.

These are the basic goals that really motivate and guide politicians, causing public investment to become diluted onto many projects that do not bring any benefits, but instead, represent just a waste of taxpayers' money. They focus primarily on increasing the number and improving the conditions of public employees, because in the end, they are voters. The result of political activity is a steady growth in the public debt of almost every economy on the planet. During economic recessions, instead of allowing the free market to self-adjust, politicians intervene generating more damage than solutions.

Central bank officials are ultimately appointed by politicians and their parties, as are the economists in key positions in the institutions on whose ideas their decisions are based. It could be possible that they are not basing but only justifying their decisions to ensure the existence of their jobs.

An increase in public spending leads to more money circulating in the economy. This in turn generates more inflationary pressure and an increase in public debt that requires more payments in interests, again accelerating the inflationary spiral. When central and commercial banks intervene in that process, they cause the creation of more monetary base (Fig.14), constituting a highly inflationary event. Visually, this economic process resembles an avalanche that grows increasingly voluminous.

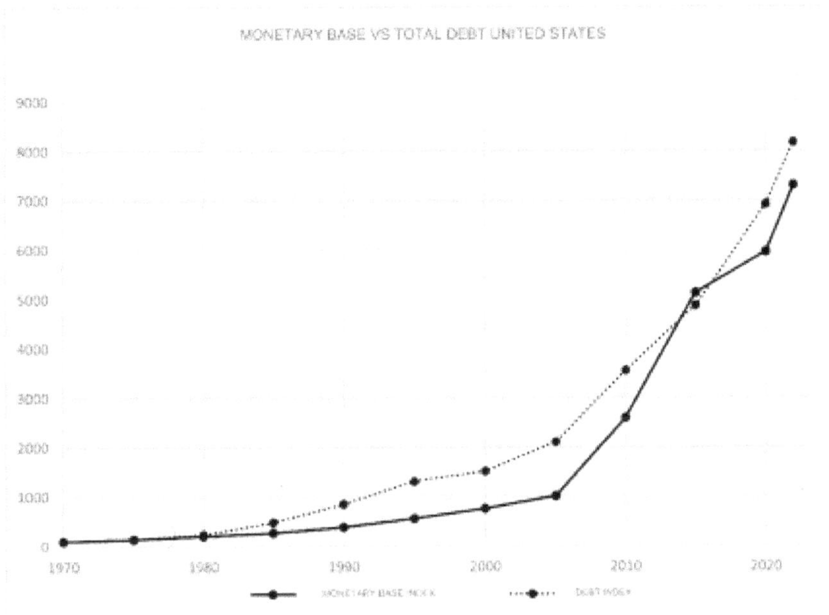

Fig. 14: Comparison chart of the evolution of public debt and monetary base, indexing both values to base 100 in 1970. Observe how the monetary base and the public debt evolve in a synchronized manner with a strong acceleration that occurs after the "Subprime" mortgage crisis (see note 10) in 2007-2010.

To return to the question: who is responsible for inflation? The answer is a bit heartbreaking, because the responsible ones are you through your representatives, no matter what political ideas you come from.

3.12.4 The role of the central bank

Central banks should normally have as their main objective the definition and management of monetary and exchange rate policy, as well as the custody and administration of the international monetary reserve. In addition to these primary functions, they have also played an active role in supporting the economies and the government's fiscal policy. For many years these institutions have concentrated and focused on the active role, neglecting what in my opinion are the main roles they should have as their guiding principle.

Does it make sense for them to play an active role in the economy through expansionary or restrictive policies? In addition to the essential functions given to the Central Bank, there is the idea that monetary policy can influence the economy. This implies that in a recessionary phase, implementing an expansive monetary policy would help the economy. On the contrary, in times when there is too much economic exuberance, a restrictive monetary policy would control inflation and the value of the currency. I wonder if the market, with its strength alone, would not be better equipped to balance itself, without the outside distortions caused by forced mechanical interventions?

Unfortunately, what we have seen across the globe is a loss of focus of the monetary authorities on the basic reasons of their existence, and instead orienting their work towards an excessive blind interventionism in the economy.

3.13 Causes of inflation

Now you can understand how explaining an economic phenomenon using a system of analysis excessively focused on the study of theoretical details can lead us to lose the vision and understanding of the problem as a whole. By this, I mean that it is necessary to study the details to understand the phenomenon of inflation, its causes and its origins. However, the mistake of many economists could sometimes be to try to explain a relatively simple phenomenon by means of complex numerical conjectures that lead to losing the vision and understanding of the phenomenon itself. Other economists, even if they understand the problem well, may not be able to speak about it, because it would be like bringing to light the reality of events by criticizing their current or potential employer, "the State".

From the obvious to the not so obvious to reach an understanding of the very complex phenomena that originated the problem.

Most Western countries were not prepared to face the post-pandemic inflationary situation; in fact, the world has been on a progressive downward trend in nominal inflation for four decades, placing it within a normal range of 0 to 5%.

What we should ask ourselves is whether this 0 to 5% range of inflation for so many years reflects the economy's real inflation or is it only a nominal representation of a much more complex phenomenon that cannot be so easily understood.

But to construct the causes and reasons that can provoke inflation, let's start a few decades ago.

3.14 The Bretton Woods agreements and the role of the dollar

It is true that history is often written by the winners, and the United States emerged as a significant victor in World War II, leading its allies to prevail against Nazi fascism. The post-war era saw the establishment of the Bretton Woods agreements, which provided many benefits to the United States as a reward for its war efforts. These agreements played a role in shaping the dynamics of the events and the global economic order that followed the war.

These agreements, in short, established the U.S. dollar as the monetary instrument for world trade exchange; in addition, they fixed a convertibility rate between gold and the dollar, as well as convertibility rates (within specific bands) between the currencies of the countries that adhered to Bretton Woods and the dollar. Thus, we see how the monetary system became quite stable, limited in its possibility of expansion by the gold offers in the system. We must also underline the fact that the United States at this time had the strongest economy and held a large part of the world's gold reserves. The Bretton Woods agreements also resulted in the birth of the International Monetary Fund, as well as the International Bank for Reconstruction and Development.

The system created by Bretton Woods came to an end under the presidency of Richard Nixon in 1971, when the United States suspended the anchoring and the fixed convertibility of the dollar to gold. This decision converted the US dollar into what we know as fiat currency, a currency that is not backed by any commodity, and whose value is guaranteed by the country of issue - in this case, the United States. However, it was not until 1976 that the Bretton Woods agreements formally ceased to exist.

The Bretton Woods agreements for the U.S. economy also meant the creation of the foundations for a strong development and further projection in the years to come. Imagine now, since the dollar was the currency of trade in all countries, central banks and companies that traded products worldwide were required to have dollars in their reserves. This was true even for countries that did not adhere to the Bretton Woods agreements, like the Warsaw Pact countries. To sell their oil, these nations had to charge it in dollars. The concept is simple. Then, that mass of dollars in circulation backed by gold finally came to support the development of the American economy. The surplus dollars ended up invested in the United States, its stock exchange, American companies, and bonds issued by that same government.

Now imagine a currency whose quantity in circulation is determined and anchored to a commodity (in this particular case gold). It would have a maximum limit of creation represented by the reserves of the underlying good. Therefore, printing more banknotes than the existing reserves of gold was not **"theoretically"** possible. Here I ask myself a question: What happens when this limit is removed or, in other words, when there is no longer an anchor between the existing quantity of the precious metal and the currency in question? **We can perhaps define this moment as the beginning of the party.** By party, I mean the possibility of easy money creation. The system created through the Bretton Woods agreements put the US dollar at the center of the world, making it the currency used internationally for the exchange of goods and services. At the same time, it generated a lot of monetary stability because all the currencies that had adhered to the pacts of the agreement were linked to the dollar, which had a fixed exchange rate of 35 dollars per ounce of gold.

3.15 The party started

There are contrasting opinions regarding the abandonment of the gold standard or fixed convertibility between gold and the U.S. dollar.

Some consider that this was necessary because more dollars were needed to finance global economic growth. Others consider that the system worked well and that it was a mistake to have abandoned this anchor. The fact is that thanks to the Bretton Woods agreements, the world was able to rise from the disasters left by the Second World War. Countries destroyed as a result of the war, such as Germany, France, Italy, England and Japan, became developed economies, engines of the world, together with the United States. and were consequently able to prosper and grow. Therefore, we can affirm that the agreements and the system were effective in achieving their intended goals until they were discontinued in the 1970s.

Furthermore, we must reflect on the geopolitical situation of those years. The Vietnam War, a costly and bloody conflict, had squandered the coffers of the United States. It has been shown quite clearly that exporting democracy was not only a costly exercise, but also an unsuccessful one, given that war had been lost.

Now, let's go back to politicians and their three basic objectives. The first refers to a very noble part of the body that complicates our lives with entangled and complex rules and regulations. I am referring to the buttocks and the fundamental objective of keeping them in their comfortable chairs, which in my opinion are too comfortable and warm. The second objective is to be reelected in the next elections. And finally, as a third objective we have the insatiable desire of men to have more and more power.

In this context, for the politicians of yesteryear as well as for those of today, having a currency anchored in a commodity that has limited reserves or that can grow slowly and gradually is obviously a major constraint. Therefore, the decision to un-anchor the dollar from the gold standard was highly tempting and that is probably how the story ended.

It is amusing to think of the way politicians sell their ideas to naïve voters. One of the reasons President Nixon used to justify abandoning the anchor between the U.S. dollar and gold was to combat inflation. Now think about it: being able to print more banknotes to fight inflation? It would be like telling the cigarette addict that to cure himself of his addiction he has to increase the number of cigarettes smoked per day. What is most interesting is that Nixon's measures were received very positively by the public opinion, as well as by his constituents.

3.16 The vacuum door

In the years following the abandonment of the gold standard, there were periods of very high inflation for more than a decade (Fig. 15).

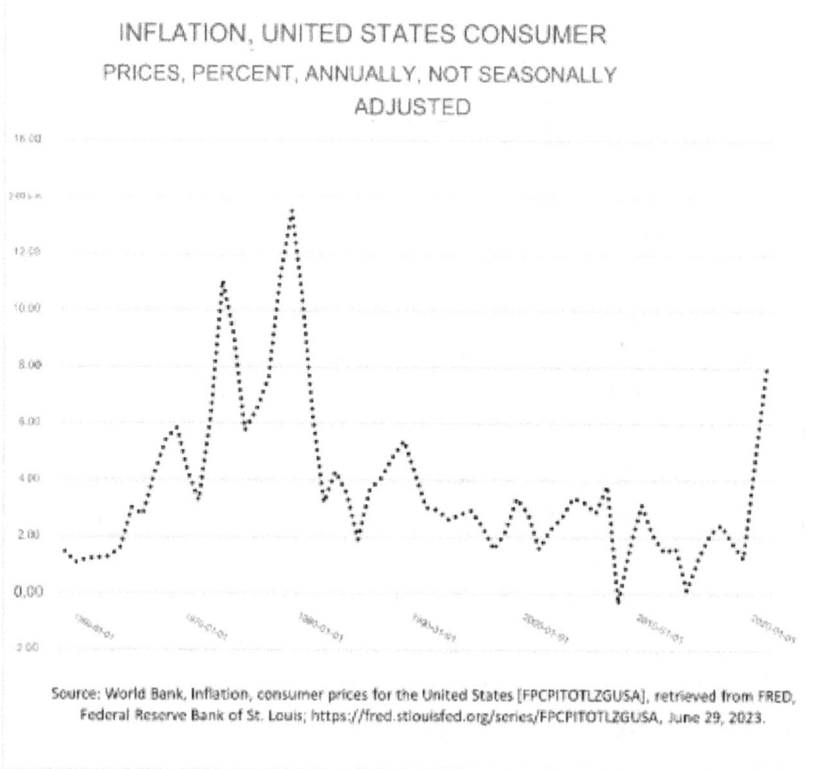

Fig. 15: Graph of inflation appreciation over the last sixty years in the United States, showing a strong inflationary turbulence around 1970 and the beginning of the 1980s. At the beginning of the 1980s, there were two important events to take into consideration, the first being the strongly restrictive monetary policy actions implemented by Paul Volcker during the Reagan administration. The second phenomenon was the change in the methodology used to calculate the "CPI" (consumer price index) calculated by the statistics institute. We refer you to Chapter 6 for a critical review of these changes.

This is quite logical to understand, because the State had been given the capacity to produce banknotes. I am not only referring to the dollar, but also to the other currencies that were linked to the dollar through the Bretton Woods agreements.

These turbulences lasted until the beginning of the 80's when, finally, under the Regan administration, inflation in the United States was "seemingly" brought under control. The end of the Bretton Woods agreements was characterized by the phenomenon of stagflation as discussed earlier, where the currency lost value due to strong inflation and at the same time the Gross Domestic Product declined.

The real objectives of the abandonment of the relationship between the US dollar and gold have been achieved: to allow the State to produce more money without it being backed by any real asset and therefore be able to spend this money through public expenditure. This also made it possible to fulfill the voracity of politicians in the creation of new projects or in the development of the most outlandish ideas.

What they did achieve was the exact opposite of everything that had been promised to the people, in other words, a loss of control over inflation. In order to understand exactly what happened in these years, imagine an alcohol addict who for a long time has had no access to bottles, suddenly finding a party with an open bar offering all sorts of liquors. The image may indeed appear lighthearted and amusing, but the consequences and aftermath it brings about are unlikely to be as ironic or humorous.

In the 1970s, the United States experienced a period of significant challenges, including high inflation and pronounced stock market volatility that persisted for several years. In the 1980s, thanks to the monetary policy of Paul Volcker and the support and determination of President Reagan, the situation appeared to be under control again. I use the term **"appeared"** because as you'll discover when you continue reading, in reality that the patient was not cured at all.

3.17 Interest rates

In their essence, or, philosophically, interest rates represent the value of money for a time frame; others may say that they represent the cost of money. However, I consider the term value to be more representative for an abstract good that everyone is pursuing. Since it became easier for countries owning their own fiat currency to produce money, or in other words to create it artificially, you can imagine what happened to interest rates. If we look at the evolution of nominal interest rates paid for government bonds in relation of the monetary base expansion (from Paul Volcker's restrictive policy until the beginning of 2022), we can observe how these rates have maintained a constant downward trend over time (Fig. 16).

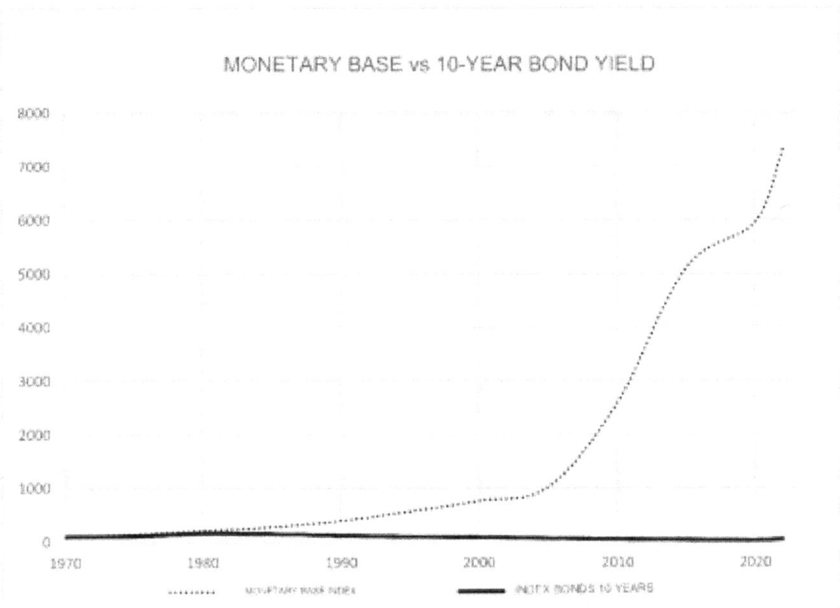

Source: Board of Governors of the Federal Reserve System (US), Monetary Base; Total [BOGMBASE], retrieved from FRED, Federal Reserve Bank of St. Louis; https://fred.stlouisfed.org/series/BOGMBASE, June 29, 2023.
Board of Governors of the Federal Reserve System (US), Market Yield on U.S. Treasury Securities at 10-Year Constant Maturity, Quoted on an Investment Basis [DGS10], retrieved from FRED, Federal Reserve Bank of St. Louis; https://fred.stlouisfed.org/series/DGS10, June 29, 2023.

Fig.16: Comparative graph of the evolution of the monetary base with the evolution of interest rates on 10-year U.S. government bonds, indexing both values in 1970 to a base of 100.

One of the main elements that determine the value of a good is its scarcity; therefore, it is easy to understand that money became less expensive as soon as governments had an easier time creating it. Consequently, we can say that the expression of its value became cheaper over time, with a constant downward trend.

In one of the next chapters, we will try to answer the question of whether the abundance of money translates into easier access to it for all citizens or whether it remains only for a fortunate few.

3.18 Public expenditure

To understand the evolution of public spending, it is necessary to analyze it from a psychological viewpoint, which is related to two of the primary objectives of politicians: to have more power and to be reelected. For a politician, access to an inexhaustible source of banknote production is and will always be extremely tempting. Make no mistake, I am not talking about conspiracy theories or corruption; I am simply referring to the opportunity to implement various programs under the guise of necessary investments for the people. By means of these programs financed with public money, politicians achieve an important personal objective, which is to show gratitude to their constituents. As an example of these expenses, one could think of providing subsidies for festivals, fairs or associations, or providing unjustified benefits to certain groups of workers, or the purchase of goods and services for some institution. When it comes to spending money, our representatives can be extremely creative. Creativity therefore becomes the guiding element of how our representatives spend money. Sorry for the bitter reality check, but that's the way things are.

The increase in public spending by countries has been a factor contributing to consistent and continuous growth over the last decades for all developed countries. The basic question I would like to ask you is: in your opinion, is this money that governments use for public spending wisely invested or, on the contrary, is it a waste of public resources?

3.19 Public debt and taxes

Public debt is another element, alongside taxes, which finally finances public spending. In an ingenious move, the State integrates taxes with the generation of public debt, because taxes alone are not enough to cover the insatiable voracity of the State. In this manner, an unnatural event occurs, represented by a blanket that fits perfectly to cover the feet and the head at the same time. This anomalous event affects the economic equilibrium of any investment plan, be it that of a family, a company, or an institution, or finally of a State, because it is simply not possible to finance all expenses at the same time. Here again, we find an intervention of the ingenuity and creative skills of our politicians, who thanks to their abilities, have managed over the years to constantly increase public spending, and bring taxes and debts to intolerable levels for hardworking individuals. When discussing taxes, it is crucial to have a clear understanding of two or three key concepts. The first is that they must be paid in full, since it will always be more costly in the long run not to do so; the second is easy to understand, nobody likes to pay them; and finally, when their level reaches very significant percentages, they become discouraging and regressive factors in the economic development of a State. This last concept is very difficult or perhaps impossible for most politicians to understand.

Many countries therefore have confiscatory tax levels. In this regard I will give you just one example that I consider quite enlightening, and relates to the VAT situation: in many European countries, this tax is above 20%, in other words, if you buy a pack of chewing gum that costs €4 in France or Italy, €1 of this €4 is represented by the VAT that is being paid to the State, this without considering the enormous amount constituted by the sum of all the other taxes that must be paid by those who produce and those who work, the people.

The final essential consideration on the level of taxes paid in an economy is that when they reach extremely high levels, they become a regressive factor for the economic development of the country. At the same time, some economists might object that they are also a deflationary factor, which would be partly true if we are referring to the reduction in the spending capacity of those who pay them. But in the total set of state expenditures which, as we have seen, have grown steadily over time, financed by taxes and by the issuance of public debt, these elements become an endemically inflationary force.

To summarize and synthesize the above concepts, think of public spending and its constant evolution, accompanied by high levels of public indebtedness, generating a cost for the states, represented by their interest payments. These are all inflationary factors. Now, we need to add a variable to the analysis of these inflationary forces, which are the high levels of taxes in a context of negative demographic evolution, and thus we have prepared the ground for a stagnation of the economy.

3.20 Monetary base explosion

The main instrument that central banks resort to in their policies to support the economy and control currency stability are interventions on interest rates. The basic limit that has emerged in the last 15 years is the ineffectiveness of manipulating interest rates as an expansionary instrument of the economy when interest rates are close to zero (Liquidity Trap[20]).

We also must contextualize this limit with the current geopolitical situation that takes into consideration the aging of the population, near-zero interest rates, and the persistently stagnant economic growth rates of Western economies. How, therefore, within this context, can governments and politics manage to maintain a growing level of public spending when we have seen that the economic, structural, and demographic conditions of a country do not allow it?

The subprime mortgage crisis that occurred in the first decade of the 21st century (2007-2010), propagated into an unprecedented financial crisis worldwide, leading central banks to adopt new monetary policy instruments. I am referring to the injections of money into the economy through the repurchase of securities by central banks, known as a "Quantitative Easing"[21] operations. These instruments are nothing more than the purchase of securities in the market with the consequent injection of new electronic money into the economy. This "monetary" creativity became necessary because the previous interest rate interventions were not sufficiently effective anymore.

Finally, in the pandemic and post-pandemic period, the central banks are acting like **"dollarinomaniacs"** and **"euroinomaniacs"**[22] addicted to economic policies without limits, initially accelerating the acquisition of securities from the market in order to inject artificial money more quickly into the economy. As if that were not enough, the Fed went so far as to reduce banks' reserve requirements to zero[23]. This practice led in the pandemic and post-pandemic period to an exorbitant explosion of the monetary base. To make it easier, they used the machine to print banknotes without limits, without any reticence, and without shame.

3.21 A dog chasing its tail: the labyrinth of modern society

Let's imagine a scenario where a sick person visits a doctor, and the doctor simply informs them that they are ill because they have a fever, without providing any further explanation or prescribing a treatment. In such a case, it would indeed be a waste of time and money to have sought medical advice without receiving proper guidance or a course of action to cure the illness.

Below you will find a summary of the mechanisms that generate the current inflation, using a simple, concrete example.

Step 1: To finance an increase in public spending, more taxes are required.

Step 2: To keep financing the ongoing growth in public spending, governments initially have easy access to the required funds through further and deeper tax increases.

This process has a limit which is defined by the very level of taxes that an economy is obligated to pay to the state. If taxes continue to increase to an excessively high level, this detracts from the economy's ability to continue to grow and thus sustain itself.

We arrive at **step 3:** The government can no longer use the instrument of taxation to finance its ever-increasing expenditures, since another tax increase would cause an economic setback. **The solution in this case will be the issuance of public debt.**

Step 4: By purchasing government debt, individuals are financing the government and thus entering this game. It resembles the game of three cups and a ball, where there are two players: a swindler who hides the ball and a player who will try to find it. If you prefer, we can also compare it to the game of three cards, and the results will be the same. In both situations it is the individuals and the collective that pay the public expenditure of the State in the first instance by means of taxes, but when the States' expenses are out of control and therefore need to finance it, this will be achieved by means of public debt that, initially, will always be acquired by its citizens. As you can see, whether directly or indirectly, the burden always falls on the taxpayers' shoulders. This game is possible until the economy grows, and taxpayers can have a real increase in their income that will allow them to invest in debt from the State. The game continues until there is a sustainable balance between debt and taxes. We have witnessed how developed economies, driven by the shifting demographic structure of their nations, have entered an economic phase that experiences a reduction of the active population. Due to the new macroeconomic conditions of lack of economic growth or eventual economic decline, accompanied by a continuously increasing public debt to sustain public spending, we reach the next step of the economy.

Step 5: Because citizens no longer have the capacity to acquire public debt and finance the states, this phase sees the intervention of commercial banks in tune and synergy with central banks through the creation of money via debt issuance. As you can see, the financing of public spending by issuing public debt results in a mere creation of money out of thin air without being accompanied by a growth of the economy.

4 Theories as causes and description of complex phenomena

4.1 Why is the keynesian economic model the preferred model?

If we were to ask ourselves, *What are the models that most governments prefer to use in their economic and monetary policies?* the answer should not be difficult to find. To find it, we need to reflect on our representatives, specifically the ones that democracies, or those we perceive as such, provide us through elections.

Let us review what we have already analyzed on the objectives of politicians. The first was to get their behinds in comfortable and warm chairs for as long as possible, or even in perpetuity; the second, which is functional to the first, to stay in office through reelection; and the last one is to have more power. In this regard, we often encounter economists who come to provide aid with their theories, offering a sense of relief, since these theories are justifications for accessing more money for the pursuit of public good and at the same time the achievement of their inner true objectives. Not bad, right? John Maynard Keynes unknowingly became a powerful ally to many politicians worldwide, as his theory was founded on the idea of public intervention in the economy. What a perfect theory! Keynes' theory was philosophically different from the classical economic thinking that had predominated for some centuries in this branch of the social sciences. Adam Smith, his illustrious Scottish predecessor, considered the market forces as the element that would have been able to balance demand and supply towards a natural equilibrium capable of adjusting on its own the economic imbalance that could arise in an economy. Here comes the contrasting perspective of Keynesian thought. In extreme summary, it views the market as an imperfect entity that is incapable of self-adjustment; therefore, it needs the intervention of the wise State to bring it to an equilibrium, in this case, an artificial one.

I don't want to be boring, but let's try to review a little theory from our most famous economist ancestor.

The aggregate demand of an economy represents the sum of the needs for goods and services of its active economic operators. The economic operators are divided into three groups: consumers, state or public sector and companies. To these "needs," the balance of net exports is also added.

To reduce inflation -according to Keynes- aggregate demand would have to be reduced. This can be achieved in the following way:

- Reduce the demand for consumer goods. This objective is usually achieved by increasing taxes.

- Reduce the demand for investment goods. This objective is normally achieved by increasing interest rates; thus, since money is more expensive, a lower demand for this type of goods is expected.

- Reduce public sector demand by simply reducing public spending.

- Reduce net exports.

If we analyze the policies to combat unemployment, we will see that they are the opposite of the policies that should be implemented to control inflation. Keynes explains that to reduce unemployment it is necessary to increase aggregate demand, and this can be achieved in the following way:

- Increase demand for consumer goods, which can usually be achieved by reducing taxes.

- Increase the demand for investment goods. This objective is normally achieved by lowering interest rates; thus, since money is cheaper, a greater demand for this type of goods is expected.

- Increase public sector demand by simply increasing public spending.

- Increase net exports.

If it is so simple, why is inflation control not easily achieved?

4.2 Monetary theory

This is where the monetary theory of inflation comes into play, which considers that it is much easier for a central bank to intervene in the control of the currency than for a government to intervene through a fiscal policy of increasing or reducing taxes and increasing or decreasing public spending.

The quantity theory of money relates in an equation the supply of money by its speed of circulation with the average price of an economy by the total amount of goods and services it produces. According to this equation, a balance exists between the quantity and mobility of money in a country or an economy and its production of goods and services in relation to their average prices.

$MxV=PxQ$ [24]

M= Money supply

V= velocity of circulation of money (how many times a year a unit of money is spent).

P= Average prices of an economy

Q= Total quantity of goods and service produced

FUNDAMENTALS OF THE THEORY

An increase in the money supply generally leads to an increase in prices within the economy. An increase in the short-term money supply can have an effect on the country's economic output and its Gross Domestic Product. The ideal monetary policy for a country and its central bank would be to accompany the increase in money supply with an increase in the country's real Gross Domestic Product. Thanks to this policy, a relative control of inflation can also be achieved.

Although it is common sense that monetary theory is *de facto* a theory with divergent views with respect to Keynesian theory, we see that in reality the central bank, by controlling the money supply, has the power to actively intervene in the economy. The difference is in the details, and it is subtle: on the one hand, we have the strong temptation of governments to fully embrace Keynesian theories, but on the other hand, we have seen the actions of central banks become more active in recent years through the expansion of the monetary base, probably guided by a Keynesian logic using monetarist type instruments through the implementation of their active monetary policies. A bit confused, aren't we? If we analyze the monetary theory of inflation and put it in the historical context of how central banks and governments have been handling this issue, a question arises, one whose answer is quite challenging to find. How is it possible to reconcile the two schools of thought?

Therefore, we conclude that if in the animal world it is neither possible nor common for two different species to mate and create offspring from their union, in economics, on the contrary, it is possible. Indeed, the interactions between Keynesian-type policies and the economy are closely linked and often intertwined with monetary policy actions. An increase in spending through an increase in public debt is normally accompanied by an increase in the monetary base, so, although theoretically in an aseptic laboratory one could analyze Keynesian-type theory and monetary policies implemented by the central authority separately, at the time of their implementation they go hand in hand due to the interrelationships between the instruments used by both policies.

4.3 Similarities between fiscal and monetary instruments

If we, therefore, analyze these theories in detail, what may initially seem like differences on the other hand could also be interpreted as similarities.

Keynesian theory considers that the government must maintain an active role in the economy by promoting full employment through public spending and fiscal policies that would support this strategy. What, therefore, would be the pillars of an active policy to reduce unemployment? These pillars would be a reduction in taxes, an increase in public spending probably financed through bond issuance, and as the granting of facilities for business investment through better interest rates. Looking at it from another point of view, these policy actions lead to an increase in the quantity of money in circulation, which indirectly sounds something like an expansionary monetary policy.

If, on the other hand, we analyze a fiscalist or Keynesian type of inflation reduction policy, its pillars would be an increase in taxes and a reduction in public spending, which would indirectly imply a reduction in the monetary base. This also resembles something of a monetary policy, perhaps not in its direct and explicit expression, but rather indirectly.

Let us now analyze a monetarist-type restrictive policy of the monetary base in circulation using an increase in interest rates. In this case, this policy takes money out of the economy, which reduces investments, contracts demand, public spending and, therefore, we can affirm that it indirectly has similarities with a Keynesian policy. On the contrary, an expansionary policy of the monetary base through a reduction of interest rates or through "Quantitative Easing" monetary expansion actions would have brought more money into the economy, facilitating business investments through better access to credit, an increased wage base, probably an increase in short-term demand, and in increased public spending, making it easier and more cost-effective for the State to borrow. This may also sound like something Keynesian.

The famous concept that states that perhaps extremes can touch each other has been shown; or maybe, instead we find that they were not so extreme despite starting from different philosophical bases, and the prescriptions end up being or causing similar results in the patient due to their interactions, turns out to be correct.

4.4 Conceptual differences of substance

At the philosophical level, in comparing Keynes with Friedman, we do indeed encounter two different philosophical conceptions: On the one hand, the belief in a wise, parsimonious, protective State that allows and is concerned about the development of its citizens from an economic, cultural and quality of life standpoints. On the other extreme, those who consider the state as a hindrance to the normal and healthy development of an economy and its citizens. Therefore, the more limited state interventions there are, the more a country can grow and prosper.

The monetary policies of central banks with interventions in the money supply are cousins (if you will allow me this poetic license) of Friedman's monetary theory. However, there is a substantial difference in the philosophical analysis of these policies that allows us to understand their operational framework, demonstrating that they have nothing to do with Friedman's ideals. By using monetary instruments as accelerators of public spending, they therefore distort his original logic, which assumed that economic growth in real terms should be accompanied by monetary growth that would sustain it and not the creation of money for the sole purpose of sustaining the resource-devouring apparatus of the government. In short, at the minimum level of analysis in social sciences, what matters is the observation of reality parting from a hypothesis confirmed by means of an eventual theory. Unfortunately, we are not analyzing a world of exact sciences where events can be explained with a formula. The mistake that could be faced is not understanding the limits of the human nature of those who are in charge, who put their personal benefits before the community they serve.

At the level of words, all politicians say what we want to hear, many times it is a manipulation of words, once they take the throne of power they are attacked by a deadly and highly contagious virus and its consequence is the forgetting of the promises made.

I leave you with some final reflections. To arrive at these considerations, analyze, however, some elements and some factors that affect daily life. First, are taxes fair in their absolute value and their percentage? Does the State spend these taxes to improve the lives of all its citizens or is it possible that these taxes are being misallocated or used inefficiently? Another important element to analyze is the number of laws through which we must live. Are these regulations and laws functional to the development of the economy and the personal development of citizens or can they become elements of confusion and hindrance?

4.5 The political perspective and how it has implemented the lessons learned from the two economic giants

I would not expect these statements to cause the two giants of economics, Keynes, and Friedman, to roll over in their graves (although I might hear bones clashing in the distance). I believe that the current political systems of almost all the countries of the world, or at least of the most important countries from an economic point of view, after apparently incorporating in their fiscal and economic policies the teachings left by these titans of economics, have instrumentally used them for their own benefit. Here, we need to revisit the three fundamental objectives of our representatives. The first is to keep their behinds in comfortable and warm chairs as long as possible or ideally in perpetuity (if possible, in some cases, they would also inherit it to their progeny); the second, which is functional to the first, is to remain in office by means of re-election; and the last is to have more power. In light of these three clear objectives, it is evident how Keynesian theories and monetarist theories can be used, not based on their philosophical foundations but as an instrumental way to achieve others' ends and denaturalize their teachings. Sadly, the ultimate objective of the political system is simply the unrestricted access to monetary resources.

On the one hand, we have the interventionist philosophical approach to the economy, which asserts that the government must actively intervene in the economy by means of an active public spending policy. This approach delivers to the political system the perfect excuse to justify its expenditures. To make the availability of money be practically unlimited, the instrumental use of monetary policies comes to its aid. Through the actions of central banks, the government manages to increase the monetary base in order to effectively have continuous access to fresh money. In other words, the ability to play at the table in an unlimited way.

I'll provide a simple example to help you visualize these mechanisms: a country wants to increase its public expenditure by 100 monetary units. There are two basic ways with which it can finance these 100 units. The first is to take it from the citizens through an increase in taxes. In this case, in extreme synthesis, the state takes away 100 monetary units from the people and spends them through state action. However, when the accumulated tax levels paid by the people are already outrageous and no further increase in the tax base is possible, the solution found is an increase in the public debt. Normally, the increase in the public debt is carried out by means of the intervention of the banking system and is accompanied by an increase in the money in circulation. It would suffice to see how the monetary base in circulation has increased steadily over the last decades. A fiscal action has, therefore, its interrelations and results in the field of monetary policy, and from there the seeds of inflation and the destruction of the value of money are sown.

I would like to expand a little on this example. The issuance of public debt in all cases entails the payment of interest that finally means an increase of money in circulation. The complexity would not go further if the governments were to place the public debt on the citizens; we would have a phenomenon similar, though not the same, to the payment of taxes because it would take money from the citizens to spend it again in the economy. The problem is that with the constant increase of public debt, to make this good a desirable instrument for the citizens, it should logically be accompanied by an increase in its profitability. We have seen that, over the last fifty years, interest rates have steadily been losing their value (Fig. 16, Ch. 3), so we should ask ourselves why. If the increase in public debt, instead of being subscribed to by citizens, is artificially achieved through the banking system (when I speak of the banking system I include the central bank) then we are dealing with an injection of money, which has constantly occurred over time. The creation of money has effectively increased its availability, making it less scarce and, consequently, cheaper. As a result, interest rates on debt have also decreased. Let us now expand to a third example: what happens when a State issues public debt in the form of Eurobonds in another currency. When this debt is subscribed in another currency abroad, the State receives this money, but in the country the legal currency is different; then the State exchanges it at the central bank for the legal currency of the country and this results in the creation again of a monetary base or an increase in it. It is surprising that all paths lead to the same result.

It is easy to understand, in the light of this perspective, how monetary expansion has been used to finance the government's interventionist actions, and at the same time make them possible thanks to a magical "Little Machine" that miraculously manages to produce money through the implementation of crazy monetary policies.

4.6 The beginning of the end

If we analyze the end of the European absolute monarchies, there is undoubtedly some common element that unites a logical thread of explanatory facts.

The first element to be considered is the lack of control of a country's expenditures; in other words, when the continuous and constant increase in public investment becomes an autonomous and uncontrollable being on the part of governments. This being as such has a life of its own, it is alive. Another fundamental characteristic is that it is self-feeding; therefore, it is not possible to control it by taking away its fuel (I am referring to public spending). In order for it to grow and feed itself, it needs a companion to make this growth possible, and the public debt is its mistress. If we analyze the evolution of public spending and public debt in industrialized countries, observe a consistent and steady increase in both over the years and decades. (Fig. 1).

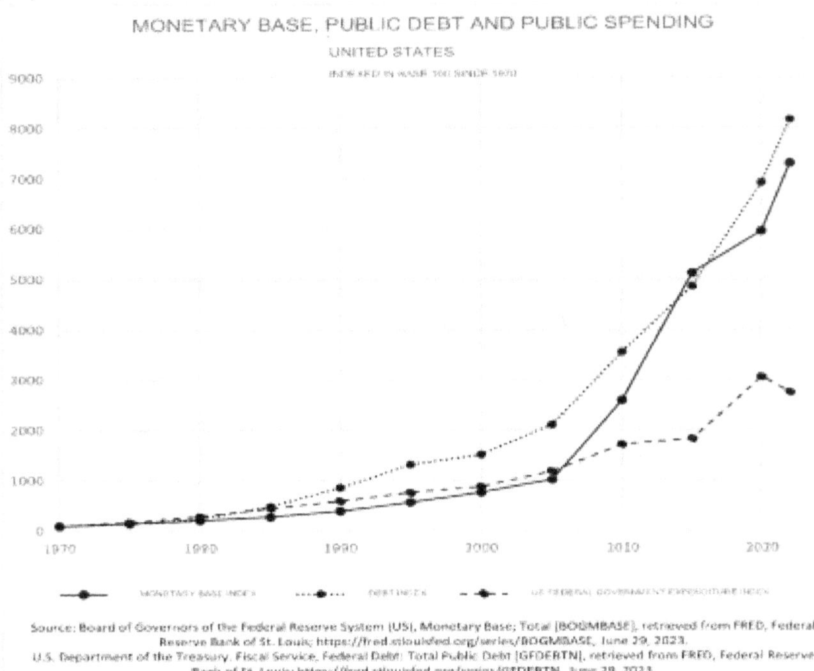

Source: Board of Governors of the Federal Reserve System (US), Monetary Base; Total [BOGMBASE], retrieved from FRED, Federal Reserve Bank of St. Louis; https://fred.stlouisfed.org/series/BOGMBASE, June 29, 2023.
U.S. Department of the Treasury, Fiscal Service, Federal Debt: Total Public Debt [GFDEBTN], retrieved from FRED, Federal Reserve Bank of St. Louis; https://fred.stlouisfed.org/series/GFDEBTN, June 29, 2023.
U.S. Bureau of Economic Analysis, Federal Government: Current Expenditures [FGEXPND], retrieved from FRED, Federal Reserve Bank of St. Louis; https://fred.stlouisfed.org/series/FGEXPND, June 29, 2023.

Fig. 1: Comparison chart between the evolution of the monetary base, public debt and public expenditure indexing these indicators in base 100 from 1970 with a 5-year periodicity. As can be seen, the evolution of these 3 items is similar over time, with a significant upward trend; however, since the subprime crisis (2007-2010), we note a strong acceleration of the monetary base and public debt over public spending. This is synonymous with a continuous and excessive monetization of the system, which over time destroys the value of money. Another important element for reflection is that since the strong expansion of the monetary base and public debt occurred at the end of the first decade of the 2000s, public spending has lagged behind, with a slower acceleration. There are undoubtedly many ways of reading this divergence between the acceleration of public spending and the other two components of the system; however, from my perspective, the first logical explanation comes from the fact that the economy, including the public intervention part of it, is not able to keep pace with the monetary explosion. It reflects the inability of the economic system to convert or keep the pace with the excessive monetization of the economic system into real growth of the economy. This inability translates simultaneously into a strong loss of the value of money and thus of its ability to retain its primary function over time.

So, yes, we can definitely affirm that these great economists of the past are rolling over in their graves. The moment we analyze how their theories have been instrumental in justifying the creation of that monster that is public spending and its wife the public debt, it can only cause them rejection. But this is the bitter reality, and in order to keep alive their memory and this theoretical screen of logical consistency, many modern economists arrive to justify this excess of governments, dusting off the old theories by adding an adjective in front of them: "Modern" to give them new validity and vigor.

Another element that characterizes the end of absolute monarchies, which goes hand in hand with the hyperbolic increase in public spending, is war. Wars do not really bring any benefit to anyone and ultimately become a futile expenditure of resources and loss of human lives. This reflection that I am sharing is not under any circumstances a pacifist discourse; I believe that armies, weapons, and the technological evolution of armaments are essential for the development of a country and for its defense, no pacifist utopia here. But if we analyze from the current economic-financial perspective the moment when these modern problems started, we cannot fail to notice that their beginning was the Vietnam War and the end of the Bretton Woods agreements[25] . When we analyze the end of the European absolute monarchies, these were also accompanied by a hyperbolic increase in public spending accompanied by wars. Here we have the elements that triggered the end of these monarchies or empires.

In order to free the world from the Nazi horror, the war that was unleashed worldwide was unfortunately necessary. Regarding the end of the Bretton Woods agreements, it is not correct to blame only the monetary policy taken by the United States but also the hostilities of the other nations regarding the boundaries imposed upon them. In my opinion, Western Europeans should be more grateful to this country. If we think about it, those who remained in the eastern part of the world were left with another unpleasant dictatorship. In the West we have had the best roof in a neighborhood of broken roofs, that is the reality and there is no reason to forget it. The countries and economies involved in the post-World War II recovery should also be grateful to the United States for the help provided in recovering their nations. Without the United States, the process would have been longer and more painful. Although Western countries have their imperfections and can be described as capitalist oligarchies dressed as armless democracies, they are certainly better than many totalitarian regimes that still exist around the world today.

4.7 The kraken monster[26]

Many economists believe that the Bretton Woods agreements and the anchoring of the dollar to gold by means of a physical exchange rate and its convertibility had become a limit to global economic development. In part, these considerations are probably also true. But we cannot hide the fact that there was a ruinous war involving the United States—the Vietnam War. That conflict caused the loss of many human lives and at today's values, its cost would be about one trillion dollars[27]. That amount of money in a context of a fixed convertibility of the dollar to gold, obviously caused many problems between the green currency and the reserves of the yellow metal of reference that was becoming scarcer.

With the end of the Bretton Woods agreements and the anchoring of the dollar to the gold, we have therefore witnessed the beginning of the party. It is similar to having a group of alcoholics in a liquor factory with unlimited access to the beverages it produces.

At the same time, it would have been limiting for the politicians of the different countries related to the Bretton Woods agreements, the fact that there was this anchor between the US dollar with gold and the exchange rate of their currencies. We can therefore understand the relief that the same politicians experienced when these agreements ended.

The end of the agreements coincides with the beginning of the party, a party that probably represents the beginning of the end of the current global economic system. Let's analyze in detail what has happened with the exponential increase in public debt and public spending by understanding how these phenomena play out economically.

As I mentioned before, the two great economists would be quite disappointed to see how their economic theories have been instrumentalized for such a bestiality. To give you a good understanding of what has happened, the basic philosophy preferred by most of the world's politicians, no matter what political party they belong to, is the Keynesian one. If we ask ourselves the reason for this preference, the answer is obvious: with the State at the center of economic development we have the perfect justification for the implementation of public policies that demand unconditional access to money or to the magic machine that creates electronic currency.

The perfect marriage between public spending and public debt has been facilitated by the instrumental use of the increase in the money supply through the expansion of the monetary base. This continuous growth of the State and its expenditures under Keynesian logic achieves a perfect theoretical justification for its actions.

4.8 Until there is war there is hope

With the Second World War, mankind should have understood that wars cause death, destruction, loss of wealth, and poverty. Let us not be fooled by the post-war recovery, since wars are always and only harmful to the economy and to human beings. As I have explained, this book is not a pacifist manifesto. I consider it regrettable how some wars in history have been necessary. We would not have been able to free ourselves from Nazism without war; however, it is undeniable that death and destruction are associated with this instrument.

Analyzing from this point of view, we could affirm that, theoretically, if the world had had instead of wars a good economic management and diplomatic resolution of conflicts, it could have achieved better development of society; however, this was not the case. If we analyze it well, the post-World War II world economies have been driven by wars. This consideration has no political connotation either. On any side of the political spectrum, wars have been the engine of society.

If we associate war with its main industry, the war industry, we can observe that the latter is arguably the most flourishing industry of the last century, whether we analyze it from a Western point of view or from an Eastern or Asian point of view.

After the devastation left by World War II, we have witnessed disastrous wars in Korea, Vietnam, and a myriad micro-conflicts and coups d'état in underdeveloped countries, followed by wars in Afghanistan, Iraq, the Middle East, Eastern Europe, etc.

Finally, the Western world managed to take many steps forward against the subculture of racism, and an African American president was elected in the United States, and the progressive Swedish Nobel Academy immediately awarded him a Nobel Peace Prize. Despite not yet engaging in any pacifist politics worldwide, he was awarded the Nobel Peace Prize.

President Obama, winner of the Nobel Peace Prize, and acclaimed by progressive leftists around the world during his eight years in office, did not bring about the much sought-after peace. On the contrary, there have been significant numbers of coups d'état in the Middle East, the Arab Springs that in many cases turned into desolate Arab winters, the rise of Isis, and finally the destruction of countries such as Iraq and Syria. The responsibility for these war conflicts cannot be attributed to the U.S. presidency; however, they have occurred under the gaze of a nice Nobel Prize awarded by an institution that has probably lost touch with reality. Although, as I have explained, the responsibility for these conflicts is not under any circumstance directly attributable to the presidency of this country. I consider that we have not seen from that administration a sufficiently consistent effort to end the wars, which was the initial expectation when the Nobel Prize was awarded. I repeat, this book is not intended to be a pacifist program, we simply must be objective and realistic in analyzing the world we live in, simply in order to recognize the reality of the facts. Wars, therefore, have accompanied us and continue to accompany us throughout history, together with the war industry and with the latent power of destruction that is the nuclear arsenal, which is already in the hands of many countries, and of which a small fraction has the potential to destroy all life on the planet.

Finally, if we analyze the issue of war, there are some elements that are important to understand in their complexity in order to situate this phenomenon within everyday life.

War, rather than an instrument that is meant to liberate peoples or restore legality in vast areas of the planet, has been an instrument for a new distribution of natural resources, snagging them from the hands of their legitimate owners. This is due to the fact that many wars are basically aimed at obtaining the natural resources that economies require for growth and consolidation.

Another aspect of war is, to a certain extent, a socialist or communist concept of redistribution of wealth. While wars lead to the destruction of wealth and patrimony, they also facilitate the creation of new wealth and patrimony.

Finally, we come to the point of cataloguing war for what it really is, beyond the instrument of death and destruction that we know it to be. Wars have become economic instruments of governments and allied nations in conflicts. As economic instruments, they are the maximum generators of public spending, public debt, and expansion of the monetary base that sustains the system.

We can affirm, therefore, that wars are an important inflationary instrument in the hands of governments. Obviously, politicians will never admit this aspect of armed conflicts, but if they think about it, in reality they end up being only an economic instrument that destroys wealth through the inflation and public debt that they cause. This is not new in history, as wars have also been the beginning of the end of absolute monarchy and the beginning of the end of many of the political systems of past societies.

4.9 How war becomes the perfect excuse

The post-pandemic inflationary spiral has been justified by many politicians and economists in a highly creative manner, where they have shown the limits of their capacity for self-criticism and analysis. Throughout 2022, the war between Russia and Ukraine has become a common justification given by politicians and economists, and spread by mass media, particularly in Europe. Many politicians and their economist companions in fact used this brutal conflict as the explaining factor that triggered inflation. Thus, we can see once again, how war is the perfect scapegoat, to fantastically solve problems for which an honest and sincere explanation should be given. The famous thought that says: until there is war there is hope, has never been more current than now. I say this sarcastically since this terrible conflict has provided the perfect justification to confuse voters, making them believe in an apparently logical reality. This conflict is in no way the justification for the post-pandemic inflationary crisis. Thus, it turns out once again that a war is the perfect justification for any occasion.

Politicians have certainly been experts in the art of offloading their own responsibilities onto scapegoats, using logical excuses at times, but always taking advantage of the people's lack of attention to economic and global order problems. At the moment the war between Russia and Ukraine started, the Western countries punished Russia with many economic sanctions and started to decrease the purchase of Russian oil and gas in retaliation to the invasion by supporting the Ukrainian position. Precisely when the availability of fossil fuels became scarcer, in view of the European winter, the prices of these raw materials soared; however, two basic considerations need to be made. The first is very simple and refers to the acceleration of inflation that predated the war; in other words, when the war started, we were already in inflation. The second answer relates to the objective analysis of how Western countries took sides with Ukraine by imposing sanctions on Russia. The shortage of raw materials has been a consequence of the sanctions and the actions taken by the governments of the European Union and its NATO allies[28]. The war alone was not, therefore, the direct reason for the increase in energy prices, as these are the result of the positions taken by the European Union in the war conflict. With these lines I am not justifying the war under any circumstances, nor the invasion of another state. I simply believe it is better that the facts be analyzed correctly, and not using pretexts to justify the mismanagement of the economic policy prior to the events in question.

4.10 Background interpretation of economic theories

Certainly, let's clarify it once and for all, economics is not an exact and natural science. It is a social science of humanistic nature that tries to give explanations related to society, its evolution and its interrelationships using also mathematical models. These mathematical models are an instrument used by many economists mainly because they give credibility to ideas and also help in the synthesis of complex phenomena, by means of visually simpler and symbolic expressions. At the same time, the strong underlying limitation of these models is that if they were applicable as formulated, everything would be simpler. This is clearly not the case and their explanatory function, instead of proving the hypothesis exactly, is reduced to logical explanations of a qualitative type. Consequently, many confuse economics as one of the natural exact sciences, which it is not. It is rather a humbler social science.

In a previous chapter, I emphasized the concept of contaminations and why these affect the result of any formula we use. This underscores the fact that chaos theory has a valid basis of application, within a chaotic and perfect universe, but within a contaminated social universe it is not applicable at all.

There is also one last factor that I would like to talk about briefly, which is the psychological factor. I would like to dedicate a few lines to explain the importance of this factor in the daily actions of human beings and the countries and governments they lead, respectively, because this is the element that interacts at a human relation level and finally allows the system to function. Talking about the psychological issue can be extremely difficult and it is like walking in quicksand, for the simple reason that many of the factors that contribute to the disorders of our society are the result of psychological explanations; that is, psychology leads finally to these same phenomena. In other words, psychology is likely the biggest culprit in the polluting factors that impact the calculation of our villain, which is inflation. As an example to enlighten the paradox, think of an economist who is very clear that some governmental decisions go absolutely against the common welfare, but he does not oppose this perspective—it's a move to ensure he does not lose his job. Then the existential force of living is stronger than the force of ideas. This is not true in all cases, because there have been very honorable people throughout history who have sacrificed themselves for their ideas. Unfortunately, most of us are not heroes, and as a result, we face certain consequences. And with this reflection, I end my psychological analysis, hoping that I have contributed a grain of sand to the sea of understanding that we need to comprehend the phenomena under discussion.

If we analyze the three most emblematic schools of economic thought, on which many nations have based their monetary and economic policies - classical economic theory, Keynesian economic theory and finally Milton Friedman's monetary theory - there is a common thread that unites the three theories. This common factor is a relatively logical and straightforward explanation of the economic world and its factors. However, it is important to note that describing a phenomenon qualitatively is not equivalent to explaining it quantitatively in exact mathematical formulas. Understanding these theories is crucial for comprehending the impacts of economic actions implemented by governments on the actual economy, real finances, and ultimately, the day-to-day lives of their citizens. I believe that governments support, for psychologically understandable political reasons, their officials' belief in Keynesian theory by using monetary policy actions instrumentally in order to access more resources without worrying about the consequences on the economic prosperity of their citizens. There are "**modern**" currents of thought, as I have mentioned previously, that only want to come up with a greater justification for the indiscriminate use of public spending and monetary expansion for economic sustainability. In my opinion, these theories are used as simple justifications without any basis and without any scientific rigor or substantive basis for their use. Therefore, I do not want to spend much time analyzing them, only a few lines to demonstrate the absurdity on which they are based.

Let's consider the **Modern Monetary Theory**, which in extreme synthesis says that public spending is not directly related to inflation. A country has to solve its employment problem by means of unlimited public investment, and this, according to this theory, would not be an inflationary action. Here a spontaneous question arises: *What is the use of taxes, if the debts of a government and its interests can simply be paid with the issue of new money.* Moreover, there is a continuous issue of new money for the creation of new works. The answer this theory gives is that taxes control inflation because the problem does not lie in government spending but rather in the spending of families, which, according to this outlandish economic theory, are probably not rational or at least are much less rational than the government. Therefore, families could potentially be identified as a source of inflation. This theory simply has no real logical foundation, because the indiscriminate increase in government spending, even when families are taxed in a controlled environment, leads to uncontrolled inflation, because it increases the amount of money in people's pockets anyway, which they spend on goods and services.

If we analyze the limits of theories, they pose two types of problems. The first is the contextualization of the theory in the period in which they were written. The second is to not understand these economic theories as explanations of phenomena and potential prescriptions, but as medicines of free use and without limits of supply.

If you think about it, this is the opposite of what the two great economists of the past would have wanted to leave us as a future legacy for a better life and management of nations.

4.11 Historical contextualization

If we analyze the great economic theories in the perspective of their historical context, we can find many answers about the logic and background philosophy with which they were developed.

We'll begin with classical economic theory, which emerged during the early stages of modern industrialization, in the second half of the 1700s. This period began with the abandonment of feudal economic models and the development of commercial economic models between continents and the changes brought about by the Industrial Revolution. England was the homeland of trade with the colonies between continents and of the Industrial Revolution with the excessive growth of urban areas. This was the fertile ground on which the concepts of classical economic theory were developed. Its philosophical basis is centered on the free market and its ability to achieve a perfect equilibrium between the forces of demand and supply, thanks to an invisible force that guides it wisely. It considers any government intervention as an interference with the free development of the market. If we reflect on this historical context and the emerging economies of that time, we can observe how classical economic theory aligns well with this structural framework.

Keynes and his school of thought arrived many decades later, when the new industrial societies were already mature, a terrible and destructive war (i.e. World War I) had impoverished several continents, and society was in crisis. Here comes the Great Depression of the 1930s, which lasted for many years, opening the doors to another war, more violent than the first (World War II). This economic depression left millions of citizens not only in the United States, but around the world without work and without prospects. What a fertile ground for a thought that carried the idea of a welfare government, capable of reactivating the economy, thanks to its immense wisdom and restoring economic and social justice, through fiscal policies that expand public spending! Finally, contrary to classical theory, Keynesian theory sees the need for public intervention in the economy as the force capable of balancing the market, reducing unemployment, and maximizing production, correcting the inefficiencies of a system of pure capitalism that classical theory advocated.

The monetary theory of inflation developed at the moment when the United States abandoned the fixed convertibility of the dollar with gold. This is a historical moment when the party had begun, the bar was open, access to liquor was free, and the economies were all drunk. They had gone through the 1970s, through times of stagflation and high inflation, caused by the flood of easy money created out of thin air without any logical basis. This is the fertile ground for someone who was finally able to understand how the use of the monetary base in an excessive and unlimited way constituted a totally inflationary and economy-destroying factor. The monetary theory of inflation correctly identifies the risks of introducing money into the economy and the dangers at the inflationary level. It was a product of its time and of the events that were occurring.

When we look at the present day, as we analyze some new economic trends, we see that these are finally taking shape strangely from the need of governments to justify their strong interventionist policy, in terms of public spending and monetary policies. Here we have the "Modern Monetary Theory", which says that the government can have a free bar in the expansion of the monetary base through the creation of money, to finance its public spending policies. The public spending and the creation of a monetary base in this particular moment of history would be actions that do not influence inflation. According to this fanciful theory, inflation control would be achieved through taxation. The government would be wise in its policy of money creation and public spending, and at the same time increasing taxes on citizens (who probably would not be so wise) and thus efficiently control inflation. Therefore, we should be happy to have to pay a lot of taxes, because the government will be able to control inflation thanks to these wealth transfers to the voracious machine of the government. A bit sad in my opinion. The theories of the past possess a logical coherence and exhibit a common thread within the historical framework in which they were developed, while this modern monetary theory of inflation represents a set of somewhat bizarre ideas because it has, in my view, the sole merit of arriving at a justification for the excessive spending of governments and the excessive increase of the monetary base, which, after all, is not a merit.

Therefore, through these examples, we can understand that economic theories do not always represent revolutionary discoveries, because they are often guided by an underlying logic that is related to the moment in which they were conceived. In other words, at the historical moment of their formulation, they made sense and represented an alignment to the times.

4.12 The key to understanding the arcane

We have seen that being able to explain and demonstrate by means of a formula the economic phenomena and in particular inflation, is not an easy exercise. Many economists have tried to give consistency in their explanations of inflation. More than just a numerical explanation and demonstration, we have to focus on the search for conceptual elements that allow us to understand the phenomenon from a qualitative logical point of view. In this respect, the observation of the New Keynesian economists on the rigidity of wages and prices within the system is intriguing. In fact, we have seen that we are not in a perfect and aseptic laboratory, where the different variables move in the expected way and to the expected extent. This concept of rigidity, therefore, comes to confirm this reflection.

The modern monetary theory, when analyzed correctly, draws many of its basic conclusions from the observation of reality, which presents strong government intervention in public spending, an increase in public debt, the consequent increase in the money supply of the system, and a relative inflationary rigidity. With these words, I do not absolutely justify this theory, although I understand some observations and logical conclusions of the current reality. Let's remember that there are several contrasting forces in the market: Globalization, demographic evolution and productivity are strong deflationary elements that have undoubtedly contributed to a semblance of controlled inflation in recent decades and have balanced the misalignments of the explosion of the systemic monetary base. The key to understanding current phenomena within the demographic reality in which Western societies live is ultimately the measurement of inflation and its accurate numerical conceptualization. This can radically change the perspectives of analysis.

5 The money production machine

5.1 Control of money supply

To understand how central banks and governments come to control the money supply, we need to review some concepts: the process of money creation, the composition of the monetary base, and the actions that central banks implement to control its supply.

Let's now analyze the processes by which governments, through the assistance of their central banks, create money. To understand how money is created, the analysis must be subdivided into two macro-categories: first, the physical money produced directly by the state through its printing press or its mint, where its coins are melted down. The central bank can be delegated by the government to print banknotes and melt legal tender coins, which constitute the monetary base of a country. Again, as previously explained, these activities are proper to the State printing press and the State foundry. This physical money represents a small part of the total money in circulation of the system, between 3% and 10%. Therefore, it is accurate to state that normally, the majority of a state's money supply is not in the form of physical currency.

The second form of money creation is electronic money, which is generated through the activity of central banks and a country's network of commercial banks. When a customer deposits his bills and coins in a bank, the bank replaces this physical money with electronic money, which represents electronic bank money. When a customer withdraws money from the bank in cash, they receive physical money from the central bank and decrease the corresponding amount in electronic form.

5.2 Fractional reserve banking

Commercial banks work under the concept of fractional reserves of deposits. I will try to explain the basis of this concept, which is so important at the monetary and banking level. Let's take a simple example to clarify this mechanism, where the citizens of a small mountain village deposit their salaries or the money they receive for the businesses they run in the offices of the village bank. The citizens of the village will not need to withdraw their deposited money all at once. Consequently, the bank does not need to keep the entirety of the deposits in liquid form, as only a small portion is expected to be withdrawn by its customers.

A part of the money received in deposit will be kept in liquid reserve, to meet the obligations of those who need to withdraw cash, and the other part will be used to grant loans to other citizens of the town who need it for their activities, or businesses.

A typical deposit of one of the citizens of that village will be split in two parts, a small part of this amount will be kept in legal reserves, but most of it (the second part) will be used by the bank to grant other loans. Normally, the banking rules define what the cash ratio is, which represents the fraction of deposit money that is not borrowed and kept in the banks' cash reserves. In other words, the cash ratio is normally set by the central bank, and in some cases, the banks themselves may require by internal statutes a higher percentage than that imposed by the country's banking rules. This system allows us to understand how electronic money is made, which in substance represents much of the money in circulation in an economy, and in a country.

5.2.1 Bank multiplier

Understanding the working mechanism of fractional reserve banking allows us to understand how easily money can be created in an economy. Thanks to its functioning, this system ultimately expands the amount of money in circulation that is available to economic players. This expansion of money is achieved through the concept of the bank multiplier. Let's analyze, therefore, the relationship between the reserve requirement or cash ratio and this multiplier factor.

Normally there is an inverse relationship between the cash ratio and the bank multiplier: the higher the cash ratio is, the lower the bank multiplier will be. Conversely for a lower the cash ratio will correspond a higher bank multiplier.

Banking multiplier formula:

- $M = 1/W$
- $MM = BM \times M$

where M represents the bank multiplier, W the cash ratio, MM money supply, and BM monetary base.

Let's examine how this process works with a practical example. Imagine a client who deposits 1000 dollars. The bank is required to keep a certain percentage of this amount as reserves (known as the cash ratio), while the remaining portion can be utilized by the bank to extend new loans. The reserve percentage is supposed to be used to meet the demand for money by the depositors that need a withdrawal. In this respect, it must be considered that the percentage of mandatory reserves varies from country to country, and in some cases the reserve percentage can reach close to zero, which would make the theoretical capacity of money production practically infinite. Let's assume that these reserves are 10%. This implies that the Bank has $100 in reserves and that it can use $900 for other bank lending operations. These $900 of borrowed money return to the banking circuit, which implies that they will be deposited again because citizens do not usually carry their bills or coins in their pockets. The result of this operation is that most of the money is converted into electronic money, created by commercial banks. Once that money returns to the banking circuit, 10% will go into reserve and the remaining 90% can be used by the Bank as I explained above. From a simple deposit of 1000 dollars in the system, 10000 dollars are finally produced thanks to the bank multiplier, which in the case of the example is equivalent to 10 (1/10%).

Now, what is the key element that enables the creation of money?

If you think about it, the key element is the granting of new debts in the market by the Bank to its customers; in other words, debts play a crucial role in the creation of money. If we analyze this from an accounting point of view, from a simple deposit in the balance sheet of a Bank two accounts are generated: the first one in the assets of the money received, and the other one in the liabilities that represent the obligation of the Bank to return the money to the client who deposited the money. Now analyze the case of the loan that the Bank grants to a client. From an accounting point of view, in the assets the Bank will have a credit to the client to whom it has lent the money. As a result, it can be summarized that the process of money creation by banks represents an increase in their balance sheets.

5.3 Money generated by central banks

Starting in 2008, central banks began to intervene more actively in increasing the monetary base; in other words, they increased the money in circulation in the system. As explained above, this process has been exponentially increasing the monetary base during the pandemic era, but, let's ask ourselves, how does the Central Bank generate new money?

The way the Central Bank generates money is through the acquisition of assets, which occurs by buying securities in the market that increase its assets in exchange for money that is produced in electronic form. Understanding this process is crucial to comprehend the precariousness of the monetary bubble in which we are floating, which represents a river of money produced by a system that has lost its shame in the multiplication of new electronic money.

Let's imagine now, this electronic money that the Central Bank has produced out of nothing by buying securities, where is it going to end up? Do you already know the answer? This electronic money ends up in the banking circuit, but let's review: What happens to the money that arrives in the banking circuit through the banking multiplier with the fractional system with which commercial banks work worldwide? **Billions of dollars of the central banks' money creation end up becoming astronomical figures after they have gone through the different steps of this system of magic money production out of thin air.**

We should ask ourselves a single fundamental question: Did the economy grow enough to justify so much money in circulation?

All the processes by which central banks acquire new assets are the basis of new money production. Out of nothing, as I have explained, new money is being created.

This happens not only with the operations of injecting money into the economy, known as "Quantitative Easing", but the permanent facilities that can be represented by lending to banks in the system when they need liquidity. At the same time, it has become very fashionable due to the abundance of securities in the market and so of unused cash in repo operations[29] and reverse repo[30] that can be creators and destroyers of the monetary base.

5.4 The state issues new debt

Typically, when the government issues new debt, part of its subscribers are also the central banks. By acquiring these new bonds, central banks increase the monetary base. With the money that the State receives from the issuance of debt, the State will make its payments and finally, all this liquidity is returned to the banking system. Consequently, this inflow of funds contributes to the expansion of the money supply as it becomes deposited in the banks. From any perspective we examine how the money creation process has been used, representing a systematic way through which the state plays an active role in the economy. The continuous growth of public spending over time, accompanied by a policy of constant increase of public debt, are the main factors causing the increase of the monetary base. A system that feeds itself, that has no limits and that is supported by economic theories that justify this evolution of public spending and public debt.

5.5 Monetary base

The term money supply refers to the total amount of money available in an economy for the purchase of goods and services. Based on this definition, there are several typologies of money aggregation, which depend on its liquidity or availability.

M0 is the money circulating in the economy and is defined as the number of banknotes and coins held by citizens, in addition to the money that banks have in their vaults and deposited in the Central Bank.

M1 is the money circulating in the economy, including M0, and adding the current deposits of citizens, that is, the amounts that citizens have readily available to spend.

M2, includes M1 and adds the existing short-term deposits that citizens have in the financial system, that is, money and its short-term substitutes, accounts that are normally defined with terms of up to one year.

M3, includes M2 and sums all deposits, including longer-term deposits.

M4, includes M3 and adds additional deposits, such as deposits held by foreigners in the country and deposits held by government ministries.

Monetary policies

The monetary policy operates through the control of interest rates; thus, by varying the interest rate, a more or less expansive or restrictive monetary policy can be achieved.

The monetary policy intervenes mainly in the money market. Financial markets can be broadly categorized into the capital market and the money market.

Money markets are based on financial instruments of less than 18 months:

- Money
- Short-term deposits
- Short-terms bonds, 0-18 months
- Time deposits of no more than 18 months

Basically, we are witnessing two types of monetary policies:

- Expansionary monetary policy, where the amount of money in circulation is increased.

- Restrictive monetary policy, where the amount of money in circulation is reduced.

These policies are characterized by a decrease or increase in interest rates.

If we analyze the evolution of interest rates and bond yields over the last fifty years, we notice that we have had an expansive monetary policy for this entire period (Fig. 1).

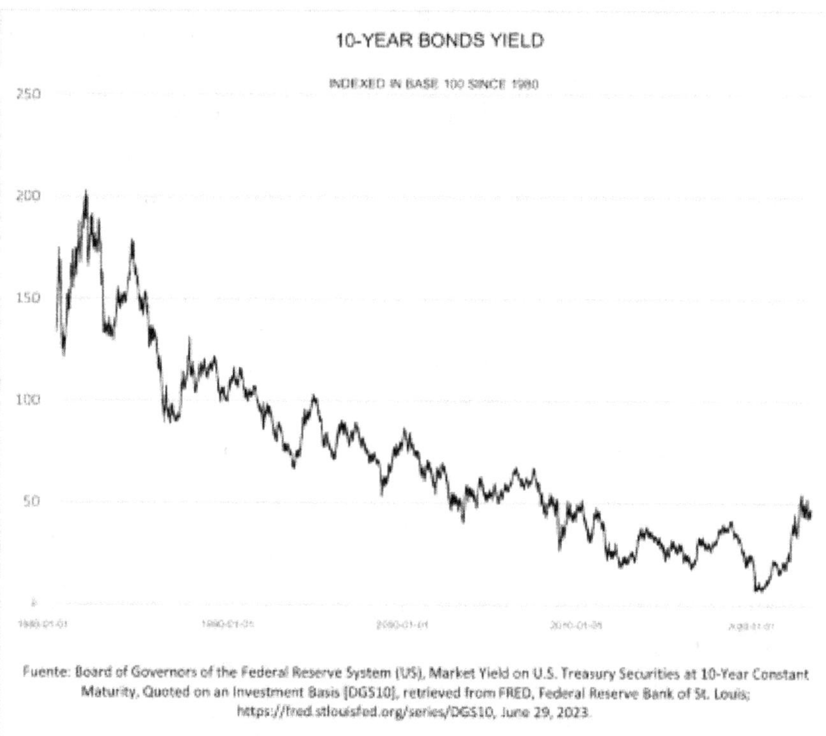

Fuente: Board of Governors of the Federal Reserve System (US), Market Yield on U.S. Treasury Securities at 10-Year Constant Maturity, Quoted on an Investment Basis [DGS10], retrieved from FRED, Federal Reserve Bank of St. Louis; https://fred.stlouisfed.org/series/DGS10, June 29, 2023.

Fig. 1: This graph plots the yield of 10-year U.S. government bonds, indexed to 1980 on base 100. These bonds had a first phase that lasted more than a decade marked by rising interest rates, which coincided with the end of the Bretton Woods agreements (See note 6, Chap. 4). These years were marked by phases of strong stagflation and inflation until the restrictive policies of Paul Volcker as chairman of the FED (1979-1987) allowed the first concrete results in this regard. The second phase runs from around the mid-1980s to the present day and is characterized by a steady and continuous monetary expansion over time, accompanied by a decline in the yield on bonds issued by the U.S. government. This phase at the end of the second decade of the second millennium brought yields to a level equivalent to zero.

At the same time, we need to understand how and if, in an environment of strongly expansionary monetary policy, controlling inflation within normal parameters would have been achievable by using regular instruments?

5.6 Quantitative easings

Central banks purchase government bonds, private company bonds, mortgage-backed securities (MBS[31]) and thereby inject liquidity into the system. The objective of this operation would be at least as a "façade" justification to push economic growth. By analyzing the development of the stock capital markets over the last thirteen or fourteen years in the United States, it is possible to appreciate that this monetary exuberance helped the constant and continuous growth of all indexes. Another aspect to consider would be analyzing the economic evolution in real terms, to be able to determine if it has indeed achieved the declared "façade" objective of helping the economy.

At the same time, this instrument has also been adopted in the European Union by the European Central Bank.

MONETARY POLICY INSTRUMENTS

- Intervention in interest rates.

- Open market operations (mainly repo and reverse repo).

- Permanent facilities.

- Minimum reserve and cash ratio of credit institutions.

- Liquidity injection.

- Extension of the list of accepted financial assets.

- Purchase of public debt and private debt securities, which is Quantitative Easing.

5.7 What is money?

When we talk about money, we often come up against an underlying belief - to me profoundly mistaken, although many economists are in the same line of thought. I am referring to the visualization of money as a simple lubricant that allows the economy to function. Although this definition is partly correct, it does not adequately frame the concept and importance of money clearly enough. In this regard I would like to provide a very simple example: Imagine you are a jeweler, and a young man comes to your store to buy a sparkling diamond ring for his beloved fiancée. Seems normal so far. It would not be that normal if money were the simple lubricant of the economy to function. In this case, you would be making a serious mistake as a jeweler by giving the diamond ring in exchange for a dose of lubricant.

Minimizing the importance of money, in a philosophical conception of it that is not broad enough to be able to describe its functions correctly, is a very serious error that can lead to even more serious mistakes. For example, underestimating the importance of inflation.

The main function of money is to implicitly represent the expression of intrinsic value (i.e., the essential element of money) to fulfill its function correctly in an economic system. Without this implicit intrinsic value, money would become meaningless. Those who underestimate this aspect of money make a big mistake, showing that they don't understand the basic function and the essential purpose for which money exists.

Starting from the main function of money, which is the representation of its intrinsic value, two additional functions complete the qualification of money as we know it. The first function is to serve as a measuring unit for goods, which allows, quite simply, to set prices to carry out exchanges of goods and services. The second function of money is to act as a lubricant that facilitates the exchange of goods and services between individuals, entities, and economic operators around the world.

It is important to correctly define the intrinsic function of money because if we make the basic mistake of conceptualizing it as a simple means of exchange, we lose sight of its essence. What sense would it make to exchange goods and services for something that is worthless and is only a simple representation of a unit of exchange? The answer makes no sense at all. However, central banks have been trivializing the essence of money itself by issuing money to subsidize uncontrolled public spending. The moment you understand this simple definition of money, you will quickly realize the importance of the production of inflation, which gradually erodes the inherent value of money, destroying its main characteristic.

5.8 The value of money

The modern monetary theory, like many economic theories, is a child of its time; therefore, it offers a theoretical justification for the indiscriminate use of monetary mechanisms by different countries to expand public spending, increase public debt, and ultimately enable the unlimited creation of money. When we examine the concepts of this theory within a logic of the value of money, we can easily demonstrate how the only academic value this theory has is that of being an end for itself. It serves as a simple theoretical chess game to justify the current world economic and monetary situation.

Events do not occur suddenly, and at the economic level, we have had different economic theories. It all began with the classical theory forged by Adam Smith, to conclude in our days with the modern monetary theory intertwined with each other. By this aspect, I am referring to the initial interpretation given by these theories and their use over time, depending on the requirements of the political-economic system to justify its actions. With this aspect, what we observe is an instrumental use of economic theories that are adapted to find a theoretical-justifying basis for the actions of our rulers. In this way, we can affirm that theories have served as instrumental tools for achieving the basic objectives of politics. The concepts developed by Keynes and Friedman have been exploited for decades to develop the modern monetary theory. To finally find a suitable justification for the actions of expanding the monetary base indiscriminately without end, the largest economies on the planet now are taking advantage of this new theory (the modern monetary theory).

What determines the value of an asset? This is the basic question to which we should give an answer. Certainly, the value of a good is undeniably influenced by both its scarcity and the costs associated with its production. So, the two basic elements that determine the value of a good are its scarcity and the difficulty in producing it, which is expressed through the associated production costs. These two elements go hand in hand with the desire of those who want to own that good, to have it in their possession. Imagine, therefore, a reality, where if we had no limit to the production of money - since we are talking largely about electronic money, which has a really low production cost - how much could this good ultimately be worth? In these conditions, where there are infinite possibilities in the creation of a good with a production cost practically close to zero, the only element that could give a certain value to it would be the desire of its users to own it. But relatively to this last aspect, owning something of which we have infinite availability, and which has no associated cost in its production, is similar to placing value on the air we breathe, which we all own to some extent without having to pay for it, so far.

The ability to create an unlimited amount of money undermines the essence of money itself since it destroys its very function, that is, to hold and maintain value through time. It is therefore easy to understand how the theories that try to justify the production of money by a State for investment in unlimited public expenditure, if applied to their extreme consequences, would lead to the destruction of the monetary economic system. A very clear example of this situation can be found in countries characterized by hyperinflation, such as Venezuela (Fig. 2).

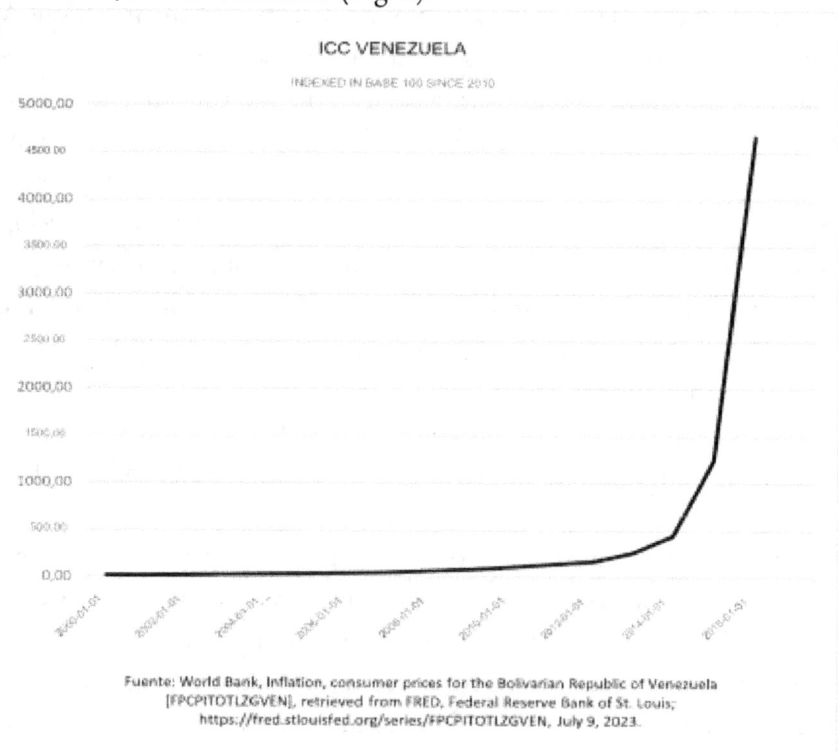

Fuente: World Bank, Inflation, consumer prices for the Bolivarian Republic of Venezuela [FPCPITOTLZGVEN], retrieved from FRED, Federal Reserve Bank of St. Louis; https://fred.stlouisfed.org/series/FPCPITOTLZGVEN, July 9, 2023.

Fig. 2: Graph showing Venezuelan inflation indexed in base 100 as of 2010. We can see how a policy of monetary expansion made to create money out of nothing, leads in a few years to the loss of the total value of a currency. In almost 6 years it goes from an index of 100 to 5000, which means that the money lost practically all its value.

5.9 In a world in reverse

If we were to take as an example an employee who gradually starts stealing money in the place where he works, the process by which these acts would occur would be through means of some repetitive patterns. A description of what could happen in this regard would be that this employee, at the beginning, would gradually take money or insignificant resources from the company, and then, as time goes by, escalate the audacity of his actions without fear of consequences. This same employee would take value from small actions to the point of stealing larger sums of money and more and more goods from the workplace. In this process, we observe that the uncommitted employee is gaining security and confidence in performing repressible unacceptable behaviors instead of improving his work efficiency, taking home or into his pocket goods or money from the company that does not really belong to him. This process of increasing the security with which these dishonest employees take resources that do not belong to them is in some cases a fast process, in other cases slower, but it always takes time for them to become more and more uninhibited in these actions.

As in the previous example, the mortgage crisis of 2007-2010, known as the "subprime" crisis[32], marked an important global difference from the past worldwide, this being the crucial moment in which the different central banks of the world lost their modesty in the creation and injection of money into the system. The solution to face this crisis, instead of taking the right path, which would have been a deep restructuring of the monetary and financial system of the different countries with stricter regulations for banks was another one. At the end of the day, we were faced with the perfect excuse, which refers to the concept of "too big to fail" and therefore every effort was needed to avoid bankruptcy. Putting past events into perspective, I believe that this was a significant missed opportunity for a new structural and functional approach to the monetary system at the level of industrialized countries and the global level. The correct cure was another, but unfortunately, to follow the narrative line of this book, it was the wrong medicine that was distributed to the patient. To make a parallel to the world of addictions, it would be like recommending to someone who wants to quit smoking cigarettes, a prescription to change the brand of cigarettes to one that has more nicotine. As in the world of addictions, the financial system addicted to the creation of easy electronic money, instead of looking inside itself trying to understand the crisis that had been generated by the mortgage bubble, decided to increase the dose of its addiction and the cure was to inject more electronic money and increase the monetary base within the system. Looking at it in perspective, I repeat, it was a great lost opportunity to put the house in order. However, putting the house in order would have implied a lot of work and sacrifice, things that are certainly not in the interest of our politicians, who, on the contrary, prefer "prêt à porter" easy solutions[33]. If we analyze the essential function of money, which goes beyond its use as a means of exchange of goods and services, but in its philosophical condition is necessary and sufficient to justify the reason for its existence, which is to be a store of value, it is clear how the representation of implicit value has been lost through the policies of central banks. When central banks introduce money into the economy without any justification and in an uncontrolled manner, and only as a palliative for an economic-financial situation that requires a profound restructuring of the monetary system, they are paradoxically undermining its essential function. If we take away the essential function of money, which is to represent value, trivializing it to something that no longer has value, it would only be an expression of a nominal façade value. When governments, through central banks, began to flood the economy with banknotes, the implicit value of the banknotes was destroyed, and an irreversible crisis of the monetary system began (Fig. 3).

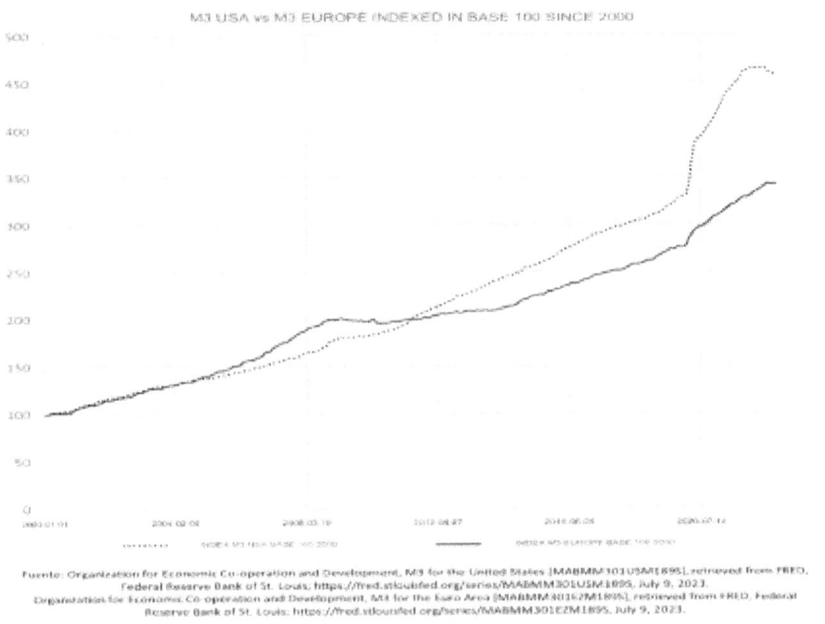

Fig. 3: Comparison chart of the monetary base indicator M3 for Europe and the United States, indexing both values in base 100 as of the year 2000. As can be seen, the amount of money in the economy for the eurozone increases 3 times, while for the dollar zone, it increases 4.5 times, the index number for the euro in the year 2022 being close to 300, while for the dollar it is above 450. Concerning this graph, we have several considerations to make: the first one is related to the important increase of money in the pandemic period, and the second consideration shows how the American monetary authority has been more aggressive in the creation of money concerning the European economic authority. However, for both zones, we have to observe that the money created is above the real needs of the economy, which could indicate that the political-administrative system uses the creation of debt to subsidize the public expenditures. If we look at the real economies of the United States as well as Europe in the same period, they do not increase at the same pace of the money supply. A similar consideration is seen when analyzing the middle class, which has actually been impoverished.

5.10 Cryptocurrencies

Cryptocurrencies have seen over true last 15 years the conditions for their birth and consolidation in the world financial system. As the first element of the flourishing of this new monetary expression, we have without a doubt the abundance of money available within the economic system. So much money in circulation must eventually find utility within the system. One such use is undoubtedly in the cryptocurrency and digital asset sector. Cryptocurrencies are in extreme synthesis electronic money backed by a complex cryptographic code. Within this logic, they can serve as an exchange for goods and services. A pizza maker can trade pizzas for digital money that he will use to buy flour, salt, cheese, and tomatoes. As you can see from this example, if different economic actors agree to use a cryptographic or electronic currency for their exchanges, the exchange system can function effectively. Doesn't it seem a bit dangerous for the current monetary economic system?

Bitcoin coincidentally saw its birth at the time of the subprime banking crisis. What more opportune time than a time when the world's central banks had removed any inhibitions to printing banknotes and creating money from nothing, to create a cryptocurrency that had a limited supply of units in circulation? This particular cryptocurrency has the unique feature of having a limited number of units available for issuance programmed into the market. But only thanks to the pandemic and the other strong injections of money and consequent monetary mass in the system, its quotations came to inflate exponentially, becoming worth close to 70000 USD per piece. If we analyze the totality of cryptocurrencies, we can count only in Yahoo Finance around 10000 of them, of which the vast majority are probably destined to be worth nothing or are no longer worth anything. Some of them, however, will have a future and a place in an economy that has an excess of money in circulation not backed by real and steady economic growth. What has made Bitcoin particularly interesting for investors is the maximum number of these cryptocurrencies that will be able to come into circulation. If we compare it to traditional currencies, we can easily understand the underlying philosophical difference.

Nowadays, the world of cryptocurrencies mostly represents a monetary system that has no boundaries or limits. It has surpassed any kind of restraint in creating new units. The basic dilemma which we should address is whether a cryptographic code has or represents any value at all because it is simply a unique and complex number. For many, some of these currencies represent digital property; therefore, if you own an apartment in Madrid and decide to move to Buenos Aires, it will be very difficult to take your home on the plane to the other city. On the contrary, you will be able to go anywhere in the world or the universe with the digital properties that you own. However, in my opinion, the basic dilemma remains without a clear and precise answer: Does a complex cryptographic code ultimately hold any intrinsic value? Or is it simply an escape valve for a monetary illusion?

If we analyze many of the bankruptcies that have occurred around the crypto world, I think it confirms a possible hypothesis that these currencies do not represent any real value and therefore are not the solution as alternative currencies to fiat currencies in the system. The case of FTX and their created token is self-evident.

5.11 The crossed arms

Certainly, the governments and the main monetary authorities will not keep their arms crossed. The system of public spending, public debt, and fiscal policy is strictly related to the currency of the State, be it dollars, euros, or Argentine pesos. I find it very challenging for the financial authorities of various countries to accept the dissonance of another system of payments and exchanges outside their control; they would simply lose all their power. On the other hand, I believe that the monetary authorities of the different countries find the possibility of creating digital currency extremely interesting. Let's imagine that a person addicted to alcohol would find a miraculous and simple way to create the liquor of his preference, just by using a magic wand. This addict would believe he had been miraculously catapulted to paradise thanks to the mysteries of the universe's spacetime. Now then, our brave political and monetary authorities would find the idea of being able to count on digital currency extremely attractive, as it would make it much easier for them to collect taxes, expand the monetary base in circulation, and finally achieve greater control of the population and its expenses. The answer is that, as time goes on, it is likely that we will have numerous digital currencies in use, which might slowly replace traditional money.

The basic dilemma remains unresolved, which is how a currency that loses its value due to its scarcity or the ease of its creation can fulfill its fundamental function, which is to maintain its value over time. To provide an answer to this dilemma, we will have to analyze the dollar's loss of value over the decades, as well as the evolution of the costs of the main financial assets and the evolution of non-financial assets available to investors.

5.12 An irreparably ill system

Is the current global monetary system. It would be a mistake to concentrate and focus our analysis only on the US dollar, even though it is the main "FIAT" currency[34] in circulation globally. The reality of things is that all currencies have some kind of relationship, and when we can see an increase in the monetary base at the US dollar level, we are most likely to see an increase in the monetary base also at the Euro or other currencies level. There is a certain level of equilibrium between different currencies, a certain level of balance, which is reflected in the evolution of their exchange rates, and which can vary over time. However, when these fluctuations are too sudden, they can have significant economic consequences. The continuous injection of money into the economy is a worldwide reality observed throughout the different fiat currencies. Some of these have probably been more virtuous than others. The economic fundamentals of some economies have justified in some ways more than others the creation of money, but the common feature of the fiat currency system is the ability of governments to be able to print and create new units of currency at the stroke of a computer key.

The advent of digital currency will undoubtedly help speed up the processes of many governments in these harmful monetary policy processes by making the process simpler and faster. What we still need to observe is how the banking system will develop within a digital fiat money scheme. But we will see how governments will handle this aspect sooner rather than later. Do not worry.

6. Consumer price index "CPI[35] " and its controversies

6.1 Consumer Price Index

Consumer Price Indexes, or CPI for short, are used by statistical institutes to calculate inflation. Gaining a thorough understanding of this indicator is essential to embrace the complexity of inflation. The objective of this indicator, therefore, is to calculate over a given period how average prices vary for consumers and households. Inflation is a change in average prices and does not refer to specific products or services, but to a basket of these. Thus, for example, the increase in oil and its derivatives does not necessarily denote inflation in a country; if they increase by 10% it does not mean that this corresponds to inflation, as it represents only certain products traded and produced in an economy.

This indicator holds particular significance as it is associated with various indexes that define an economy's performance and, ultimately, a country's state of health. Among these, we have the variations of the Gross Domestic Product, which is a crucial indicator also related to inflation for a country's economy. To eliminate the effect of inflation on GDP performance, its nominal value is corrected by a deflator[36] which represents the inflation of the period under analysis. Likewise, the level of inflation is associated with a country's social security expenditures. Therefore, governments will decide how much to increase the amount of social assistance they consider for their citizens in the state budget, depending on the increase in inflation.

In the United States, this indicator specifically pertains to consumers in urban areas, and is divided into two components: CPI-U[37] which represents more than 90% of the consumer spending pattern, and CPI-W[38] more focused on consumers who base their income on urban wages such as clerical workers. This component of the indicator is important because it is more related to social security. Statistical institutes also offer us other indicators more related to the industrial area, such as the "PPI"[39].

The calculation of inflation is, therefore, an average of the changes in prices paid by consumers in urban areas for a basket of products and services. The exact calculation of this average price change is extremely complex - if not impossible - because of the enormous quantity of goods and services exchanged in the market, where finally the basket of goods and services for some individuals does not coincide with the typical basket of another group of individuals.

We are going to analyze the first group of frequent criticisms of the way CPIs are calculated, although, as you will see, in my opinion, they refer to minor elements. As always happens, the seriousness of the problem could be lost if the focus is oriented on minor aspects and details that do not describe the complexity of the situation. It is my impression that perhaps there may not be a real desire to look for the real origins of inflation. However, the only way to face this disastrous phenomenon is by starting on the right path by measuring it correctly. If it is not measured correctly, it is causing an incomplete description of the reality that will never delineate its seriousness, nor will it help us find the necessary solutions to correct it, when possible.

Some limitations to how consumer price indexes are calculated:

GEOGRAPHICAL AREAS. The first limitation refers to the fact that this indicator is calculated in urban areas and not for rural areas; therefore, it is representative of inflation for certain areas of the country, while for others it is not representative. While it is true that most people live in cities, excluding rural areas makes the indicator less reliable and accurate.

There is another criticism regarding SUBSTITUTIVE GOODS, which says that the indicator may overestimate the evolution of the price of some products, not considering cheaper goods that consumers could acquire by substituting those that have become more expensive. In my opinion, this second aspect does not apply, because including a change of products in this case due to an increase in the cost of others would be a way of distorting the data provided by the indicator.

INTRODUCTION OF NEW PRODUCTS. The incorporation of new products is not automatic in the calculation of the CPI; therefore, before a new product is taken into consideration, a certain amount of time passes, which sometimes takes years. This criticism has an objective valid basis, since with globalization the number of products and services available on the market increases significantly every day. However, in my opinion, there is not yet an adequate statistical synthesis or methodology to measure this phenomenon.

QUALITY OF PRODUCTS AND SERVICES. Another criticism is about the difficulty of including the quality of products and services in the calculation of the indicator. The concept of quality and related correctives can be a bit misleading since the evolution of products or services constantly includes those changes. Eliminating the quality effect, contrary to common opinion, would be a form of inflation manipulation. This is because "quality" is mainly a qualitative attribute, and it is an element very difficult if not impossible to measure and therefore translate to quantitative terms. On the contrary, trying to introduce the qualitative effect in the calculation of the indicator may provide us with rather inaccurate data.

INDIVIDUAL VERSUS TYPICAL CONSUMER. The CPI calculation refers to a typical consumer and not to individuals; therefore, it can sometimes be misaligned to relate the evolution of inflation to individual expenditures, as these two spending patterns are sometimes completely different.

6.1.2 Harmonized Consumer Price Index[40]

In the case of the Eurozone, things get a bit more complicated, because many countries are using the same currency; therefore, the European Statistical Office must come up with an indicator that summarizes inflation in the area. This indicator is obviously quite complex, for the simple fact that it must compare realities that are profoundly different from each other, as well as spending patterns that are influenced by important cultural differences between countries.

If we compare the index and its construction, which is done in Europe, with its analogous index in the United States represented by the "CPI", we can see how the weights of the different components change. From this point of view, it is understandable that the differences exist since the indicator needs to be adapted to the specific geographical region of reference.

What must be kept in mind is that the construction of the inflation index for Europe in itself presents many challenges, considering the different countries and the varieties of expenditure typologies associated with different local cultures. By comparing the European indices and the U.S. one, the result could lead to a weak consistency as a quantitative representation of the problem, for different reasons that must be understood.

First, it referred to different goods and services aggregations that are being measured, in other words, the products used are not the same.

The second consideration refers to the observation of data on goods with different relative weights. The costs related to rents and houses in Europe do not coincide with those in the United States, and so many other items.

Thirdly, when comparing the two calculation methodologies, considering the corrections provided by the different statistical institutes (like the geometric mean among many) might not be the same. In this case, an additional variable is added that ultimately detracts from the quality of the comparisons between countries and continents.

Finally, it is easy to visualize that measuring different goods, in different ways, with different weights, would be the same as comparing apples with oranges. In general, that does not give an accurate picture of the phenomenon.

However, we should not underestimate the concept of inflation comparison, because it is still valid to describe its trend. If inflation is increasing on both continents, it means that inflation is increasing as a trend in both areas. Analyzing the absolute values of the numbers on the contrary leads to a loss of homogeneity. In other words, it may not be appropriate to compare inflation by stating that it is 10% in the United States and 8% in Europe.

6.1.3 How it is measured globally

The complexity of inflation and its calculation poses a major challenge at the level of the different countries, as spending patterns change, as well as the typology of products in the reference basket of goods. However, similar guidelines can be found at the level of OECD countries[41] , which can ultimately lead to the same errors of underestimation of the inflationary phenomenon. Since OECD countries are related by trade exchanges among themselves, having similar benchmarks would help to compare data. If the calculation in the same currency and geographical area is extremely complicated, when comparing data between countries the exercise becomes even more difficult and with even less significant numbers. As I have explained before, when comparing Europe with the United States, even if the numbers we get about inflation are not the exact reflection of reality, they have some background importance, as a description of a trend. Finally, their value is squeezed under a trend logic; on the contrary, according to my criteria, the absolute values that compose the index are quite questionable in their accuracy.

Considering the selection of products considered for calculating the index, we should expect that it might include the correct brand and type of cheese. Which is why I have strong doubts about the accuracy of the calculation. At the end of the day, I prefer to focus on major errors rather than getting lost in minor details. This helps by maintaining a better understanding of the problem at hand. To focus on minor details in the end may lead us to lose sight of the complexity of the problem, which is usually the case when talking about inflation.

6.1.4 The PPI indicator

Refers to the measurement of the calculation of price increases or decreases from the point of view of producers or, rather, companies. It measures the inflation that companies face due to the increased cost of production. The difference between the CPIs is that they measure the expenditures of individuals.

The purpose for which the two indicators are used is somewhat different, as PPIs are used to measure the real sales performance of companies, while CPIs are used to make cost-of-living adjustments. Social security uses inflation indicators to intervene in the increase of pensions and miscellaneous benefits through cost-of-living adjustments (the "COLA"[42]). To achieve these adjustments, Social Security relies on CPI data. It's clear that if these data are not accurately represented, the adjustment made will be insufficient to uphold the purchasing power of households.

6.2 Household expenses (Tab.1)

If we analyze how household expenditures are composed, it can be observed that their predominant part is determined by the concept of housing represented by the "shelter costs"[43]. The main component of the expenditure basket is represented by the costs related to the household where one lives. This expenditure indicator is represented by three main components: the first, is the evolution of rents ("Rent of primary residence"[44]); the second is a data equivalent to rent, but for the owners of the house ("Owners' equivalent rent of residence"[45]), and the third represents the expenses incurred while traveling ("Lodging away from home"[46]). Since 1983, the value of the price of houses is not included in the calculation of the "CPI" and has been replaced by the concept of Equivalent rent. The explanation given in those years was that the costs of houses were constituted by two components, one of which is attributable to a rent paid to live in it and the other part would be the representative portion of an investment. The CPIs do not take investment into account.

Table 6. Percent distribution of total annual expenditures by major category for all consumer units, 2018-21

Spending Category	2018	2019	2020	2021
Average annual expenditures	100.0	100.0	100.0	100.0
Food	12.9	13.0	11.9	12.4
Alcoholic beverages	1.0	0.9	0.8	0.8
Housing	32.8	32.8	34.9	33.8
Apparel and services	3.0	3.0	2.3	2.6
Transportation	15.9	17.0	16.0	16.4
Healthcare	8.1	8.2	8.4	8.1
Entertainment	5.3	4.9	4.7	5.3
Personal care products and services	1.3	1.2	1.1	1.2
Reading	0.2	0.1	0.2	0.2
Education	2.3	2.3	2.1	1.8
Tobacco products and smoking supplies	0.6	0.5	0.5	0.5
Miscellaneous	1.6	1.4	1.5	1.5
Cash contributions	3.1	3.2	3.7	3.5
Personal insurance and pensions	11.9	11.4	11.8	11.8

Tab. 1: Source BLS[47] , Table representing the weights given to the different categories of expenditures for the calculation of the CPIs.

The most important expense for many families is the purchase of housing. Now, if we read the explanation given by the "BLS" (See note 13) on the reasons why it was eliminated, it seems to me that it was a decision made with the intervention of several economists and that finally, at the "OECD" level, they share the similar conceptualization of this type of expenditure.

In my opinion, this explanation is not convincing, as it shows a crucial conceptual flaw: How is it possible that the most important household expenditure is not included in the inflation calculation? If such spending was included in the calculation of the consumer price index, the inflation data would be significantly different from what we have been used to seeing in recent decades. Inflation does not look good. Perhaps for someone it would be better if it appears lower than what it really is? To answer this rhetorical question, it seems to me that, rather than wanting to address the inflation problem as such, it has been easier to find ways through which the numbers come out more favorable than the reality.

Reading the justification given by the "BLS" and analyzing it critically in retrospect, it seeks a justification that in my opinion lacks sufficient consistency. By simplifying the concept, we are told that the change was made because it is better. The picture is equally discouraging for many of the other "OECD" countries, where few analysts dare to question the inflation numbers, perhaps because they do not understand the essence of the phenomenon. When analyzing the BLS's response, one might be tempted to think that they are on their own. In conclusion, it is quite disappointing to acknowledge that we are confronted with a barren and desolate outlook.

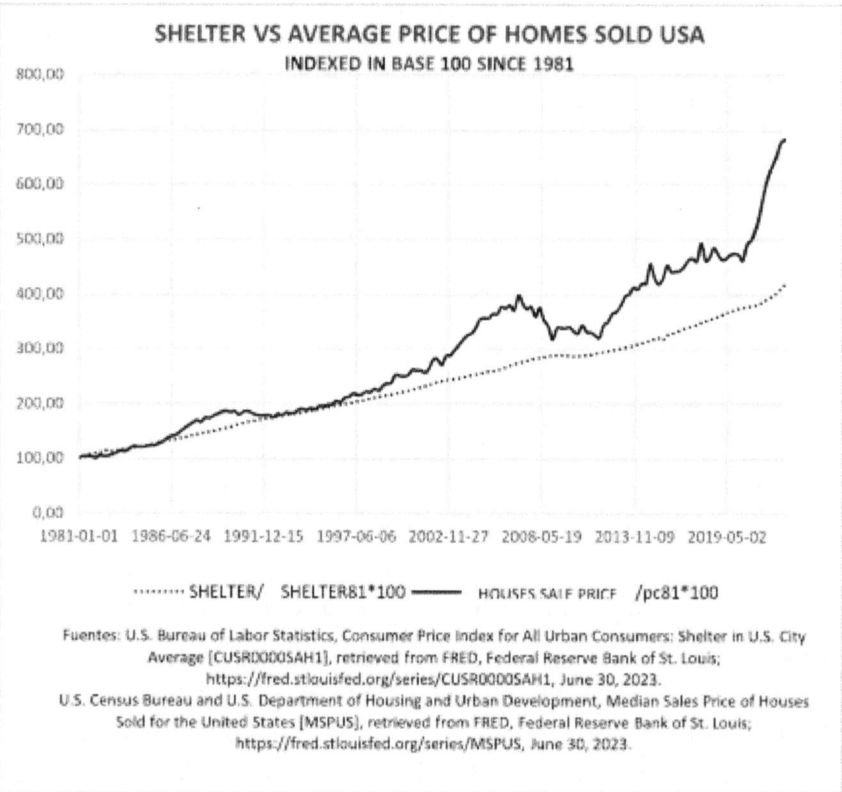

Fig. 1: Comparison chart of the housing cost component included in the CPI calculation, known as "Shelter", vs. the historical evolution of the sale price of houses. Both values are indexed in base 100 from the year 1981. The result shows how the component used in the calculation of the Consumer Price Index underestimates the increase in these costs. The "Shelter" component arrives at an index number of just over 400, when the index number for the increase in housing costs is close to 700.

If we compare the evolution of housing expenditure from 1983 to the present day (Fig. 1), with the cost of housing at the same time, we see that the evolution of expenditure grows at a significantly slower rate than the cost of housing. As I have explained previously, the most important expenditure of families is the purchase of their homes. Analyzing the comparison between the evolution of housing costs and the evolution of the costs represented by the "shelter" index included in the CPIs (Fig. 1), we see that the value of housing has increased significantly. This confirms that thanks to the removal of the cost of housing from the calculation of consumer price indexes, a lower inflation rate was achieved. While it is often considered a mistake to think incorrectly, there are instances where it can guide us towards the correct path.

6.3 COGI versus COLI [48]

One of the first important elements of doubt about how inflation is calculated is the concept of the "Cost of goods index"[49] versus the concept of the "Cost of living index"[50]. Historically, to calculate the price evolution, two equal baskets of goods were considered in each period. The calculation of inflation was thus extrapolated on two baskets of products that did not vary over time, remaining the same (COGI). Over time, this basic concept on which the calculation of price increases was based, evolved towards a constant standard of living over time (COLI). Now, we have seen that with the increase of the monetary base and without restriction in the production of money, inflation has gradually become an endemic uncurable disease in the economy of the nations. To the increase in price, indexes is anchored in social spending, we can therefore understand that an out-of-control inflation implies consequently an out-of-control social spending. This conceptual evolution, although seemingly harmless, implies a radical change in the philosophy with which inflation is conceptualized. Instead of attacking the causes of inflation, that are merely attributable to erroneous monetary and fiscal policies, this new vision began to circulate in the U.S. Congress. The new philosophy embraced by the U.S. Congress is based on the idea that when faced with higher product costs, consumers choose to replace them with cheaper alternatives; for example, if they used to buy Swiss cheese, they would substitute this cheese for a cheaper one, even if they like it less.

This conceptual change implies the evolution of the concept of the two equal product baskets "Cost of Goods Index, COGI" towards a concept of "Cost of Living Index, COLI," which leads to considering product changes in the reference basket due to price increases under a substitution mechanism. Consumers would thus exchange more expensive products for cheaper products. It is therefore important to understand the conceptual difference between these two ways of calculating inflation. According to the explanation provided by the BLS, this change is necessary in order to eliminate calculation elements that could overestimate the level of inflation. In particular, the cost-of-living price analysis considers two important elements of the purchase of products: the first is quality; and the second is substitution. When this change occurred, many economists supported it, while others realized that the new way in which inflation would be calculated would inexorably lead to underestimating it. Someone mischievous might draw a parallel between military conflicts, where ideals sometimes take a backseat to a logic of mere expediency. I wonder if the government-related economists who supported these changes were truly convinced that they were correct.

To understand this conceptual change, let me give you a simple example: imagine two products in a basket of goods, chicken wings and drumsticks. Wings cost 9 USD and drumsticks cost 10 USD; both increase by 10% bringing the cost of the wings to 9.9 and the drumstick to 11 USD. Under a "COLI" cost of living index concept, there is no inflation because consumers will stop buying drumsticks to buy wings, which are slightly cheaper. This substitution logic could lead to a minor decrease in the relative inflation of these two products, creating a paradoxical situation. Another example to understand: in 1970 the purchase of a ROLEX brand watch was accessible to virtually all consumers with an average salary; however, with today's prices a watch of the same brand could probably take about 30% or more of what would be the average salary of a professional for a year. According to the logic of the cost-of-living index, instead of the ROLEX, consumers could purchase a TIMEX or a CASIO, and therefore no price increase would be recorded in these items of analysis of the basket of products. Finally, let us imagine an increase in the price of sirloin steaks in the butcher's shop. For the economists of the Institute of Statistics, this product could be replaced by hamburgers which are cheaper and, therefore, although there is inflation, the index is adjusted so that there does not appear to be so much inflation. The CPI index under this logic would no longer represent a sufficiently correct measure of how much purchasing power consumers lose in real terms due to inflation, significantly underestimating it in its manifestation[51].

6.3.1 Hedonic changes in products.

Another crucial element in the methodology for calculating CPIs is the concept of hedonic quality change, which refers to a method for adjusting the prices of a product that has increased in price due to innovation or the introduction of qualitative improvements. The Statistical Institute uses a formula with which, by means of regression, studies the evolution of changes in quality[52] for a broad category of products[53] . This methodology eliminates cost increases due to changes in product quality. On the contrary, if we read the justification given by the Bureau of Labor and Statistics "BLS", we notice that it tries to justify the use of this type of correction and its scientific basis and rigor[54]. If we analyze the essence of the concept of quality, it is, in my opinion, a little more difficult to understand. However, let's consider an example of a product that experiences a notable increase in value over time. According to this logic of quality, increases resulting from qualitative changes in the product should not be included in the calculation of inflation, as it would understate the inflationary phenomenon. This justification is inadequate in my opinion; in the context of the complexity of the technological era in which we are living, we see how cell phones are constantly changing their specifications and features. Under this logic, qualitative improvements are hiding cheaper material used to reduce the cost of the products made. The same example could be made with cars, where we would conclude that the prices of cars of a particular brand owe their increase to some optional improvements. In this highly technological era, where technological changes are constant, it would be incorrect to allow these new tech advances to compromise the consistency of the inflation calculation index, thereby providing an inaccurate representation of the phenomenon. The misjudgment comes from an incorrect qualification of quality changes at the philosophical level. These changes are more related to the state of the art of technology evolution than to the "eventually real" quality improvements.

6.3.2 Geometric mean.

In order to understand the magnitude of the changes contributed over the years to the methodology for calculating consumer price indexes, there is another concept used by the Statistical Institute, which involves using the geometric mean[55]. In short, this method subtracts the importance of items that have experienced greater increases, giving more weight to items with smaller increases. This is based on the premise as explained before that consumers change their spending according to the evolution of the price of the most expensive items, opting for cheaper alternatives. However, the practical evidence for how this happens is not well understood. Meanwhile, the only certainty is that the introduction of this new method of averaging the data gives the appearance of lower inflation when it is not the case. I am very struck by the justifications given by the Bureau of Labor and Statistics for these controversial elements. In extreme synthesis they state that the logic of the changes does not reduce a measured inflation, when in practical reality it seems to me that this is the result they achieve[56]. I consider that the use of the "COLI" system is a way of artificially deflating the data, representing a downward estimation of the phenomenon, with the result being the opposite of what the Institute of Statistics seeks to justify. Thanks to this system, the results are estimated lower than they really are. According to this logic, consumers would lower their quality-of-life standards to make ends meet with their salary.

Economist John Williams has a website and a newsletter with a lot of information and comparisons between nominal inflation and a more realistic representation of inflation (Fig. 2). Analyzing these data is particularly interesting. It allows for a comparison of inflation in the United States from 1980 to the present using the two calculation methodologies.

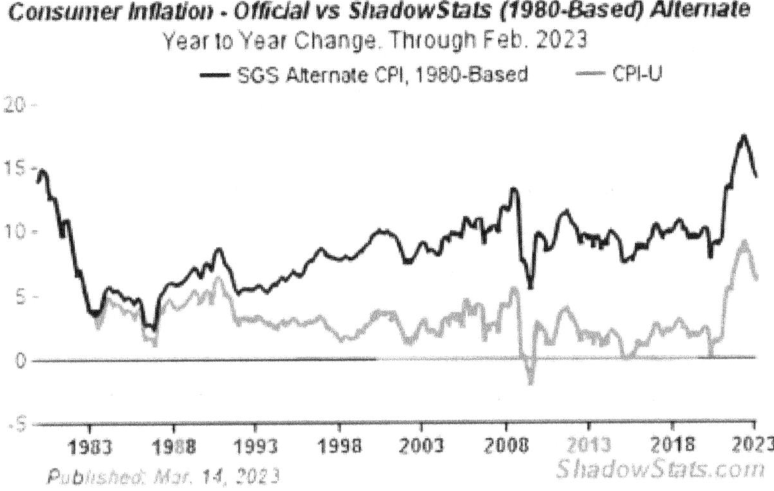

Fig. 2 Source Shadow Stat: Graph of inflation evolution. It shows how this phenomenon has been constantly underestimated in the last four decades by the new calculation methodologies of the statistics institute.

6.4 Consumer goods and services

The effects of globalization have brought the market to an ever-increasing level of competitiveness, allowing consumers access to cheaper goods and services. More companies compete with more products at a lower price level. The effects of this competitiveness that has been growing and increasing over the years are a powerful deflationary element in consumer products, goods, and services. At the same time, to stay in the market, companies have been forced to implement cost reduction plans and, the effects of their strategies are in some cases quite evident. Think of the millions of jobs that have been lost in Western countries as a result of cheaper products coming from economies with much lower labor costs. The companies that have survived are, to some extent, fortunate, as many others have closed, leading not only to job losses, but also the dissolution of entire industrial clusters.

We can see all the aspects that globalization has generated, the first of which has been a relative control of inflation. I use the adjective relative because we have seen that the inflation calculation system used does not fully reflect its magnitude, in reality underestimating it. This means that, despite globalization, inflation has been widespread in the economies. On the other hand, this has encouraged the search for and a strong focus on productivity. An increase in productivity often goes hand in hand with the automation of processes and the consequent loss of direct and indirect labor; therefore, we have had economies that have seen an increase in unemployment. Lastly, there is a third aspect that cannot be fully quantified or comprehensively analyzed, which is the decline in the quality of products and services provided to consumers to compete in the market. In order to explain this phenomenon in detail, I would like to use the example of the airlines. Over the last few decades, airlines have undergone profound restructuring to remain competitive in the market with prices accessible to a middle class that has been increasingly impoverished, losing much of its purchasing power. To remain in the market, airlines need millions of passengers; consequently, they need what used to be the middle class. In a reality where the middle class lost purchasing power, a very concrete threat was generated to affect the livelihood of the airlines. Frequent flyers have noticed how airlines have constantly lowered the quality of the products they offer, from a reduction of food on international flights to its elimination on domestic flights. But the cost-cutting actions, or actions in search of increased revenues, have been so extensive that nowadays checking baggage is very expensive. In some cases, the cost of checking baggage can even be comparable to the ticket´s value itself. Therefore, we have a cost for a service that has not varied much. However, by analyzing the decrease in the quality of the services offered in terms of food, new costs for checked bags, or the costs to change departure data (when allowed), it can be observed that the true value and cost of airline tickets has skyrocketed over time. A clear manifestation of the inflationary phenomenon in its pick. Indeed, this decline in service quality or reduction in the overall quality of services is not captured in the calculation of inflation.

We can extend the examples with cars. If we compare the quality of a car of the same brand built in the early 2000s or in the 1980s with the quality you can see in vehicles produced in 2023, it is easy to understand how it has been deteriorating. This exercise can also be extended to consumer durables, such as a washing machine or a clothes dryer. As a last example, I would like to analyze the clothes we bought in a store 20 or 40 years ago. The most frequently used materials were legitimate cotton, wool, linen, silk, and synthetic fibers of very low value. Today the same garment is mostly produced with synthetic fibers or blends of them. These fabrics have improved in quality, but at the same time they are much cheaper than the natural fibers I described before and, at the end of the day, they end up being modern plastics. Perhaps we could also look at hyper-massive consumer products, such as cell phones, which seem to be made to last no more than a couple of years due to programmed obsolescence. Thus, cellphone sellers help consumers by means of exotic financing plans to buy new models with some extra function and at a significantly higher cost. Companies, therefore, have used technology, pretty colors like make-up to hide wrinkles, and a constant reduction in the quality of their products, to allow them to stay in business and compete with cheaper products that arrive thanks to globalization. Statistical institutes widely and opportunistically use the quality increase of the products and their changes to lower the price of the products that lead to understating inflation; but at the same time, they do not recognize the quality changes in the opposite direction that I have just described, which in reality are much greater with respect to the others.

6.4.1 Gross domestic product.

An economy affected by inflation will therefore present Gross Domestic Product data that will incorporate this effect. In order to arrive at the correct measurement of Gross Domestic Product, a deflator is used as an expression of the total inflation affecting the country in question. This deflator takes into consideration the prices of raw materials, as well as the prices of goods and services produced within an economy. If we compare, therefore, the deflator with the data provided by the consumer price indexes, the deflator is normally comprehensive of more products and services than those considered in the calculation of the consumer price index.

6.5 A slow process

The methodology by which the U.S. Bureau of Labor and Statistics has been calculating inflation over the years has undergone many changes. We go from the evolution of the value of housing to the concept of "shelter costs". Finally, we went from the logic of a fixed basket of products or "COGI", to the concept of maintaining the quality of life or "COLI", which introduced changes in the basket of products, depending on the evolution of their costs. With the adjustments related to the evaluation of product quality, as well as the use of geometric averages, new analysis paradigms have been introduced over time for the calculation of the "CPI". These changes have led to the evolution of the methodology in new and unexplored directions over several years. Commissions of experts, and perhaps strong political intervention by the government, have gradually succeeded in bringing about these far-reaching changes in the philosophy of calculating inflation[57]. If we analyze the documents and the abundance of information on the subject, we can conclude that there was a strong debate guided by a clear and precise underlying will.

The governmental apparatuses were the ones that guided this debate, pressing for the need to migrate towards a new calculation system. The objective was seemingly to achieve a purportedly more precise estimation of the inflationary phenomenon.

Let's think about it: if you were proposed to have a more accurate measurement of inflation, who would dare to oppose such a logic, which would undoubtedly be beneficial for the whole community?

The many changes coincidentally give us a lower view of inflation than we would have if it were calculated using the traditional methodology. In order to understand the magnitude of the problem and how it arose, it must be analyzed from the perspective of the socioeconomic context in which these changes were implemented.

In conclusion, it is important to recognize that there is not a universally perfect method for calculating inflation. From this perspective, some of the criticisms of the previous model of calculation undoubtedly had logical foundations. Another conclusion that we have been exploring throughout the book in many chapters, refers to the interests of politicians in pursuing an increase in public spending, a factor that is highly inflationary. This aspect is also implicit in the reality of things. Finally, the factor of analysis. I would dare to say that inflation does not look good, since it is a calamity that directly affects most of the population. Following this reasoning, a slightly underestimated inflation, on the contrary, largely benefits the centers of political and economic power, even if it harms the majority of voters. However, due to its lack of popularity, this viewpoint cannot be openly expressed as it may have costly consequences during election time.

If we analyze the process through which the changes in the inflation calculation methodology have been implemented, over time we see that these changes have been based on an excessive abundance of data and information—thousands of pages and reflections that went largely in a certain direction. Therefore, someone with incorrect thinking could conclude that it was a fine way of directing the debate towards the expected result. This, in layman's terms, would be nothing more than coordinating the writings according to how the centers of power wanted the inflation numbers to be seen.

If we think about it, we have a certain dualism: on the one hand, a large number of mathematicians, statisticians and politicians who have justified changes through their writings. That could -according to the wrong-thinking- be instrumental to have inflation appear as a lower level than it really is. On the other hand, we have a few who consider that it has not been a completely correct way to implement such changes for the simple fact that these were going to cause, as they have been de facto, an underestimation of the reality of things. This can be summarized in the image of David facing Goliath; that is, a few without power against many with power. Thus, to reach a logical conclusion from the discussion, we must analyze the descriptive philosophical bases of the concept of inflation because many times formulas and numbers are expressions, and depending on the paper on which they are exposed, usually as an inanimate element, they can stand anything. On the contrary, simple logical and linear reasoning would explain things much better.

In short, inflation represents the loss of the value of money. However, the definition that I like, because it is more down-to-earth, would be: **The average cost difference that households pay today for exactly the same things (goods and services) that they had acquired in the past.** If we use the essence of this definition, we have the possibility of demonstrating whether the reported inflation reflects reality, and if the changes in its calculation project a lower indication of the phenomena than the reality. The loss of value refers to the amount of the same products and goods sold in the market that cost more money, causing a reduction in the purchasing power of the households.

Analyzing the changes implemented by the statistical institutes, and sticking literally to the linear definition, we conclude that they could be functional changes that reflect a lower level of inflation than the actual reality. Starting from the simple concept of a consumer who, due to price increases, changes his purchasing pattern towards cheaper products, we can draw two basic conclusions: the first, seen in the universe of expenditures of an economy, is irrelevant, but in this specific case the products have changed cost and money has lost value. Utilizing a different product in this manner, based on the assumption that this consumer has changed his purchasing pattern, is an important conceptual error that consistently diminishes the result of the inflation calculation and leads us to error.

Quality is another important aspect to consider. The quality of products is constantly changing as the economy evolves over time. Technology plays a big role in these changes, as do many other factors.

Trying to disincorporate these technological changes from the value of products leads to an underestimation of inflation, because products have increased their costs and money has lost its value. It is incorrect to justify these price changes by the quality factor because this largely represents the natural technological evolution of the economic environment. When we analyze the geometric mean, these try to give greater weight to products that have lower price increases against those that have increased in price in a more sustained way. We see again a distortion towards a reality different from the one that should be represented correctly. Which is simply a decrease in the value of money and due to an increase in product costs. In conclusion, the moment we critically analyze the changes to how statistics are calculated, it's clear that they were implemented to describe an inflation different from the real one. This does not mean the experts' past criticisms are completely wrong, but the best way to deal with possible differences would have been through a different calculation method.

When discussing quality, we must distinguish between two concepts. First, an evolution of quality due to technological advances. Second, new products with different uses. For example, in 1960 a car did not have GPS; nowadays it is likely that most cars include GPS, but this would not justify for any reason to decrease the value of current cars for this extra option they offer, being the result of a natural technological evolution due to the time that has elapsed between 1960 and today. GPS for sports is different. In 1960, items like that didn't exist, but today they do. That means they're new things, not just natural improvements resulting from technology. The issue of quality has finally become so complex that it is sometimes difficult to frame it within measurable parameters. We have seen how globalization and the increase in competition between companies worldwide force them to look for strong cost cuts. If we take the example of automobiles, for example, we will see the introduction of new extras such as GPS, but at the same time a reduction in the quality of the materials used. Statistical institutes are very good at identifying the correctives for possible quality increases. The basic question to be answered, however, is whether the quality has really increased simply because of the GPS or, on the contrary, has decreased due to the use of cheaper materials.

Speaking of product quality, the statistical institutes in the different countries have failed, in my opinion, to incorporate the sharp decline in the quality of economy-class seats. We can conclude that adjustments made to account for changes in quality largely led to significant conceptual mistakes.

As you can understand, the answer is not simple, but the current way of measuring inflation significantly underestimates the phenomenon, and most of the adjustments made during its calculation, instead of leading to improvements, have been increasing the deficiencies in its measurement.

6.6 The missing link in inflationary evolution

We have been able to demonstrate how the calculation of inflation tends to underestimate the phenomenon. Reported inflation is lower than the actual inflation faced by economies. For governments, we have some important advantages in underestimating the inflationary phenomenon. Inflation reported as lower than actual inflation allows for the control of public spending on social security. Another important benefit for governments is a lower interest payment to sustain the country's debt. Also, inflation leads to an increase in wages and automatically an increase in the tax generated by the system thanks to more bills circulating in the economy and higher tax brackets into which taxpayers fall. Finally, when analyzing the benefits of an inflated economic system, the loss of value in public debt is an important factor to consider also.

But by analyzing the data, we are still facing a reality to which we have not yet found an exhaustive answer. I am referring to a missing link in the calculation of inflation, which is normally not considered when calculating inflation and which therefore leads us to radically underestimate this disastrous phenomenon. We have seen throughout the chapters of the book how inflation is caused by an uncontrollable level of public spending, which, due to the mechanisms of monetization of this spending through the expansion of the monetary base of the system, generates inflation. However, if we analyze the expansion of the monetary base of the system and the levels of inflation that economies have been facing, we can notice that something is missing that has not been taken into consideration. On the contrary, this missing element must be considered in order to arrive at a correct estimation of the inflationary phenomenon.

Let us review the expenses of a family that uses its money to buy perishable and durable consumer goods to eat and live. Human beings are somewhat more complex than animals, which only need to eat, reproduce, and shelter from the weather. The description of consumer spending is much more complex and encompasses various other factors. If the spending environment under analysis were limited to only this aspect, it would be too narrow in scope, and we would be forgetting a section of family spending that is essential to the life of individuals: investments.

The limit in calculating inflation is to focus only on perishable or durable consumer goods and services and not on investments. Investments represent an essential spending pattern of rational consumers. Without investments, we would have billions of people in the world working without a vision for a better tomorrow, with only a limited view of life that would bring us too close to the other components of the animal kingdom. To have a successful life, consumers have investments as the main expense to focus on. It is only through long-term investments that consumers can improve their quality of life over the years.

This concept is not simple and should not be underestimated, we are comparing a conception of living from day to day versus a much broader vision, which is to build a future through their work and investment goods that the consumer and his family can acquire over their lifetime and pass on to their children. Understanding this concept in its maximum expression is fundamental and essential to be able to explain the inflationary phenomenon in its entirety and not superficially and inadequately.

What are the reasons why the inflationary phenomenon is underestimated? This is the basic question to which we have to find an answer.

7 The empire strikes back. A war of false powers

7.1 The role of the U.S. dollar

At this point in the story, we should ask ourselves: Why do we primarily focus on the role of the U.S. dollar when discussing inflation? The answer lies in history and in how the United States has consolidated its economic, political, and military hegemony after World War II. History is told by the winners, not the losers.

Humanity throughout the centuries has been characterized by the birth, consolidation, and decline of empires. Some of these empires were more powerful than others, sometimes with a more favorable geographic location than others, and other times very extended along different continents. We can agree that perhaps the greatest empire of the past has been the Roman Empire[58]. Since the decline of the Roman Empire the world has seen the birth, consolidation, and decline of many other empires and so has been the history of mankind, which has manifested repeatedly in various forms of domination and supremacy over the centuries.

With the Second World War, the United States managed to place its currency at the center of the Western world. Also, the blocs and empires antagonistic to the American one, I am referring to the countries belonging to the Warsaw Pact and China in the years and decades following the end of World War II, were required to use the US dollar as a means of global exchange of goods and services.

Our analysis is about the US dollar, since it is the currency used in global exchanges around the world, the currency on which the world financial system is still built. However, any monetary policy related to the dollar automatically has repercussions on all the other currencies of the world, which are forced to adjust their monetary policy following the evolution and decisions that accompany the dollar. A monetary policy applied to the dollar, whether restrictive or expansive, is almost automatically accompanied by similar policies on the part of the other currencies. In this process, there can be a certain inertia, but if the other currencies do not respond to the monetary policy actions of the United States, an imbalance will be generated that will be reflected in the balances of payments among different countries and may even cause some unwanted adjustments within national economies. The dollar is the leading currency in the world monetary system and the other currencies are linked together with it in a more gregarious manner. This is why we talk so much about the dollar, because it is the most important currency; and the others, even if they don't like to admit it, must follow the leader.

As a final example of these reflections, we have the changes to Japan's monetary policy rules, which were forced to raise interest rates at the end of December 2022, following the US dollar's interest rate hike and breaking with the decades-long pattern of interest rate reductions. Japan was forced to raise interest rates to slow the decline in the value of the yen. The entire herd sooner or later follows the Shepard, this is the actual reality.

7.2 "Weaponization[59]" of the U.S. dollar

There is hope if there is war, war as an instrument of conflict resolution, creation of public spending and debt, creation of monetary base, enrichment of some, and impoverishment of others. After World War II ended, all of the countries agreed that they did not want any more conflicts, but looking back on it now, there were very few days when the world has been without conflicts or battles after this terrible war.

Empires consolidate their power through wars. Sometimes, very rarely, to be precise, there are just wars. Thus, we have witnessed the export of democracy and the Western way of life to evil countries that are not fortunate enough to be in the right political, economic, and social system. But are we sure that the others are truly evil, and that we are the good guys? The US dollar has thus become an instrument of war, or in other words a weapon of war. I repeat again, this book is not a pacifist manifesto, nor is it a political writing -politics do not interest me- it is a work on economics. The political situation must be analyzed to be able to come up with a correct explanation of the economic phenomena the world is currently experiencing and will likely continue to experience in the future. Therefore, do not misunderstand the writing, there is no judgment, just simple reflections and observations of facts and the consequent reality. The basic question is, if diplomacy had been used instead of war as an instrument of conflict resolution, would planet Earth be in a happier and more prosperous situation? Have wars been an instrument of democratization of society or have they finally resulted in something different?

We have seen in recent years that the use of the dollar as a weapon of war extends to many conflicts. I am thinking of the economic sanctions against countries such as Cuba or Iran, and finally the very structured package of measures against Russia for the invasion of Ukraine. Greenbacks are the world's currency of exchange; at the same time, due to their role, they have also lent themselves to this type of action, which would normally have nothing to do with the conceptualization of money or currency.

7.3 Advantages for the U.S. economy

Let's try to analyze what kind of advantages facilitated for the United States, the role of its currency as world reserve money, and its role in global trade.

First, there is a very important concept to understand about the currency used in trade between countries. This role implies that reserves are generated in the central banks, in the banking system, and in the companies of the world's largest economies. This abundance of dollars worldwide indirectly facilitates access to credit and capital markets for the U.S. government, as well as for companies listed on the U.S. stock exchange. The most important stock exchanges of the developed economies are in the United States and if we compare the market capitalization of these stock exchanges, we see that they easily represent a predominant portion of the Earth's finances. In other words, global finance is driven by the US dollar. It is crucial to understand the central role that this currency played in supporting the revival of the hardest-hit economies of World War II because, without the help of American dollars, I don't think the recovery would have been as rapid.

Another significant advantage has been the cost reduction for U.S. companies in acquiring raw materials, which are paid directly in dollars. The price of these goods has remained unaffected by exchange rate fluctuations and there has been no need to pay commissions for currency exchange or exchange spreads.

Ultimately, if we review a little of what we have studied about the expansion of the monetary base and the ease with which money can be created after the end of the Bretton Woods agreements, it is clear that the dollar-owning economy has had significant access to a vast majority of the world's resources using a simple action like the clicking a computer button. Finally, the ease with which it has been possible to increase the monetary base in dollars is reflected at the banking level. By comparing the proactivity of the American banks and the credit facility of these institutions with European or Latin American counterparts, it can be observed that access to credit facilities for a business activity in the United States is faster and easier than in other continents or other latitudes. Therefore, without a doubt, the magic machine for producing money is more efficient in North America than in the rest of the world. If a system demonstrates high efficiency in the production of new banknotes in physical and electronic form, these banknotes will eventually finance business ventures as well and therefore industries and companies. In this place, business ventures will be able to prosper more than in other places where credit is more difficult to access.

If we take as an example the real possibilities of accessing sources of financing in countries such as France, Italy, or Spain and compare them with the United States, we see that the financial systems in these countries are much more cumbersome and slower than those of their greatest ally. Whether we choose to acknowledge it or not, this translates into reduced entrepreneurial dynamism and, consequently, the creation of fewer companies. Finally, by analyzing the employment rates of these old European countries and comparing them with those of their main colleague on the other side of the ocean, it is clear that American dynamism has been able to create more jobs over the years.

Two questions arise here: How has the dollar managed to maintain itself over so many decades as a currency used in global exchanges, and why have countries that are not so friendly to the United States continued to use the dollar? The answer is not so difficult to understand and confirms the fact that despite the criticisms that can be made of the dollar, it has inspired more confidence than other currencies. The US dollar serves as the best roof in a neighborhood of broken roofs. If this was not the case, economies around the world might have migrated to use reserves on other currencies instead.

7.4 Competitive advantages and disadvantages

have to be analyzed in order to explain this description of the broken roofs; it would be wrong not to make some economic reflections on its main trading partners.

European countries are often entangled in useless regulations, complicated in many cases by completely dissonant tax policies within a union that is only an appearance. On the one hand, in the old continent, we also have highly regulated countries where it is almost impossible to start a business activity, which prevents them from making necessary new investments, and all this comes seasoned perhaps with a bit of corruption. Moreover, these countries compete with tax havens within the European Union itself. When we look at Europe we have many additional complications, which make it very difficult to synthesize the level of chaos that this political monetary union represents. It has a centralized bureaucratic apparatus, with a lot of deep state power and with little influence from the citizens of this union. This bureaucratic apparatus is guided by big bureaucrats, who in the end are not elected by the people but by coalitions of political parties united only by the interest of staying in power, but with ideals often opposed to each other. Therefore, bureaucratic Europe as such represents an important cost that has to be financed by the different countries that are part of it. This bureaucratic cost is a crude way of subtracting resources from the real economy, to create political posts and feed the various starving parties throughout the different European latitudes. Remember, politicians love high-paying jobs as well as power. Within this Orwellian design, we have a European Parliament that has very little power and that represents in the end a facade of democracy for the voters of the different countries. In reality, it represents a highly hierarchical and impenetrable oligarchic castle.

Within this disorder, not all countries possess equal power; on the surface, all members of the European Union are equal, but in reality, certain countries hold more power than others. Therefore, the second-level countries have no option but to remain silently submissive in front of those in charge. When politicians come home to visit their voters, they usually make proclamations their about how nice it is to be submitted in this dysfunctional union which is nothing more than the restoration of oligarchic form of a past empire. In the European hierarchy, the nations that economically rule and therefore count are Germany and its satellite allied countries. France still believes in its influence being a veteran of the Napoleonic imperial vestiges, and it still considers itself to be a great military power, without realizing that throughout history, it has probably lost more wars than it has won. All others could be divided into two groups: the first being the beneficiaries, and the second, those who ultimately foot the bill after all the others have had their fun and enriched themselves.

Among the beneficiaries, we have many countries of the former Warsaw pact, which by the simple fact of having joined this coveted club are waiting like beggars to receive economic aid. These countries are the real beneficiaries, and thanks to their membership in the European Union, they have received and continue to receive substantial amounts of money, enabling them to achieve exponential growth in their economies.

On the other hand, we have waiters and servants. I would not like to name in this line any particular country, but those who are in Europe can easily understand who I am mainly referring to. We can, however, give you a hint by saying that they are blessed by a warm Mediterranean sun, which makes their winters a little bit more pleasant than the Nordic and German ones. What is slightly surreal is the fact that, in addition to being waiters and servants, their politicians try to sell their citizens the idea that this nice club is something beneficial for them. Surprisingly, their loyal voters have been believing in this narrative so far. These countries are tied up in an inexorable press, represented on the one hand by the desire for French grandeur and on the other hand by German austerity, which is really the economic ruler of the European Union. When their leaders travel to the periodic meetings of the heads of state, with their tails between their legs, have no choice but to say always and repeatedly say "yes sir" to the wishes of the one who rules (i.e. Germany.)

7.5 Is the euro the future or the fruit of failed imperial vestiges?

The European Union, if analyzed properly, should lead countries with very deep cultural, historical, and idiosyncratic differences to form a new nation, which could be defined as the United States of Europe. This is undoubtedly a project under construction, which makes it difficult to predict with certainty its political and economic outcome.

By critically analyzing the facts and what we have seen so far, instead of moving towards a political-monetary union, it has been in a way a dusting of old imperial vestiges, where, by means of democracy, Germany would finally come to control the continent. At this point, the first conflict arises with France, which undoubtedly also misses its imperial and colonial past, putting on a happy face and a bad game to German economic power.

As I said in the previous chapter, I will give you a small example to demonstrate the bureaucratic costs of this project. These costs are enormous; just think that, with the European Parliament's headquarters in Brussels, to satisfy the French desire for grandiosity, one week a month the institution and its representatives also meet in Strasbourg. In other words, there is a redundant duplication of resources. Which company in the world doubles its office expenses in this way? The answer is simple: only those that want to go bankrupt.

Finally, the politically weakest in the European Union are the ones who end up paying for this bureaucratic party to a large extent; I am referring to those places blessed by the climate and the Mediterranean sun. The politicians of these countries sometimes cannot even express themselves correctly in the languages mostly used in the palaces of the European power, since they can barely communicate in their native dialect.

The monetary union project is the expression of a failed project from the beginning; for some of the countries it has been beneficial, but for others it has been nothing short of a catastrophe.

It is therefore evident how the monetary union project has not been successful. In the end, the British, thanks to Brexit, were able to catch a glimpse in time of the undesirability of belonging to such a project and therefore managed to save themselves from that inexorable press. If we ultimately arrive at this conclusion, we have no choice but to view the euro as a currency that remains subservient to the dollar, with limited prospects for future success.

7.6 The dollar in perspective with other currencies

It is therefore interesting to compare the U.S. dollar with other currencies that have experienced excessive reproduction. In this regard, I am considering the Japanese yen and the Venezuelan bolivar. The central banks of these two countries have implemented, over the years, a policy of almost unlimited money supply expansion. In some cases, despite these monetary actions, the currency manages to preserve a certain level of intrinsic value, I refer to the US dollar and the Japanese yen, and in other cases, the currency loses almost all of its value, as in the case of the Venezuelan bolivar.

Japan's yen has had its backing in a highly industrialized country with an extremely orderly population, if we compare Japanese culture with the "Venezuelan Latin American" culture, we can perfectly understand the differences between one and the other. The other important element to take into consideration is the productive and industrial structure of the country. Japan, at some point in its history, was the country with the highest per capita income level in the world and, I repeat, a highly developed and articulated industry—things that Venezuela does not have. The complexity and structure of its economy have allowed even the unbridled monetary policy to sustain the economy, whether it be in the case of Japan or the US dollar. In the particular case of the US dollar, used globally as a currency of exchange, we can affirm that a strict relationship has been made between that currency and the world economy, making a case of analysis even more interesting (Japan) because in the case of the US dollar we are talking about the global economy. On the contrary, the case of Venezuela is very emblematic, because the process of printing banknotes has not been leveraged by industry, which is almost non-existent, by trade, or by agriculture, only through the exploitation of raw materials and some primary process of refinery. It is easy to understand how, in a country with a disorderly spending pattern, as well as a poorly developed industry and economy, the production of banknotes has caused hyperinflation and the rapid loss of wealth.

There are limits to the production of banknotes, also for countries with a more articulated and complex industrial and commercial structure. If these limits are exceeded, we will see the potential destructive impact of this monetary policy activity.

To further support the foundation of our reflections, we should examine the currencies of industrialized countries in the Western area. I am referring to Canada, Australia, or perhaps smaller countries such as Switzerland or Norway. In all these cases there are economies that form the basis of these currencies, which are quite active; however, they are not large enough to become an eventual alternative to the US dollar. Thus, within the hegemonic hemisphere of the empire, no currency truly competes with the US dollar, since this is the only currency that has all the characteristics to be and remain, I repeat, the most important reference currency, especially in the western hemisphere.

7.7 Limit to the use of monetary expansion

If through the creation of electronic money, a country can have access to natural resources, imported goods and services, then what is the problem? What would be the limits to this activity? Undoubtedly, it would be a much simpler society if we did not have to worry about money and if it were possible with the simple click of a key to solve the needs of the scarce good of money. In this order of ideas, we understand that taking this process to its maximum consequences eliminates the scarcity factor of good money. Thanks to this magical little machine of money production, we could miraculously solve social problems, and economic inequalities and finally live in a fairer society, where we could all consider ourselves rich with the ability to print the money we need to live well in abundance.

If we take this analysis to its fullest extent, we can affirm that it is not necessary to work, because to get the money we need to live would require a simple gesture that does not require much energy expenditure, such as pressing a button on a computer.

Here comes the answer to our questions: money serves to be able to buy goods and services. **To fulfill its primary function, money must possess intrinsic value. Therefore, the intrinsic value of a currency is lost when its production becomes an unlimited activity, transforming it from a scarce good into a readily available commodity, which can be reproduced without a production cost.**

Therefore, understanding the limits to the use and expansion of the monetary base, it is difficult to understand how these limits could have been coupled with the events of the last few years.

7.8 The roman empire and its decline

We have seen that the beginning of the end of the great absolute monarchies has been characterized by a pattern of uncontrolled public spending which was further accelerated by wars. Wars, therefore, act as an element of final acceleration towards collapse.

Let's set the clock back a few thousand years and analyze one of the first cases of inflation in history and the consequences it had on the economic, social, and political structure of its time.

The dollar of the Roman Empire was a coin called "denarius", which served in the exchanges just like today's greenbacks. This coin was a casting of a few grams of silver (about 5). Silver was a scarce commodity, and suddenly there was not enough to be able to produce the necessary quantity of coins to cover the empire's expenses (mostly represented by military costs). As you can see, it is a situation like what we experienced with the end of the Bretton Woods agreements. The Roman emperors proved to be good and ingenious students of modern economic and monetary theories, and they thought well about reducing the amount of precious metal to clone more coins. Is this similar to the process of detaching the dollar from gold? In modern words, they increased the monetary base of the system.

Maintaining an empire costs money, the lifestyle of all the powerful, armies and wars. So, in Rome, thanks to the brilliant idea of cloning more coins, reducing the quantity of precious metals in them or changing the casting league, they found a way to meet all their expenses. With this brilliant economic and monetary policy idea, the system ended up having more money available to waste. It was the emperor Caracalla who better understood this game of multiplying money, and in a short time he kept reducing the amount of silver in the denarii. But this emperor was particularly ingenious; he introduced a new coin called the "Antoninian", which was supposed to be equivalent to 1.5 denarii, but with time it also came cloned with less silver than established until it became bronze at a certain point in history.

Well, we know: the emperor Caracalla had a small ego problem. Between the cost of the army, the wars, and the public works, there was a great need for money. Among the public works, the Baths of Caracalla are particularly notable. Those who have been able to visit Rome may know them.

However, this additional money available in the system was not accompanied by a corresponding increase in the production of goods and services; it was simply more money supply for the same amount of goods and services exchanged within the system. The demand for more money for the system was solved by reducing the amount of precious metal in the coins, so over many decades, the amount of silver in the denarii was less and less. The result of this monetary policy operation was that merchants began to demand more coins for the same goods and services. In other words, the same amount of goods and services exchanged had a higher cost. Because of all these factors, hyperinflation plagued the empire.

We can perhaps affirm that the beginning of the end of the Western Roman Empire began with the mandate of Emperor Diocletian. Although Keynesian economic theory was not written during the long years of the ancient Roman Empire, nor did anyone imagine or write about the modern monetary theory, the de facto taste of politicians and the powerful for access to inexhaustible sources of money was exactly the same as it is today. Thanks to the telepathic and premonitory power, the great Roman emperors knew Keynes' theory very well, just as they had perfectly understood the modern monetary theory. Thanks to their wide level of knowledge, they easily managed to apply these principles to the monetary policies of their time and to the empire. We can undoubtedly affirm that Diocletian was one of the many scholars of modern monetary policies of the ancient past. This emperor had to face the negative effects of so many years of monetary flood. So, he intervened directly in the economy by controlling wages, trying to control prices, and with a bit of creativity he started some monetary reforms. You see, in the past politicians were also presumed to be wiser than the market and its natural force. With all due modesty, if you look closely, this treatise, in addition to studying the phenomenon of inflation, manages to demonstrate definitively that telepathy and premonitions exist and are real facts.

Perhaps we can attribute the decline of the Western Roman Empire to this phenomenon, considering it a major culprit. A few decades later the glories of the Roman Empire were only transcribed in history books and anecdotes in schools. We cannot believe that the cause of the end of the Western Roman Empire is attributable to inflation alone. However, there is certainly a common thread linking the end of absolute monarchies with the end of the Roman Empire: a pattern of uncontrolled spending and public debt accompanied by social inequalities.

If we think about it, there is once again a common line between the end of absolute monarchies and empires. This similarity is characterized by spending patterns that result in an uncontrollable outflow of money for these misguided governments.

Wars have historically been one of the primary causes of wealth destruction and fuel for times of high inflation. Waging wars was a way of demonstrating power. Wars, if we think about it, are only a cause of death and destruction. When I speak of destruction, I am referring in part to the destruction of property, villages, cities, and crops. I am also referring to the most troubling part of these wars, which is the twisted use of money represented by its burning in acts of death, instead of being used for useful things.

Another interesting element of the end of the great absolute monarchies is related to the spending pattern of these monarchs or emperors, which was often irrational and crazy. In the specific case of Caracalla, we have the construction of the baths that bear his name, which are developed in an area of more than 200,000 square meters, a crazy work for his time. We can consider how the kings of France transformed a hunting lodge into what we know today as Versailles. These monarchs usually had an acquired idea: they had probably convinced themselves that they were the direct descendants of God. Therefore, ego was certainly one of their prominent traits. Now, let's imagine how someone with ego and absolute power could spend the money he wanted without logical limits.

In the past, as in present days, public works were carried out by means of public money; when this was no longer sufficient, they proceeded to clone more currency or to print more banknotes, depending on the time. Today, they would be electronic banknotes, at the time of Caracalla they were coins. The Baths of Caracalla and Versailles, both serving as examples, were entirely useless to the people who paid the bill, but not to the ones in power. These structures solely catered to the imperial or monarchic ego.

Finally, we have the last great element that destroys wealth, which is the cost of bureaucrats and state employees. Here we come to an infinite list of characters, depending on the era to which we refer, but the first source of expenditure of an empire usually ends up being the army. I suggest you check how much the United States spends on its current annual defense budget and there you will find many answers in this regard. Things surely do not end with the army. In ancient times there were the courts, which were represented by several characters indisputably skilled in the arts of gossip, but of dubious practical capabilities. Today the bureaucratic apparatus of the different states grows continuously and constantly over time. I'm not sure if there are any parallels in this respect, but the common factor is that in both cases, the past and the present, these apparatuses cost a lot of money.

Now, if we analyze synthetically what could have happened to the ancient Romans, we can conclude that the issue of inflation was a problem caused by several emperors up to Diocletian and Emperor Constantine. This process took decades to develop, where the government would simply print more money to finance public spending. Inflation in the past, as in the present, is initially generated by a monetary phenomenon, where the amount of money in circulation becomes detached from the economic reality and its intrinsic value, causing serious imbalances in the economy.

History constantly repeats itself, like a scratched vinyl record that spins and spins producing dissonant sounds.

7.9 What about other world currencies?

After reflecting on the various currencies' potentialities, we continue to recognize the importance that should be given to the dollar within Western economies. We have seen how the euro ends up being an experiment destined to fail, an experiment of the colonial and imperial vestiges of Germany and France, proving to be the currency of economies in deep demographic decline, made only to the measure of Germany. Finally, I find it very difficult for some countries, due to their profound cultural differences, to integrate in the future. Unfortunately, the European economies are old, just as their population, with antiquated ideas and are predestined to a continuous and inexorable decline, since it is the evolution of a continent that has lost its ancient glories for a senile destiny.

The other major economies of the Western group of countries, such as England, Canada, and Australia, although they are modern economies with a vision of the future that has overcome the old ideological barriers to which the European states are still largely anchored, are still relatively small economies so that their currencies cannot provide competition for the US dollar, which remains the absolute king in its area of influence.

Well, believe it or not, the world does not end here, finally on planet Earth we are billions of people and coincidentally the economies of the American area of influence, apart from some cases, represent the senile and geriatric side of the planet. Among so many things, the destiny and demographic evolution of these countries is quite evident proof of what I am saying, given the permanent demographic decline of these nations. As you can imagine, when a being enters geriatric age, its capacity to generate progeny diminishes. This is due, among other factors, to hormonal changes that occur within the organism.

If we look to the East, we find large industrial blocs, which, unlike the Western economies, still have demographic growth ahead of them. These two great blocks are China and India. These two great powers, however, are not alone since a new club of developing countries with great future potential is being formed. I am referring to South Africa, Brazil, Russia, and Saudi Arabia. Together, they possess a significant share of the world's resources and have growing populations. Additionally, they maintain positive relations in other areas of the third world with strong prospects for population growth, such as Africa. Unfortunately, crystal balls exist only in fairy tales and fictional movies, they are not yet available on Amazon, and surely if they are found they do not work as they are intended.

In the future we will witness many monetary evolutions worldwide, especially in developing countries with a currency that will probably gradually become an alternative to the dollar as a means of global exchange. This process will take place over many decades. Those who anticipate a swift transformation, however, may be mistaken again.

8 The failure of keynesian economic policies

When we analyze the evolution of public spending over the last decades, we see that it has increased steadily over time, a feature that can be found in all developed economies. Governments have embraced the Keynesian philosophy in its entirety. I have already explained the reasons why politicians feel much more aligned and comfortable with that philosophy than with other more austere ones. According to Keynes' reasoning, we would ideally live in a society where full employment is achieved, where there is a fair distribution of wealth, and where its citizens live happily and contently.

Things are not like that, because the problem of employment has never been solved thoroughly given that many of these economies have high levels of unemployment. As far as wealth distribution, the results are even more disconcerting; in fact, we are witnessing the disappearance of the middle class. It's important to mention that when it comes to the happiness of citizens, defining this quality of a society involves considering various factors that have as a main denominator the subjectivity of its measurement, and as a consequent result its inutility at a practical level. We can conclude that the procedure used in measuring it is probably even less precise than the formulas used by economists to prove their theories.

We have the plastic result of the failure of Keynesian philosophy and logic in the management of the economy. This theory achieves opposite objectives to what the notable English economist sought if his teachings were achieved. However, let me make it clear from the beginning that if Keynes had seen his philosophy being used to justify the improper public resources, he would have been the first to recognize such shortcomings.

8.1 Reasons why keynesian policies cannot work. theory of the irrationality of the public expenditure

In this chapter we will examine some of the reasons why Keynesian philosophy cannot work and remains one of the many unworkable theoretical utopias.

If the behavior of various mammal species were observed, the result might conclude that they exhibit a rational logic within their environment. This logic is the search for food to feed themselves, and the search for protection against the natural elements of the climate and the seasons. Reproduction occurs at the most opportune times, to guarantee the highest survival rate for the offspring, and thus the cycle repeats itself over the years, which allows the species to survive over time.

Within this logic, Keynes probably imagined the rationality of the government or public entity in the management and orientation of public spending or public investment. This pattern does not occur here, what can be observed is that public spending and investment are instrumental to themselves and totally irrational in their logic. Public spending is often used to increase spending itself, rather than creating wealth and welfare for the people. You can see that this scheme fits perfectly with the goals of our elected representatives, who are elected to do our interests or, so they have us believe, but the objectives they pursue are many times opposed to our interests and oriented to their individual welfare.

In this regard, I would like us to think about the investments that occur for an important sporting or social event, such as the Olympics or the world soccer championships. Countries compete to host these events and the first requirement for the organizers is the commitment of heavy investments. Normally the assigned country invests billions of dollars in infrastructure, which once the event has ended, is most likely never to be used again. Another example I would like to take is the World Expo, which Italy hosted in 2015 in the Milan area. Millions of dollars were invested in preparing for the exhibition. Once the exhibition was over, many of these works had already lost their purpose and the money that was used was a waste of funds and nothing more. Politicians cleverly sell the idea of these events as unique occasions for the country and for its development. However, these supposed investments destroy wealth and only benefit a small group of fortunate individuals that take advantage of that money being spent. Meanwhile, the vast majority of people are left with the debts that the country incurred to finance them.

Another example I would like to take is the number of public institutions maintained by a small country like Costa Rica, in the middle of America.

This small country, which likes to define itself as Central American Switzerland, maintains more than 330 public institutions, while it would probably only need a few of them for its operation. Each of these institutions has extremely complex administrative structures, and their activities are not well defined. This leads us to think that they seem to exist only for their own sake and contribute very little to the welfare of the people, who must pay with their taxes the salaries of their officials and the expenses generated. All elected governments over the years have been clear about this problem of the public sector; however, none of them have taken the bistoury to correct it.

If we go to the United States, to conclude with our examples, and analyze the composition of public spending in this country, naturally, one may wonder why, with such a large amount of dollars invested every year in its operation, the streets of its cities are full of homeless people, many of them human beings with mental problems. I ask to myself, how is it not possible to attend them with a basic level of dignity that any society with such a large budget to spend would be able to afford?

The answer to all these examples is very simple: the pattern of public spending by governments is not rational and its objective is only to maintain the status quo, which is self-feeding. Therefore, when considering public spending, we must envision an abstract entity that lacks self-regulation and perpetuates itself, incapable of setting limits, incapable of focusing the orientation of its actions towards the public welfare, focused only on itself. The result of this sadly ends up in a waste of public resources, which should be invested in the welfare of the society, but end up being spent without any logic. This is the reality of the situation, and this is the simple explanation why Keynesian theories and modern monetary theory are simply a mere theoretical exercise and totally ineffective in achieving full employment and socio-economic well-being for all in modern societies.

Theory of the irrationality of public spending: public spending cannot achieve the objectives it sets out to achieve, because what guides its operation is not a logic of rational spending and investment. Public spending and its financing through debt are not a rational exercise but are instrumental to the maintenance of the political-administrative system as it is. They are, therefore, an exercise that is focused internally within the public administration, in its sustenance as such, and not

externally, through the creation of wealth, representing to a great extent the subtraction of resources from the economy. Irrationality is explained by the fact that the individual objectives of public administrators, as well as those of public entities, differ from what should be the objectives of public welfare, understood as the section of society where the public sector provides its service.

In conclusion, the error of the great economists was to suppose that the State and the public administration represent rational entities capable of making reflexive and logical decisions, when, on the contrary, what should be their primary focus is the maintenance of the bureaucratic structure as such.

8.2 The role of the state and its limits

The mismanagement of public resources occurs because the limits of state intervention in the economy and society are not well defined. This poor delimitation of responsibilities also leads to the granting, by the State, of services in its essential areas of intervention, which are insufficient and poor. At the same time, its activity is focused also on areas that are not important or not necessarily under its responsibility.

What would therefore be the essential areas in which the State should play its role? The list I am going to describe now is not necessarily conclusive, it is simply and in summary what I consider to be the most important areas in which the State must play its role.

HEALTH: All citizens should have access to health services.

EDUCATION: Any country that excels in this area can successfully compete on the global stage. Education should be accessible to all. It should be an education of quality for all, not just for those who can afford a good private institution.

SECURITY: The government should guarantee security for its citizens and businesses. A safe country becomes a place where people live well, and its citizens can prosper and grow. A safe nation is also an element of tourism development and foreign currency inflows that support the economy.

DEFENSE: All countries should manage international security through its military and armaments, this is another area of investment for a nation that wants to be successful on the world stage.

JUSTICE: The efficient and speedy management of the judicial system is another essential element for a State to ensure its citizens a home with development prospects.

INFRASTRUCTURE: A country's success depends mainly on infrastructure.

These are the six pillars on which successful countries focus and constantly strive to improve for the purpose of bettering the lives of their citizens. All institutions should be functional for these six pillars to work well and be efficient. If we examine the pattern of public spending in our economy, or in our countries, we observe a significant amount of dispersion concerning what is necessary or important.

This dispersion of activities ultimately leads to a waste of valuable resources, it is a subtraction of necessary resources to throw them away. It is also the main culprit for the poor distribution of wealth among citizens. The root of poverty lies in the misuse of public resources, which are subtracted from the economy to be spent on unnecessary things.

A simple example that we can all understand is the case of a family that has the money to buy food, but instead decides to buy a new watch for the head of the family. This approach, in a nutshell, is what developed economies do with the management of public spending. They simply waste resources by making their voters believe that these resources are wisely invested. Necessary public spending involves funding activities that the private sector doesn't find worthwhile to undertake on its own. This definition, however, is not broad enough of what should be necessary spending. For example, let's look at the health sector: if healthcare is completely in private hands, this would discriminate against the most vulnerable segments of the population in a way that marginalizes them even more. Given this example, I believe that after analyzing public spending, there is not a strict barrier between what is necessary or unnecessary, as well as between public spending and private investment. In other words, there are sectors of the economy where the presence of the public sector along with that of the private one is justified and others where it is not.

The basic ideology that we should adopt is that all citizens should have the same opportunities for fulfillment in modern society. If we think about it, this does not clearly define the areas of intervention of the public sector or where it can coexist with the private sector, ultimately opening the possibility for the State to intervene in many sectors, perhaps too many. If we try to extract the minimum essential areas in which the State should be involved, these are: health, education, infrastructure, justice, security, and defense. During one of my recent trips to a big city, I noticed many homeless people on the streets. It's not acceptable for a country with exorbitant public investments to have this problem, any self-respecting society should take care of its less fortunate citizens. In this case, I realized that many of these people probably had some kind of mental disorder; therefore, the health sector has to be probably the main sector to ensure a decent life for its citizens. Having made this reflection, it is a sector that can coexist with private investments, the State simply has to guarantee access to good health to its citizens who do not have the money to pay for private health or to pay for health insurance. It is disheartening to witness individuals living on the streets who deserve better, they are human beings worthy of the same rights as others.

The education sector represents another crucial area of human development, where both types of investment can coexist synergistically. Equal opportunities, essential for all citizens to reach their full potential, are provided through education. Within this scheme, public education is important because it allows everyone to be equal. A state governed by the rule of law should give all its citizens the possibility to achieve success in the same way. In this field, we can observe prestigious private universities alongside public educational institutions, and they may even collaborate and interact with each other.

Infrastructure is another area where the private and public sectors can coexist. A country with state-of-the-art infrastructure will have a better chance of success than a country with a lagging infrastructure.

Critical public services must be exclusively managed by the government to ensure impartiality. Private intervention in those areas might jeopardize the essence of the services delivered to the citizen. Among these areas we have justice, internal security, and defense, understood as military bodies and not as a defense industry which, after all, is a private activity. These activities, precisely because of their level of criticality, fall into the public domain, to guarantee their operation in the most impartial way possible.

8.3 The honey-coated hands of public administrators

If you apply honey to your hand and handle bills, an interesting event occurs, the bills stick to your hand. If you like honey as I do, you will have noticed this phenomenon, maybe not with money bills but with paper napkins, which easily stick to your fingers.

To explain this concept, imagine a senior official of one of the international humanitarian organizations. When they travel to Bangladesh, Pakistan, or Sierra Leone, do they travel in the economy class seats near the toilets or do they travel first class? At the same time, I would like to ask: How much will their annual salary be, or what hotels do they stay in when they are operating in some area of the world? Do they look for a clean three-star hotel or maybe stay comfortably in a five-star lodging?

Surprisingly, much of the money is spent on salaries, benefits, medical and pension plans, secretaries, and small luxuries in travels, and what actually reaches the needy is not what we imagine when we make donations. With this, I am not saying that you should not donate money for humanitarian causes; on the contrary, when you donate money for humanitarian cases, you have to control very well how much the association that receives money spends on administration costs and how much reaches the final purpose. It is a valid question to consider whether balance sheets are audited or not, but we are already going into smaller details. Warren Buffet donated a large part of his wealth[60] , on the condition that Bill Gates himself would manage the funds of his foundation. This great businessman knew that Bill Gates was a good administrator as well[61] .

In this regard, I have an interesting anecdote to share with you. A few years ago, while having breakfast in a restaurant in a rural area of a Latin American country, I found myself seated with the director of an institution that helps women in that country and two of her assistants. After seeing the lady several times (almost weekly), I asked her what they were doing in that area. I learned that they were going to visit a case of a minor who had been abused, to give her support. I asked how much the support was in monetary terms, and they told me that there was practically no significant money involved; it was simply going to listen to her and talk to her. These three ladies were traveling in a luxury car, which at the time was worth around 100,000 USD, the restaurant where I saw them having breakfast was the best in the area and therefore expensive. I kept thinking a lot about this event, and in the end, the conclusion I came to was that so much money had been wasted for just a caress on the back of the one in pain. Reflecting on that situation, you eventually reached the same conclusion: that a significant amount of money is often wasted on gestures that provide little or no substantial help to those in real need. Much of the money that we pay in taxes or that the State generates through the issuance of new debt ends up enriching an administrative machinery that produces nothing but costs, and the neediest receive only the crumbs of a hypocritical solidarity that is just a mask to justify the lifestyle of someone lucky.

8.4 Ineffectiveness of fiscal policies and the fable of wealth redistribution

In the collective imagination it is thought that thanks to fiscal policies, governments can increase their income and thus work towards social equity through the redistribution of wealth. Our rulers would be the heirs of Robin Hood and with great courage, thanks to arduous policies and implementation of new taxes, they would manage to take resources away from the selfish rich to finally distribute them among the oppressed people. Politicians usually express noble ideals that are difficult to criticize, but suddenly once in power, they often fail to take the right actions to address these imbalances, even if they had initially highlighted them.

This fable, or perhaps urban legend, must be framed for what it is: an example of the failure of Keynesian ideology, which, among other things, is nothing more than a breeding ground for inflation.

In the decades following the end of World War II, the United States was subject to moments of hyper-taxation with periods in which the highest level of taxation reached 90%[62]. In this context, one could argue that this nation was in an ideal period where Keynesian ideology could finally reach its pinnacle, and through higher levels of taxation, a fair redistribution of wealth could have been achieved.

Unfortunately, things were not like that. First, at that time there were exorbitantly high levels of taxes; however, the tax codes were comprised of thousands of pages with numerous exemptions. An example for everyone is that of the Hollywood producer LOUIS B. MAYER, who was paid 2.7 million dollars by check and hired a lobbyist, who succeeded in getting an exemption for him and his associates included in the tax code (See: note 3). According to the tax law of the time, this gentleman would have had to pay close to 90%.

The concept of wealth redistribution is simply one more utopia that proves instrumental to justify high levels of taxation, of government spending, and ultimately of public debt. This utopia caters to certain sectors of voters who desire the realization of these ideals, but at the same time fail to understand that what such redistribution achieves is more fiscal injustice.

Those who can afford to pay more taxes, thanks to sophisticated exemption systems or to international trade rules, manage to avoid paying taxes, and the percentage of what they pay could end up being much less than what the middle class or the poorest end up paying.

The European Union, despite being led by theoretically left-wing and progressive governments, often fails to uphold its stated ideals in practice. In the EU, some countries have high taxes, exorbitant public spending, and growing debt, while others are known as tax havens with favorable tax environments, such as the Netherlands and Luxembourg. With great surprise, the rich have moved their companies to tax havens, where they pay little taxes; some of them at a personal level, have their residences in other jurisdictions where there are more reasonable tax brackets, such as Switzerland or England. As a result, the burden of taxes in poorly managed countries often falls on the middle class and the poor, as those who could afford to pay higher taxes have chosen to reside in more tax-friendly locations. The result, or the paradox of this situation, is that those who could really pay do not pay and those who cannot are the ones who have the greatest burden on their shoulders.

8.5 Not everything is visible at daylight

At this point of the analysis, we can understand the complexity of the inflationary phenomenon. This unfortunate calamity goes beyond the simple basic analysis with which it is usually explained and turns it into a complex monetary and economic phenomenon due to its interrelations with its political system.

However, the problem is even more complicated than we can imagine, I am referring to the conceptualization of politics as such. In our imagination, representatives stand for election, and those who are elected take office. Once they are in power, the political landscape is complicated by the influence of lobbyists, who represent the intricate web of economic and political relationships.

When we analyze lobbyists, we can imagine a set of interests that are represented very well with a spider's web, some of them in line with others totally antagonistic, and as in a spider's web each one pulls the rope on his side.

Finally, lobbyists fight for the interests of their guild or the guild they represent; if they are the pensioners, they fight for the interests of the pensioners, if we talk about the pharmaceutical industry they fight for the pharmaceutical industry, if we talk about the environmentalists they fight for some ecological interest and finally we come to the miners of the coal industry who will advocate for the interests of the coal. It is a picture seen from the outside that appears extremely complex, something like a Pollock painting[63] or even more complex.

The common denominator that lobbyists have is that, directly or indirectly, their requirements need money—resources that they are mining in the right place because it is at the political level where money is produced by a "small yet miraculous machine", through the expansion of the monetary base, so we could say that if they were gold diggers they would be in the right river.

The work of lobbyists does not take place in the sunlight; on the contrary, what most of us see is the result of their work through the decisions made at the political level. Sometimes, there are decisions that we are unable to explain within a logic of common sense or common convenience;

however, there will probably be some particular interest in the background that a lobbyist group managed to get through.

Finally, in the monstrous inflation-producing machinery, it would be a major conceptual error to analyze politics as such on its own. To fully appreciate the complexity of the system, we must also come to understand the role played by the interests of the different power groups and how they directly, or rather indirectly, influence the final decisions of our representatives.

We can undoubtedly state that lobbyists contribute to and are largely responsible for the generation of inflation, because they are an integral part of the political system, although unlike our brave representatives, the latter are not elected and are simply there, working in the shadows.

8.6 Taxes: inexhaustible surprises

Taxes have a never-ending ability to surprise us. After a deep analytic analysis of them over the centuries, understanding their true nature from a critical point of view could prove to be a really hilarious exercise.

The French nobility before the French Revolution did not pay taxes, they were exempt. In a very transparent way, the people knew that they had to work to pay the taxes imposed by the fortunate lords who were busy at gala dinners and balls, and in dangerous sports such as hunting. These nobles had plenty of free time and were delighted in the difficult art of gossip and storytelling in the salons of Versailles. People grew tired, leading to a revolution, but eventually supported the restoration of the past through Napoleon's coronation as emperor. History can be stubborn in its resistance to learn, to change, and to finally progress.

If we analyze today, we see that things are done in a slightly more sophisticated way; for example, the poor are still the ones who largely pay the taxes. Now, some of the taxes are also paid by the rich, as in the 1700's in France the new democracies delight in wars and spending without measure, the money paid mainly by the poor and by the middle class, which is getting poorer and poorer.

With this analysis we must reflect on an important issue of taxes, which are in their quantity, form, and expression established by governments, which have managed to introduce countless of them, decorated with infinite complications. Taxes most of the time serve just to finance the bureaucratic machine rather than improving citizens' lives, limiting development opportunities for the middle class and the poorest. **THIS BENEFITS A COPROPHAGOUS SELF-CONSUMING SYSTEM.**

8.6.1 A stealth tax

To describe what I want I use the word FURTIVE, since it is an obscure tax that hits us daily without mercy. It is the most important tax that we are paying without really knowing about it.

I am referring to inflation. Inflation, then, acts as an instrument of destruction of the middle class. It silently eats away at the savings and purchasing power of the less well-off. In fact, it works as a reverse redistribution of wealth, it takes resources away from the middle class and the neediest to redistribute them among those who can have better access to electronic money, the rich and the wealthiest.

Paradoxically, those who advocate, with their left fist raised to the wind, for redistributive policies through Keynesian philosophy and new monetary theory, actually achieve the opposite effect: a strong redistribution of wealth from the middle class, small entrepreneurs, and the neediest to the wealthiest in society. The explosion of the monetary base facilitates access to resources for the wealthiest and, as I explained, paradoxically takes money away from the poor to be redistributed to the rich. In this perspective also, if we analyze the unions and how they act, in their interrelationships between the just and necessary protection of workers and companies, we notice that many times they do reach some collective contract. If we analyze these contracts, we can finally notice that the most benefited are the employers, and unfortunately many times the workers see their remunerations flattened, with no possibility of growth for those who are willing to work. This can also be considered a redistribution of resources to those who need them the least.

From the government's point of view, inflation is convenient, because it does not look good, since the voters do not want it, but it is convenient for the government as an inflation-generating entity. Inflation reduces the size of the debt and then becomes food for the system which is self-generating it. This is a very important concept, pay close attention. Modern political systems rely on high public spending, heavy taxation, and ever-increasing public debt that is self-feeding the same system. **Therefore, this very system is endemically inflationary, and it feeds ultimately on the very inflation that it produces. The system is coprophagous because it has the capacity to feed on the inflation that it inexorably produces.**

This characteristic can be explained and understood very well by examining the effects that inflation generates. As a destroyer of value, inflation reduces the size of public debt. In other words, an inflation of 10% per year or in real terms higher than this in a decade could significantly reduce the size of the public debt. The government as an abstract entity would be well served if it could control inflation from growing to hyperinflationary levels. The disastrous results of this situation are passed on to those who have to pay this nefarious hidden tax, the citizens.

Now, let's understand the concept of tax: a tax is the percentage of the amount of money earned that citizens transfer to the State so that it can maintain itself and invest in social spending. It can be well understood how inflation, by destroying the value of money, destroys families' savings, as well as the value of assets. In this way, the State furtively introduces a patrimonial tax on something for which its citizens had already paid what was due.

8.7 Every excuse is a good one to get drunk

Let's take as an example an alcoholic or someone who suffers from some kind of addiction. For them, any excuse is good to fall back into the addictive substance. The alcoholic who has stopped drinking for some weeks now, in the face of a difficult moment, will probably be tempted to get their hands on a bottle of liquor; and someone who is giving up cigarettes, in the face of a difficult moment, will be tempted to buy a pack of cigarettes and smoke. If we analyze the mental process of these people, it is quite simple to summarize. In difficult moments, people may initially think of having a small drink or smoking a couple of cigarettes to cope. However, it often doesn't stop at just one sip or a couple of cigarettes. It can escalate to consuming a whole bottle or smoking multiple packs, leading to a vicious cycle of addiction again.

The perverse economic policies of expanding public spending, through fiscal actions or the creation of monetary mass, reveal the problems of an addicted patient. Our representatives and their bureaucrats are aware of the underlying problem that our society faces with inflation and the loss of asset value. They know very well that the only prescription to cure the sick patient is to remove the addiction. To remove the addiction, the only solution is austerity in spending, which involves reducing it and enduring a period of suffering in order to improve afterward. At this point we should ask if this would be possible with so many forces at play. The answer is probably no, but the prescription is clear.

There is always a good excuse to fall back into the circle of addiction. When we fall back into the circle of addiction, it often returns with a greater force of dependence on the agents that cause the same disease.

8.8 The case of silicon valley bank and credit suisse

Without going too much into detail, both banks have gone through a process of serious economic problems, probably due to an unintelligent management of their investments and funds. The purpose of this chapter is not to explain what happened to these two banks, but rather to examine the political and economic consequences of their crisis.

A small premise at the time of the creation of this book. We are in an era of inflation control, through actions by the Federal Reserve and most of the OECD central banks in the developed world, such as increasing interest rates and implementing quantitative tightening. Through the sale of securities in the market and raising rates, central banks are trying to remove liquidity from the system and thus reduce inflation.

The "SVB"[64] goes into crisis with some other regional bank. Immediately the Federal Reserve makes funds available to support the banking system by discounting assets[65]. A few days later, Credit Suisse,[66] a global bank and Switzerland's second-largest bank, also enters into crisis, after many years of losses and many failed attempts to inject capital. Immediately, the Swiss National Bank (which is the Swiss central bank) intervenes with 50,000[67] million Swiss francs of credits to this bank through asset discounting.

At a time when the world is struggling with high inflation, at the first sign of economic crisis, the response of central banks and therefore of governments is finally again to create more monetary base. Instead of seeking to restructure an inefficient system. This process of electronic money production is done by discounting the assets of the banks in crisis, in exchange for cash, which, as you will recall, is the creation of currency out of thin air. The result of this is that in the face of any financial economic difficulties, the medicine is always the same, injection of money into circulation. Perhaps some analysts or economists may think that, thanks to the intervention of central banks, the risk of contagion has been limited and this banking crisis has been contained. Well, they are incorrect, because these actions are incapable of curing bad management and only contribute to the destruction of the middle class that finally pays for the party.

Another perspective would involve allowing poorly managed banks to go bankrupt. In such cases, the remaining resources could be used to compensate savers and limit the intervention of central banks only to the part of insufficient resources, to reimburse taxpayers' losses. Another possible solution might be to keep the banks under stricter rules, among which perhaps a greater contentment of the monetary base could be achieved to make these institutions safer. As you can see, there are many alternative paths, but we end up taking the monetary addiction route every time.

8.9 If we look up at the sky on a starry night, we will get the answer

The example of addictions I gave in previous referred to those that can affect human beings. With willpower and the support of trained personnel, it is possible with much effort to be cured of these addictions. Human beings have shown in many cases to be stronger than these addictions and ultimately manage to overcome these destructive behaviors despite the challenges they face.

Monetary addiction, on the contrary, is not curable. I will explain the reasons why I consider it to be an incurable disease. When analyzing how the monetary system of the industrialized countries evolves, we can conclude that we are facing an endemic, sick system. In the previous example, we have seen how the first action taken by central banks was to issue a monetary base to face the crisis. Like all addicts, the imaginary body of the State and its economy required its drug to be able to function and to feel better. Governments, unlike individual bodies, are highly complex entities with strong interrelationships among their components. The system of industry and private banks, in many cases, is symbiotically connected to the state, leading them to become dependent and addicted to the continuous creation of money.

A starry sky could be artistically represented by Van Gogh's famous painting, but, if we raise our eyes to the sky, the number of stars that our eyes can see on a moonless night is much more numerous. When considering the State and all its dependencies, from the main entities to the most peripheral ones, directly or indirectly, they collectively represent an intricate web of interconnected stars, each reliant on one another.

Let us imagine the State as a universe of interrelated entities, starting with the first level, which includes the ministries and the offices directly dependent on the governmental system. To these first levels, we add a very important number of dependencies represented by institutions of the most varied names, some of them very exotic, another countless number of governmental offices up to the mayor's offices of small mountain villages. Numerous smaller entities, including rural schools in remote villages, depend on the State, both directly and indirectly.

Then come a myriad of companies connected to the state, with the state as a shareholder or in equity participation. Some of them will be non-profit, others will be for-profit, like the companies that manage water and those that specialize in garbage collection or public transportation. These companies include cooperatives and other organizational forms that have the State as a partner or as the main client.

Countless other companies probably provide services to the State or to companies in which the State is not a direct shareholder. We can also find an entire system of non-governmental organizations that are financed thanks to state aid, through which they manage to survive. It is possible to observe the government intervention in various areas such as: garbage collection, defense, internal security, commercial offices, or embassies in other countries.

Governments constitute the most intricate and complex systems that are the foundation of society. However, the complexity doesn't stop there. From this level, a whole series of interrelationships with the interests of private companies and their lobbyists are born, and thus the system becomes exponentially more complicated. We are facing a highly complex system that is almost impossible to visualize and understand completely.

Do not be fooled, although at first glance when we try to go into the details of this system, we keep finding new and more complex relationships that we need to understand, if we abstract from the details that make up this system and try to synthesize its operation, things become very simple to understand: a matrix of power as an abstract entity. Money and its transfers from the central entity to the more peripheral entities are the glue that allows the life of this abstract entity.

The big surprise is that this multitude of entities are eager to receive money or economic benefits, with the mere objective of paying salaries to their employees. In other words, the main objective of this structure is the economic maintenance of itself through salaries. At the same time, we have the explanation of the endemic inefficiency of the State actions in most of the areas where it is present, since its objectives often become intertwined with the primary need to pay salaries. Please note that my intention is not to be misunderstood, there are extremely efficient institutions that work well, but globally, while it is true that there is efficiency, there is more inefficiency and more waste.

Understanding this level of complexity, it can be comprehended that any administration that comes to power, even with the best intentions to restructure public spending and put order in the State's finances, will more often than not be just another failed attempt. There are too many underlying interests, too many magnets that pull, require, and demand money. If we analyze this perspective, this matrix, we can conclude that it is capable of living and feeding itself within an inflationary system that becomes its lifeblood. Taking into perspective the objectives of the representatives we vote for, within this complexity, we can perfectly deduce that the system can function in a logic of continuous spending that is permanently increasing. **This degenerates into an endemic inflationary system.**

8.10 Why central bank monetary policy actions are doomed to fail

Let's try to link the events to get a broader view of the problem. The first element is public spending, which is financed by increasing public debt and a complex system of taxes. If we analyze the evolution of public spending and public debt, it is not self-contained. Public spending and debt are constantly evolving at a higher rate than the country's economic growth (Fig. 1). At the same time, through the issuance of bonds and the intervention of the central bank in the process, an exponential increase in the monetary base of the system is generated.

When central banks finally want to control inflation, we have at the level of government entities a strong conflict; on the one hand, there is an increase in interest rates and some timid measure to reduce the liquidity of the system through the actions of "QT"[68]; but on the other hand, the political system continues to ask for money and is not willing to stop the continued evolution of public spending and public debt. The system can significantly address inflation only by combining monetary policy with the reduction of public spending and debt.

Unfortunately, if we study the evolution of public spending and public debt, at the levels of OECD countries (Fig. 2), we see that it is practically impossible to control public spending and public debt; they are two monsters totally out of control. To be more precise, they have taken direct control of their own destiny and are self-feeding by creating and feeding themselves from the inflationary spiral.

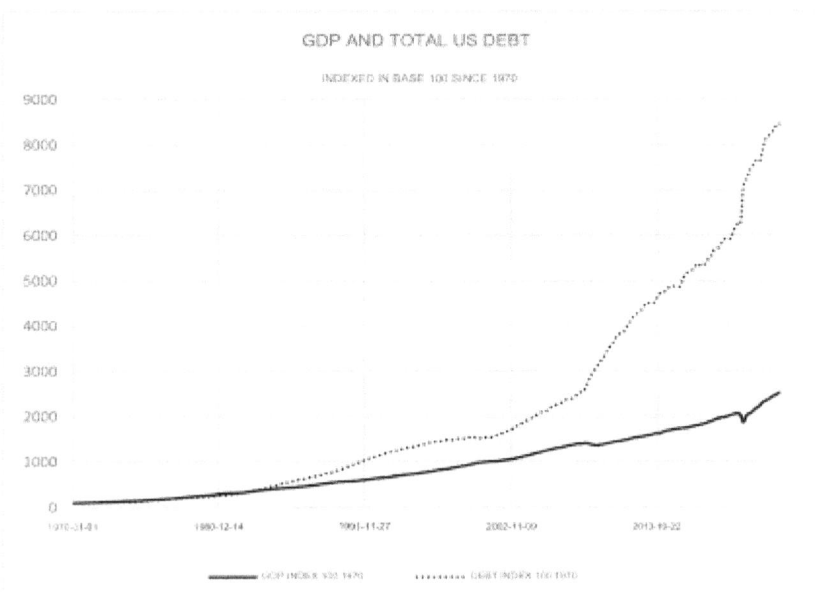

U.S. Bureau of Economic Analysis, Gross Domestic Product [GDP], retrieved from FRED, Federal Reserve Bank of St. Louis; https://fred.stlouisfed.org/series/GDP, July 1, 2023.
U.S. Department of the Treasury. Fiscal Service, Federal Debt: Total Public Debt [GFDEBTN], retrieved from FRED, Federal Reserve Bank of St. Louis; https://fred.stlouisfed.org/series/GFDEBTN, July 1, 2023.

Fig. 1: Comparative graph of the evolution of U.S. Gross Domestic Product (GDP), starting in 1970 with the U.S. debt. Both values were indexed to base 100 in 1970. It can be seen how public debt increases significantly with respect to the country's Gross Domestic Product. This simple numerical analysis shows how the monetization of an economy does not translate into more wealth for its people. In the following chapters we will be able to evaluate other indicators, which show how the increase in public spending and public debt destroy the purchasing power of the middle class and redistribute wealth as we have defined in this book in an inverse manner.

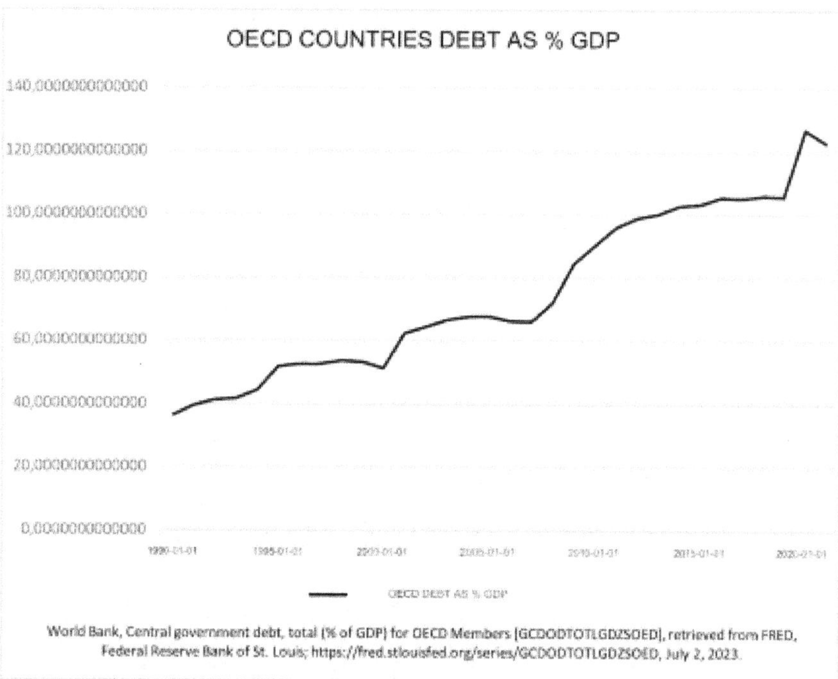

World Bank, Central government debt, total (% of GDP) for OECD Members [GCDODTOTLGDZSOED], retrieved from FRED, Federal Reserve Bank of St. Louis; https://fred.stlouisfed.org/series/GCDODTOTLGDZSOED, July 2, 2023.

Fig. 2 Representative graph of the evolution of public debt as a percentage of the Gross Domestic Product of OECD member countries. It shows how it has continuously and steadily increased over the last decades. In this respect, we can conclude that public spending and the debt that accompanies and sustains it, end up being a common feature of the Western economies of the planet.

The complications do not end. If we also wanted to achieve real control of inflation by means of fiscal and monetary instruments, this would lead the target country into a recession or perhaps a few years of economic depression, which could lead to the loss of nominal value of financial and non-financial assets. An example of this would be the stock market crash and the loss of nominal value of real estate. Such an event would be highly improbable, because it would imply that the government would place limits on its activity, which it has amply demonstrated it is unable to do. In the case of the implementation of restrictive policies, once they affect the economy, it would immediately change course, which would again push the inflationary phenomenon in the country. This is a clear example of how the State, as an abstract entity with all its direct and indirect ramifications, can feed itself and at the same time become an almost unmanageable entity. Public administrators, even if they have the best intentions of correcting the problems for the common good of society in the face of this complexity, have their hands tied because the system advances on automatic pilot and it is not possible to stop it except by assuming costs and responsibilities that no one wants to assume.

9 The irrationality of public spending causes and effects

9.1 From the decline of the great ideals to the loss of control mechanisms on politician activity in the great democracies. The origin of the irrationality of public spending

The irrationality of public spending has among its main causes the political system, and the real priorities that influence the practical decisions of its mandate. Within this scheme, it is important to visualize the role played by citizens with their ideals, their systems of control over government activity, and their values. We have seen in the previous chapter that, within this cauldron that represents the State and its socioeconomic environment, in addition to the citizens, we also have all the other private entities. These entities have their expectations, their interests, and the power to substantially influence government activity.

If we analyze the participation of citizens in the electoral processes, in the main democracies we are witnessing a process in continuous decline. The people are losing the charm of participatory democracy; instead of going to vote, they prefer to use their free time in other activities and are not willing to waste even an hour of their time at the polls, to elect those who will govern them in the years to come. Surely, this does not reflect an anti-democratic drift, as you have surely heard from the mouths of the parties that have lost the elections, attempting to diminish the victory of the party that won. These are simply stories that the losers, or those who were not elected, use to justify their electoral defeat. What is the real reason for this lack of interest in the politics of the persons that will guide our destinies in the years to come? As in all things, there is no univocal answer. Undoubtedly, one of the main reasons for the world's current state of affairs is people's lack of interest in politics. If there were interest, we would see greater participation and more control. The underlying reasons are reflected, however, in the simple and crystalline reality of the facts.

Our representatives, those we have elected in the elections, those who remain in power, will always do things differently from what they promised in the campaign. Once in power, they become miraculously infected with the very dangerous and contagious virus of forgetfulness, which will lead them to forget all their electoral promises. We should take into consideration that politicians suffer from a very labile memory, even though some of them stood out in careers that involved years of education. One would expect that they would have retained something from the time spent at the schools and universities where they obtained their degrees. What we have in the end are representatives who end up doing the very opposite of what they were elected for. They were infected by the virus of oblivion, but they did not lose the ability to speak because they will always find reasonably good excuses to justify their actions, especially if things do not go well. They usually place blame on the previous ruling party, the opposition, or maybe the press.

The noble ideals that have accompanied the progress of modern society have remained in history, as didactic cases to study. Their actual application in society looks different from what the idealists of the past had imagined. Concepts such as liberalism or Marxism are just words, painting a nostalgic reality of a long-dead and buried past. The great ideals of labor of the defense of workers have died, drowned in the indifference of a digital reality guided by artificial intelligence. Globalization has significantly impacted numerous modest job positions, focusing companies on an unlimited search for economies of scale, which reduces the quality of products and services offered. In a world were competing by cutting costs proves to be the only hope of life for many old businesses.

The world at this moment is once again facing a new revolution, even more important than those of the past, new technologies and robotics guided by a new form of intelligence and self-reasoning. They will come to impose more radical changes to many of the fundamental aspects of our lives without us realizing it. Perhaps those changes will occur when people are half asleep, in a safe virtual reality that does nothing more than make us dumber human beings than we would normally be.

The true concern surrounding artificial intelligence is not to take jobs away from mankind but rather to make hominids unaccustomed to thinking and finding solutions using their own intelligence. The greatest danger that humanity faces, therefore, will be to turn us into automatons because any type of problem will be solved by our computers. A bit sad, isn't it?

The great ideals of the past have faded away, existing now only in the history books, where the only thing left is to remember them in a sad nostalgic wake that certainly will not bring these ideas back to life. For those who enjoy raising their left fist or using other political symbols, remember, and do not be offended, these no longer exist and actually in fact never existed. It's important to ground ourselves in reality and find purpose within it.

9.2 The complot theory: how citizens do not understand what their administrators are doing.

The proliferation of plot theories, thanks to the accessibility of the Internet and information, has mushroomed in recent years. The basic issue that we should come to understand is how politicians and the representatives we choose come to change their minds and act differently than their promises. Finally, the answer is more linear and simpler than you can imagine, without uncomfortable reptilian thinking or similar ideas.

When we talk about the public sector and its complication as a starry sky, where the stars are interconnected with each other, we have described with a simple image the visual reality of what the public sector represents from a small mayor's office to large countries. How many interests and how many interrelationships are there between the different forces that move the politicians' decisions? Some of these forces will push in one direction, others in the opposite one. Within this complex scheme, all of them will engage in a power game to achieve certain benefits for certain interest groups.

The power of interest groups is what really moves the decisions of politicians. Those in power must balance their decisions between those who want one thing and those who want the opposite. Many times, the outcomes that we will see embodied in laws are the result of compromises rather than solutions. The great disinterest we see in politics of an increasingly larger part of the population that has lost faith in the electoral participation is largely due to the understanding of these voters that their vote will change very little anyway. Voters believe that the results achieved finally are predetermined by powerful groups representing other interests.

The power of lobbyists moves many decisions and achieves results that are sometimes surprising. The decisions made at the political level do not come from nice and pure ideals, but rather from the balance of interests between lobbies and the ruling authorities. It is a twisted and opaque process. Within this dismaying picture, there are public spending decisions that often end up in the misuse of funds by financing projects of little or no use.

In the face of these great divergences between electoral promises, which are usually not kept, and the practical results that governments implement, voters have inexorably lost interest in the system. This is something deeper than a simple loss of interest; it is alienating citizens from politics. They no longer believe in politics and consider it a waste of time because they do not have enough power to change things. These feelings that citizens are experiencing are particularly dangerous because they imply not only a distancing of the people from their governments, but also a loss of control over the economic and fiscal system and how resources are being used. Regarding the control mechanisms that people should have over the actions of politicians, let's consider a simple example: imagine that you are a jeweler, and you have all the jewelry displayed with many customers inside your store. In this situation, you would not leave them alone for a single moment. You would stay with them while they decide whether to buy. Similarly, citizens often leave politicians alone throughout their term, and as a result, they lose control over their actions and decisions.

Society is divided into those who hold power and those who do not, where the majority is of the latter category. The former manages to convince the latter that what they are doing is going well and is good. The middle class and the majority of voters make up the second group. As they come to realize how little influence they have, they become disinterested in participating in the electoral process.

Therefore, the causes that explain the theory of the irrationality of public spending are as follows:

- Divergence of the objectives of politicians with the needs of the community.

- Voter disinterest in politics, its mechanisms, and results.

- Discrepancies between the interests and the power to influence the community and the interests of the power groups.

- Lack of adequate mechanisms for citizens to control public spending.

9.3 The irrationality of public spending, new inflation theory

Public spending plays a significant and direct role in the rise of public debt and inflation because it increases the amount of money in circulation. To finance their government activity, countries use the issuance of public debt which increases the monetary base of the system. When this debt is acquired or subscribed by the central bank, it contributes to the creation of new electronic money, which ends up expanding by means of the bank multiplier. This new money gradually destroys its intrinsic value. Upon reviewing the definition given in the previous chapter on the public spending system, we come to this conclusion:

The economic and monetary system is endemically inflationary and ultimately feeds on the same inflation that it is producing. This system is coprophagous[69], because it has the capacity to feed on the inflation that it inexorably produces.

Understanding this aspect leads us to a new theoretical view of inflation:

Inflation is a monetary and economic phenomenon, endemically related to the public spending of government systems, which leads to the loss of value of money in relation to consumer goods and investment assets.

It is not possible to intervene in inflation without intervening in public spending and debt, which are the main cause of the inflationary phenomenon.

Intervening in inflation using only interest rate control policies or other monetary restrictions does not allow the monetary institutions to control the phenomenon. Evaluating the inflationary phenomenon only from the point of view of consumer goods is the cause of underestimating its dimensions. It is essential to explain by the relationship between the value of money in relation to the consumer goods and investment goods. Therefore, analyzing inflation solely from the perspective of consumer goods is a significant limitation that does not describe the phenomenon correctly and does not allow intervening to correct it.

9.4 How public spending is used

Venezuela (Ch.5, Fig. 2) and Zimbabwe (Fig. 1) with their currencies have achieved this destruction of value in a theoretically perfect and fast way. We must understand this crucial aspect of the economic policy of most of the governments of our planet. What is the real need for public spending, or in other words the percentage of it that is necessary for the country to function well? Once the necessary percentage of public spending has been quantified, we must understand what effects the other part of it causes on the economy. This other part finally represents a waste of public resources.

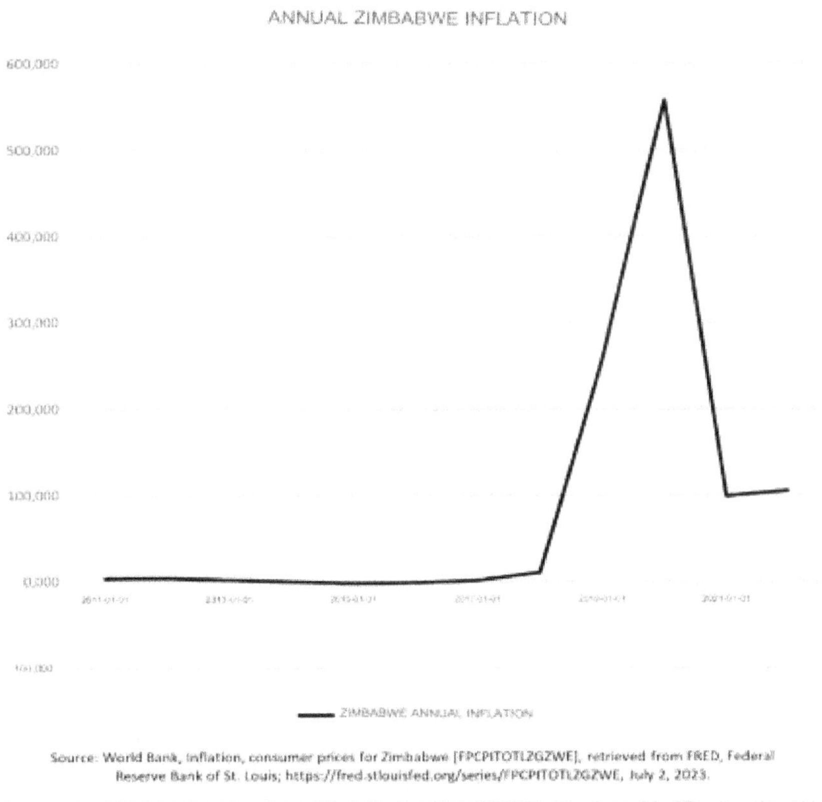

Source: World Bank, Inflation, consumer prices for Zimbabwe [FPCPITOTLZGZWE], retrieved from FRED, Federal Reserve Bank of St. Louis; https://fred.stlouisfed.org/series/FPCPITOTLZGZWE, July 2, 2023.

Fig. 1: Chart depicting Zimbabwe's inflation. How the stratospheric level of inflation can destroy the value of money with an explosive speed and bring its ultimate effects on a country's economy. This process begins at the monetary level but ends up causing severe economic imbalances that require many years of order and discipline to heal.

To identify which public activities are unnecessary, we need to ask ourselves a basic question which it is not so difficult to answer. The question refers to the efficiency that a private entity can achieve in its business compared to what can be expected from the public sector. People who have witnessed some privatizations of public services in Latin America will agree that the quality of the services provided by private entrepreneurs normally has improved at a lower cost for the community. A private investor puts his whole life at stake with his activity—his savings, hopes, future, and the future of his family. On the contrary, a public entity that performs the same activity beyond the façade reasons for it which exists represents only a few offices and some extra employees without a real underlying inner objective. If we can solve this intellectual puzzle, we can comprehend how reducing public intervention in the economy can create better opportunities for success and employment for its citizens. Faced with this reflection, we should ask ourselves: What is the role of the public sector? The answer is simple: the public sector must be the arbiter, the one that dictates the rules to make life easier for companies, to protect private interests, and to guarantee a minimum level of necessary services in the system. Ideally, therefore, we have an active public sector that provides some activities that cannot be delegated to the private sector, present with a role that promotes social equity within the community, and finally, as the arbiter so that the system flows well through its laws and regulations. All other interventions of the public sector hinder and cause inefficiency, delays, and backwardness in the economy and at the country level.

Irrational public spending has two negative consequences: inflation and waste of resources through misallocation. To understand this aspect, we have to divide public spending into a part that is essential for the proper functioning of a country and another part that is unnecessary. It is easy to understand the unnecessary part because it is a simple destruction of resources, but when we analyze the necessary part of public spending, we must ask ourselves: **How efficiently are these resources used in these necessary areas of intervention?**

9.5 The productivity of countries and public administration

Globalization has significantly intensified competition among private companies, which, to cope with these pressures, are obsessively seeking to reduce the costs of their products and services. As a result, there is relative price control over consumer goods, while inflation has had more detrimental effects on investment assets.

But how has the public sector experienced the phenomenon and the external competitive pressure? To answer this question, we have to use some examples and I apologize, from the beginning, for what you will see as an oversimplification of the concepts presented. I hope you will understand that I am using simplification as an instrumental tool to enhance comprehension.

Let's take the example of a private entrepreneur with a limited budget for their business. They need to make strategic decisions to achieve their economic and financial goals. The initial steps that will guide them in their decisions will be the evaluation and rationalization of expenses and investments according to the expected profit, since the resources available are limited.

The objective of any business is to produce profits. Decisions are made based not on pleasing anyone but focused solely on producing results.

Finally, within this process there is the possibility of errors that, once understood, will be immediately corrected to prevent wasting more resources. Normally, this economic activity will remain the property of this entrepreneur until it is sold, inherited by its children, or enters a bankruptcy process.

In the public sector, there are significant differences. First, the investment budget does not belong to individual managers; it is allocated through a budget approval process. This means that obtaining additional resources can be relatively easier compared to a private company. Once a private company exhausts its available funds, it may have limited options for obtaining more capital. Finally, errors do not hit the managers' pockets. In the case of public companies, these errors hit an abstract entity, the public sector itself, which has neither names nor surnames. The main objectives are usually not to generate a positive economic result, but to generate jobs that will be limited to strict office hours. Unlike our private entrepreneurs, the public sector normally enjoys a certain exclusivity; therefore, there is not much competition, which is totally the opposite of the private sector's need to constantly attract and retain clients. Another substantial difference between the public sector and the private sector is meritocracy, a word that is practically unknown in public employment. In the private sector, high-performing individuals are typically rewarded with higher salaries and greater opportunities for career growth. In the public sector the main meritocratic element is to belong to the right party at the right time, and dismissals are a rare occurrence.

If we compare the two examples, we see that productivity in the public sector will never be more than a few lines on a purpose paper.

To describe plastically the sad reality of things, picture a scenario where the mayor's office hires a man to paint the streets. On the first day, he managed to paint three kilometers, on the second day two and a half kilometers, and so on until Friday, when he does less than 500 meters. The administrator of that entity calls him concerned and asks him the reasons why he painted so little on the last day, as well as why his productivity dropped so much. The new employee explains to him that he has to walk further and further between the paint pot and the area where he is going to paint, and this is the reason for the low productivity. In this scenario, the manager, in a considerate manner, approaches the employee and appreciates his efforts and dedication to the job. The manager then warmly announces that he will propose a salary increase for the employee, recognizing that it is well-deserved. What the story omits is that this public employee found the job because he supported the mayor in the elections that had just taken place. This is the graphic view of how things are going in the sector.

We, therefore, have to come to some conclusions regarding productivity in the public sector, which is often a destroyer of resources and is not prioritized like the private sector. Imagine that there are countries in which getting angry with a public employee, and talking to them in a higher tone, after they have given you a bad service, can be punishable even with jail[70].

As an illustration of the perceived lack of productivity in the public sector, one can observe the continuous growth of public spending itself, which represents the money spent by the State in its activities, its companies, and its projects. This spending is a voracious monster that increases every year without any tendency to decrease. Within this continuous growth of public spending, the government has evolved creatively in the way it finances itself. There have been different steps in this process. First, a scheme strictly focused on taxes, towards a scheme focused on public debt. As a last step, we witnessed a leap in quality, at a point where finding new acquirers of state debt becomes increasingly difficult. And now we come to the printing of money, in order to continue financing expenditures that are totally out of control. To summarize the process there are basically three steps: the first one on taxes, the second one evolving into debt, and finally the last one which is the printing of paper that gradually loses value.

The last decades have been an important competitive challenge for the private sector, due to the forces of globalization and technological evolution. Meanwhile, the public sector has consolidated a continuous increase in its expenses, as well as in public debt, and we would dare to say a continuous and constant decrease in productivity.

To answer the question posed in the previous chapter, the public sector, in the area of its activities necessary for the proper functioning of a country and the economy, will use public money inefficiently due to its own systemic weaknesses.

9.6 How the inefficiencies of the public system cause a poor distribution of wealth and the impoverishment of that country

Understanding how the irrationality of public spending comes to influence government fiscal policies and the wealth redistribution system is very important to be able to qualify the actions of governments.

Many economies in the Western bloc seek the redistribution of wealth as an instrument to create equity and achieve social justice; it is important, therefore, to make some reflections on such a noble purpose and its practical results at the economic level. The redistribution of wealth is undoubtedly a noble and just cause, but questionable at the same time. However, we should question its functionality and whether it is merely a facade action promoted by our rulers and trade union associations.

Wealth redistribution means sharing wealth from the rich to be reassigned to those in need. However, this redistribution process does not consist of taking money out of one current account to pass it to others; achieving this implies a whole series of bureaucratic mechanisms (Fig. 2). Coincidentally, in countries where wealth redistribution is prioritized, these are the same states where there is a very low floor for most wages.

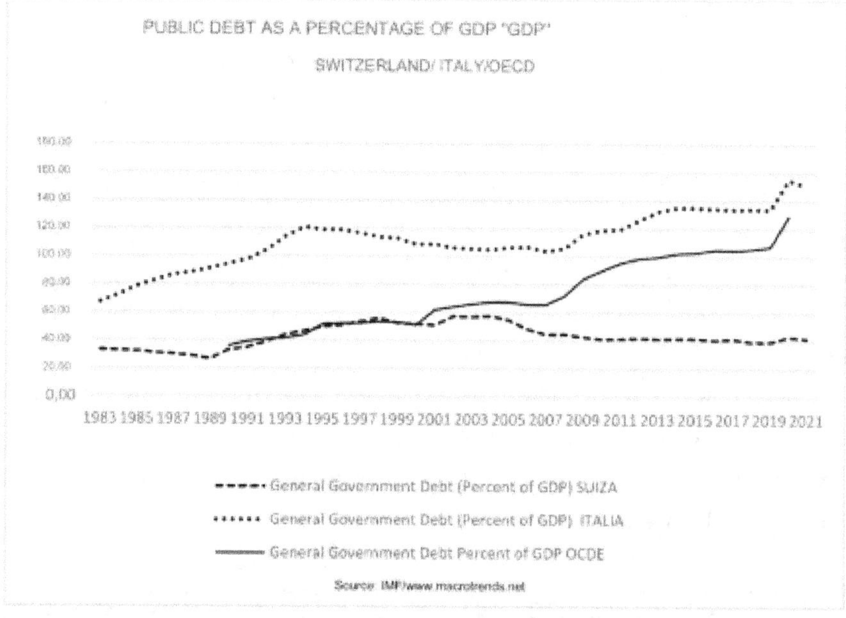

Fig. 2: Graph analyzing public debt as a measure of state interventionism in the economic system and comparing its evolution in relation to the Gross Domestic Product of: Switzerland, Italy and the OECD average. The basic question it tries to answer is: Is Italy well managed or, on the contrary, does the level of indebtedness represent the waste of public resources of a partitocratic system, oriented to the distribution and redistribution of electoral gifts, instead of seeking the welfare of its citizens? This analysis does not refer to any political party, nor to any political tendency, it is a dynamic view that covers almost four decades of history where all parties have been responsible at a certain point in time. As can be seen in the last forty years, Switzerland's public debt as an expression of its public spending increased moderately. In contrast, in Italy it increased almost three times, or in other words in an exponentially significant way. In the next series of graphs, we present the social spending and evolution of GNI (Gross National Income) per capita, thus we will have an answer to whether income redistribution policies and highly public interventionism work. Or on the other hand, they are just a failure of the system that only impoverishes the population by destroying economic resources.

To achieve these redistributive policies, governments typically follow a consistent set of actions. They begin by increasing taxes on companies and higher income levels, to implement a series of governmental plans that should achieve this goal. In the particular case of Italy, many of the companies that used to pay their taxes in that beautiful country, the land of pizza and pasta, have abandoned it in order to legally transfer their headquarters to other places in the European Union with important tax advantages. At the same time, many high-income individuals decided to move their residence to countries with important tax advantages. Ultimately, the human being could be a bit selfish and in a European framework of already very high tax levels, he does not understand the reasons to pay more taxes than necessary. Finally, we have the big global groups that are very well advised on taxation and manage to pay and optimize their tax outflow every year.

The other more dramatic aspect of wealth redistribution is the modalities by which politicians usually plan to achieve these objectives. These extra funds collected in taxes finally end up in the machinery of public spending. You can draw your own conclusions about how this story might end. What is surprising is the innocence of many politicians and many trade unionists, who have not apparently understood after so many years how the economy works. The way they usually implement wealth redistribution has no hope of working, and consequently leads to a waste of public resources.

The answer is obvious, there will be a clear explanation of that in the chapter that analyzes how the middle class has been crushed by inflation throughout the various latitudes and longitudes of the planet. However, there is a fundamental conceptual error when talking about wealth redistribution that comes from the basic objectives that guide our politicians in their actions. From a political perspective, wealth redistribution is seen as an opportunity to invest; but, on the contrary is just a way to spend public money. Politicians believe that by spending more resources, they can increase their power and influence. To understand what kind of result extra public sector expenditures, given a correct redistribution of wealth, could bring to the economy, it is crucial to comprehend how the public sector ends up investing the resources it collects in taxes. The efficiency of its use and therefore whether these expenditures represent a higher productivity or just an expression finalized in themselves is clear.

From this perspective, the various wealth redistribution projects, cannot prosper since the public sector by definition is inefficient and is not rational in its spending pattern. Consequently, the additional funds intended for redistribution may not reach those who are most in need, and probably end up in a complex system of electoral handouts.

The government should focus on redistributing wealth by providing tax facilities to the most unfortunate sectors of the economy and through the implementation of ideal conditions for the creation of companies. That strategy would finally be able to commit the resources to be invested correctly. The waste of resources ends up being the main reason why governments cannot achieve a redistribution of wealth, and this is due to the inefficiency of the public sector itself. By reducing its taxes and the size of the government, a country can foster the growth of more companies that generate more jobs, and better salaries and finally contribute to a true redistribution of wealth by creating the conditions for its nourishing.

Due to the inefficiency and waste of public resources by governments, any action related to the redistribution of wealth does not achieve these objectives and paradoxically leads to unintended consequences, capital flight, an increased tax burden on the middle class, occasional impoverishment of the population and a rise in unemployment.

Fig. 3: Graph comparing the strong redistributive interventionism of the Italian government versus the behavior of Switzerland and the other OECD countries. Italy manages to almost double Switzerland's social spending in percentage and at the same time invests about fifty percent more than the other member countries. According to common logic, therefore, in the beautiful Mediterranean country, the land of poets, sailors, pizza, and good wine, we should have more social equality and a better redistribution of wealth. The next graph will analyze whether so much public interventionism translates into better per capita income for the people, or whether all that money turns out to be inefficient in redistributive terms to its citizens. But this heavy spending is very effective in terms of retribution of wealth to political parties and bureaucracy of a highly politicized and at the same time endemically inefficient system.

Resources are limited, and when they are misused, they deprive the economy of the opportunity to create jobs, better salaries, and more wealth for the country. The inefficiency of the government sector, instead of healing itself, infects the healthy economy and does not allow it to develop competitively in the world. This result is seen in the most indebted countries in Europe compared to the others. For example, Italy, because of its high level of public debt and its confiscatory tax system, does not create the conditions for the enrichment of the country. On the contrary, it is the cause of worsening the living conditions of its middle class, causing, on the contrary, an impoverishment of its population in comparison with the rest of its European partners. The misuse of its public spending is responsible for its inefficiencies. None of the right- or left-wing politicians that you hear from this country will be able to recognize this because the favorite sport of both groups is to blame the country's problems on others, instead of looking for solutions so that the country can prosper.

In conclusion, it is necessary to develop a theory that explains this phenomenon, as well as the impossibility of achieving a real redistribution of wealth with the instrument used by politicians and governments over the decades.

9.7 Inverse wealth redistribution theory

A system unable to control its public spending and financing within sustainable parameters causes an inverse redistribution of wealth, impoverishing the lower-income socioeconomic class to the advantage of the higher-income socioeconomic classes. (fig. 4).

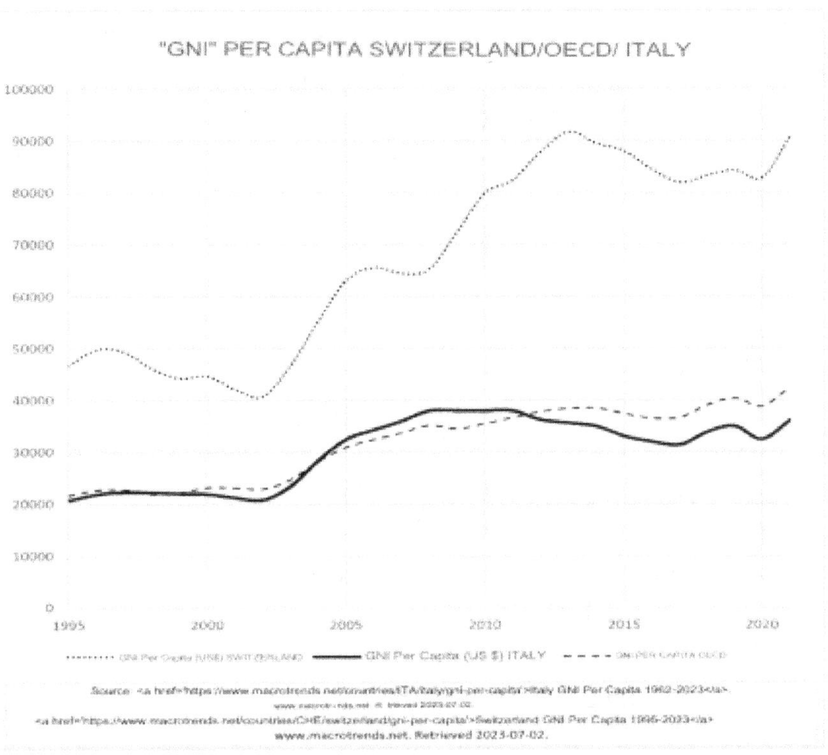

Fig. 4: Comparative graph of Switzerland's gross national income "GNI[71]" per capita from 1995 to 2021 versus the same indicator for Italy and OECD member countries at the same time. Italy supposedly invests a large part of its citizens' resources in social and public spending, its politicians and citizens believe in this method to redistribute wealth and build an economically fairer and more egalitarian society. The results are reflected in the analysis of these two countries: Switzerland uses the instrument of public spending and public debt moderately and maintains high levels of welfare and income of its citizens; on the contrary, we see how government interventions in Italy destroy the wealth of its population. Please note that in the last 20 years, Italy's GNI remained practically unchanged, while on the contrary, Switzerland's increased significantly (doubled), and that of the OECD countries increased moderately. This leaves Italy in a lagging position. This Mediterranean country has been guided by redistributive logic since the World War II, and remains trapped in the past, gradually destroying its middle class and impoverishing its population.

If we examine the distribution of resources in Western economies in recent decades, they all show an impoverishment of the middle class, de facto implicitly demonstrating the above theory. It is important to understand the central factor of this theory, which is intrinsically linked to the theories of the irrationality of public spending, as well as to the new theory of inflation.

Paradoxically, when governments pursue wealth redistribution through traditional means such as increasing taxes and redistributing them to the lower socioeconomic class, governments achieve exactly the opposite result. The key concept that explains this dystopia is the sustainability of the fiscal economic system.

Normally, when a government increases taxes, this action is governed by noble purposes, and many times the increase of taxes or the creation of a new tax is subordinated to certain objectives to ensure that society can live better. Such objectives may be an improvement in road infrastructure, health services, and public education. Once these resources reach the public administration system, which is known for its insatiable voracity, they are promptly used for purposes other than those for which they were intended. Very rarely are taxes spent for the noble reasons for which they were created. Normally taxes, although sometimes conceptualized for a short period, end up on a constant stable base by the voracity of the public sector.

When we think about resources to help in emergencies around the world, a similar thing happens. Much of this money ends up being used by the public sector of the recipient countries. Due to the high corruption of the recipients, only a small fraction of these aids ends up being used for the initially intended humanitarian purposes.

To understand the complexity of this theory we must think about how a society is capable of restraining itself and what not overflowing squandering resources would be like. A society of this typology does not seek to spend what the fiscal administration of its country collects through taxes. The logical guide would be the opposite of just spending for its own sake, but it will be focused rather on the investment of resources for common welfare. By spending money in the right way, the objective would be to generate the conditions for the less fortunate social classes to have access to educational and entrepreneurial opportunities that radically improve their quality of life. The sustainability of the system is its capacity to limit itself by reducing and controlling the voracity of its public sector and channeling resources where they are really needed. But taxes can't just keep going up without limit. There have to be some controls and priorities. Getting this concept is key.

Taxes are an essential and fair requirement in society; they should be designed and paid appropriately. There is a fine line of demarcation between levels of sustainability and the opposite that leads to the destruction of resources. This fine line should be demarcated by our managers. I leave it to you to analyze whether they apply this basic logical concept or do not fully understand it.

A society that knows how to limit itself in the expansion of its public sector understands this concept very well and usually has fewer economic discrepancies among the socioeconomic segments that make up the population of this country. **Failure to understand the concept of sustainability leads to the inverse redistribution of resources, which is a common characteristic of most of the modern societies in which we live.**

9.8 Inflation as a monetary and economic phenomenon

According to many schools of economic thought, inflation is often regarded as a purely monetary phenomenon with limited economic significance. The way inflation is viewed under this logic has been limited due to a lack of understanding of the complexity of the inflationary phenomenon. Although, indeed, the direct causes of inflation are mainly attributable to monetary expansion, its effects have repercussions and consequences that go far beyond a simple monetary phenomenon.

Inflation creates an imbalance within the system; which in turn has various implications for the valuation of consumer and investment goods. These changes are a consequence of the imbalance that inflation causes at the monetary level; as an example, we could think of a variation in the exchange rate of the currency of a country affected by inflation; this variation in the exchange rate has an effect on the import of goods and services and therefore on the local economy.

Another area where the economic effects of inflation become evident is in the inverse redistribution of resources within a system, and the loss of value and purchasing power of some social classes that are hardest hit by this phenomenon. These effects of inflation can be classified as economic and extend beyond the mere monetary effects.

Lastly, I would like to conclude this reflection with a concept of the chaos theory which, although not directly applicable to the study of inflation, can demonstrate how the events within a system cannot be viewed in isolation but rather as interconnected with the causes and effects they produce. Within this line of thought, important variations in the money supply in an economy in the systemic framework indirectly affect the economic part of the system itself.

9.9 Corruption in a resource-wasting scheme

Through a critical analysis of the irrationality of public spending, we discover a sad vision of the future, and see how public resources are used inefficiently. Inefficient management of public resources leads to waste. Resources are limited, and when they are wasted, they have lost their economic and social function.

Poor management of public resources, accompanied by high taxes and a system of crude state regulatory intervention, are the main causes of the inequalities experienced by our modern society and of unemployment. The scarce outlook for growth for the poorest and the struggling of the middle class is the direct responsibility of their own representatives. Regardless of the political ideology from which our representative is coming, the results are the same. The different political tendencies do not matter because they have an owner to be pleased with greater power than the voting masses that vote for them. We can define modern societies as appearing democratic, but they are de facto classist and oligarchic, where the same system rewards and shields itself, and thus takes away the chances for most people to truly succeed.

We are facing a highly complicated, imperfect economic and socio-political system, where many divergent interests, sometimes inconvenient for most of the people, fight for the allocation of economic resources, but we have not yet touched on the last variable that makes this system even more disorderly, which is the corruption factor.

When we look at corruption, we see it hurts different countries to different extents, and finally, the result that it causes on the economy is even more waste of resources that are added to the problems of the public sector itself. Therefore, in the total scheme of analysis, we leave it as an uncontrollable external variable, which, depending on its incidence, can be more or less harmful to the overall performance of an economy.

Having made these clarifications, we return to the concept seen at the beginning of the book of chaos theory, where an extremely complex reality such as the universe has a logic that it is possible to formulate mathematically representing a perfect system. At first glance it gives us the impression of a complex and disorderly reality, but deep down it is the expression and fruit of perfection and systemic order. When we delve into the analysis of socioeconomic and political systems, we are faced with an imperfect reality. This reality is plagued by elements that harm the environment and deplete its resources leading to an inflationary reality, with problems of employment and distribution of resources that have no solution and cannot be summarized in a formula that explains them correctly. We must reflect and analyze very well the real effects of inflation, since it is the most harmful and dangerous variable of the socioeconomic systems in which we live.

10. How inflation has destroyed the middle class

10.1 The great financial bubble, myth or reality?

If we analyze the evolution of financial assets, we should agree with the thinking of many observers and analysts who describe the phenomenon as a big bubble. Indeed, this analysis has some basis of truth and is therefore partly correct. However, I believe that they may not take into consideration the key element of this phenomenon, which is inflation. In other words, if financial assets increase exponentially in nominal value, this increase could be more correctly described as a loss of value of the reference currency due to inflation. To be able to estimate the value of assets and their evolution over time, we need to consider the impact of inflation.

As the famous song by the well-known Panamanian singer-songwriter Rubén Blades says: "Life gives you surprises." If we remove the inflationary factor from the nominal value of financial assets, we will surely have some surprises as well. Perhaps we would discover that, in real and not nominal terms, some assets increased in value while others lost them. The bubble effect, as defined by many, may simply reflect the devaluation of the reference currencies that caused the nominal cost of the assets to increase.

These nominal values of financial and non-financial assets, from the value of houses, trough the stock prices of the SP 500[72], have increased at a constant pace throughout time with only small pauses. We see how they inflate, becoming a bubble. If we analyze the concept of inflation including in its study the evolution of prices of these assets, we can explain the phenomenon linearly and simply for what it is. The valuation of some goods by means of more monetary units is therefore an expression of an increase in their nominal value that does not represent necessarily a real value increase. For that simple reason, it is not a bubble. The financial and non-financial assets have increased their cost because of inflation where their real value is much lower than their nominal one. **Welcome to the world of autotrophic endemic inflation.**

10.2 Growth of economies

One of the big significant questions we can ask ourselves when presented with economic data is: Why is there such a strong emphasis on the growth of the economy? In other words, the expectation of continuous growth of economies, what is the underlying necessity for continuous growth? To explain I give you a small example: imagine a family, which could be the microscopic representation of a nation, if this family manages its expenditures without debts and saves part of its income, in the face of a reduction in wages it does not go into crisis. Why? Because it will have the savings and probably, even if its income has declined, it will be more than enough to cover its costs, and perhaps it will have some left over to continue saving. Imagine another family, which lives with credit card overdrafts and constantly increases its debts. They are forced to generate new debts to cover their expenses and the interest on the existing ones. If you compare these two cases, an income reduction could be catastrophic in the second one. However, in the first example, it would not generate a major problem.

Most developed countries have a pattern of spending that is reflected in the behavior of family number two; for this reason, they constantly need an increase or growth in the economy to sustain part of the increase in their spending. However, this constant growth of the economy is not enough to maintain the imbalance in which they live. If we look at these entities from an economic point of view, we see that they need the creation of more debt and inflation. These measures are necessary to prevent the system from collapsing and to maintain an appearance of equilibrium.

To understand how inflation plays into this exponential spending and debt scheme, we have to go back to the stagnation in which many of the developed economies find themselves. The main reason for this stagnation is seen in the evolution of their demographic structure. As I explained at the beginning of the book, the spending pattern of a 27-year-old professional is not the same as that of her 75-year-old grandmother. Western economies are coupled with a shrinking labor force and an increase in the number of pensioners who need their pensions. To face this reality, a well-managed state with no debt and with resources it has been saving over the years will simply draw, if necessary, on its savings. The only way in which a poorly managed state will be able to cope with the continuous and growing demand for expenditures is by creating new debts and thus increase of monetary base. This creates a need for a continuously growing economy because in this way more money will pour into it allowing the system eventually to maintain its balance. The subtle part to understand is the role of inflation because it can give us the artificial illusion of economic growth. The real Gross Domestic Product is debugged by the inflation effect. If these effects are higher than what has been measured, a Gross Domestic Product in positive nominal territory can perfectly become a decreasing indicator in real terms. In this way, inflation becomes an instrument of the system, so that it manages to stand on its feet in a situation of strong imbalance. In this complex reality, inflation plays a not very clean stealth game, through the redistribution of wealth, and this is the most present force in the market. The final problem lies in the fact that this wealth redistribution is not equitable, because, on the one hand, it destroys the real purchasing power of the middle class, their savings, and their investments and takes resources away from the poorest to finally benefit those who do not need this redistribution of wealth.

10.3 The great paradox of taxation according to current ideology and its practical results at the socioeconomic level

When engaging in discussions with politicians regardless of the tendency they have, whether they are conservative or of extreme left, both agree on the fact that paying taxes makes it possible for governments to provide their services to the people and thus support the weaker socioeconomic classes through the social programs put in place. If we were to read the transcripts of some speeches given by politicians from various ideological backgrounds, without knowing who gave them, the big surprise is that (apart from some ideological reference to identity in the background) they all say the same things. Finally, if we think about it, when we go to vote we elect representatives who say the same things as their opponents with some subtle differences in the background.

Theoretically, governments can spend the money that citizens pay them in taxes. These transfers of money from the people to the State finance public spending. However, the administrative system of the states has to tackle two challenging paradigms. The first one is the public expenditure in constant and continuous growth accompanied by an operational incapacity to effectively implement strategies to reduce it. The second paradigm is very simple to understand, starting from the fact that citizens do not like to pay taxes; this obviousness must be contextualized with the confiscatory tax levels that the main OECD countries apply to their citizens, as a result, there is no room for maneuvering to increase them to higher levels. In addition, we have to consider that when taxes are too high and unjustified, they ultimately have a dampening effect on the economic growth[73]. Our politicians often showcase remarkable talent in finding solutions to budget problems, in order to spend more money and due to the strong constraint of very high levels of direct and indirect taxes, the instrument used to finance themselves is debt issuance. Through extensive analysis, we have observed that public spending and debt are mainly responsible for inflation.

Let us now analyze what public debt means in its theoretical essence. The State through its representatives, in other words, we, indirectly get into debt to invest money for a better world. However, in many instances, this money is ultimately wasted or rather squandered. Therefore, we are responsible for inflation. When we look in the mirror, we must be aware that, through the electoral system, we contribute to inflation. It is important to analyze what public debt represents at a theoretical-philosophical level. Said in a folksy way, they are debts that sooner or later we will have to pay. A debt that we as a collective have to pay off is, in synthesis, a debt that is engraved on us at an individual level as well. Therefore, the debts of the State end up being our debts. Indeed, the situation becomes more intricate than what meets the eye. On the one hand, there are the taxes that you pay directly and indirectly; while on the other hand, the increase of the State's debt decreases your individual patrimony a little every year.

The tax and debtor system of the public administration is a brilliant way to mask a tax increase through the instrument of debt issuance. As increasing direct and indirect taxes has real and concrete limits that make the instrument unfeasible due to the level of taxes we are at, thanks to the increase of public debt in an indirect and camouflaged way, you pay more taxes, believing that the tax level is the same and the State miraculously manages to finance itself. Milton Friedman understood this concept very well. It is important not to be naive and to critically evaluate the narratives we are presented with. We simply have to be clear and know how things happen to be able to exert the right pressure on our representatives.

Other effects of inflation are at the tax level, which can ultimately increase your tax bill. As an example, if we think of someone who was earning $100 because of inflation they are now earning $130, but in addition to the loss in real terms of purchasing power, this individual also faces a higher tax bill, which ultimately detracts even more from the value of his or her wealth. What is greater in terms of value is the liability you have for your country's debt. Things, unlike the fairy tales we are shown in the movies, do not end here and they do not end well. The devastating effect of inflation is measured in the loss of value of money and in the irrational nominal increase of financial and non-financial assets, which are not worth more money and are not an expression of anything other than how much money has lost its value. In this scheme we are witnessing the continuous destruction of the middle class using a tax system that achieves the exact opposite objective for which it was created, in other words, the reverse redistribution of wealth. The poor and the middle class become poorer and the rich end up being the beneficiaries of this completely unbalanced monetary economic system.

To correctly understand the inverse redistribution of wealth, we have to bring together several key concepts: first, the taxes we pay to the State; the second, which we have extensively discussed in this book, is inflation; the third is the main inflationary element of the economy, which is the production of monetary base; and the fourth key element to understand this delicate mechanism is the capacity to access the production of new monetary resources. In this complex labyrinth, we have three socioeconomic forces that sustain the system: the dominant socioeconomic class together with the bureaucratic administrative apparatus of the State are the beneficiaries of the system itself. Numerically speaking it is the minority of the population. However, this group holds power, influences decisions, and controls the economy directly or indirectly through regulations. Finally, there is a third group represented by the middle class and the poorer social classes that represent most of the society in terms of votes, but when it comes to decisions and the distribution of economic benefits, they count for almost nothing.

In a society where the production of electronic money is highly abundant, which finally decreases its intrinsic value destroying wealth, what makes the difference is who manages to hoard more of this resource that is worth less and less. The one who has the biggest hands and the biggest pockets will be, at the end of the day, the one who benefits the most from this scheme.

The dominant social class is the one that has the best access to credit; therefore, for any type of investment, they will have the banks that will open their doors to them, which is different from the rest of the third group. Having understood and well - structured the logical reasoning basis of how the public sector works within the socio-political reality of a country allows us to theorize the inverse redistribution of wealth: **the expansion of the monetary base leads to a loss of value of money due to inflation, the waste of resources due to the imperfections of the administrative public system, accompanied by the subjective difficulties of the middle and lower socioeconomic groups to access credit contribute to the impoverishment of these groups and an inverse redistribution of wealth.**

10.4 The nominal value of financial assets

When we study the data on the monetization of the economy, where money creation is utilized to support the public spending system, and analyze it in terms of nominal inflation, we find that the information provided by the statistical institutes gives us an incomplete perspective of the inflationary phenomenon.

The underlying question is where does all the printed money end up?

If we look closely at the economy, we have the answer to our question. The explanation comes from the evolution of financial asset valuations.

A significant turning point in the analysis can be identified with the mortgage financial crisis that occurred in the late 2000s (2007-2010). From this moment the central banks began to support the economy by creating a monetary base (Chap. 3, Fig. 1,2). If we compare the flood of easy money in the economy with the evolution of the main stock market indexes, we have the answer to this action of the central banks on how it affects the value of money and the impoverishment of families (Fig. 1).

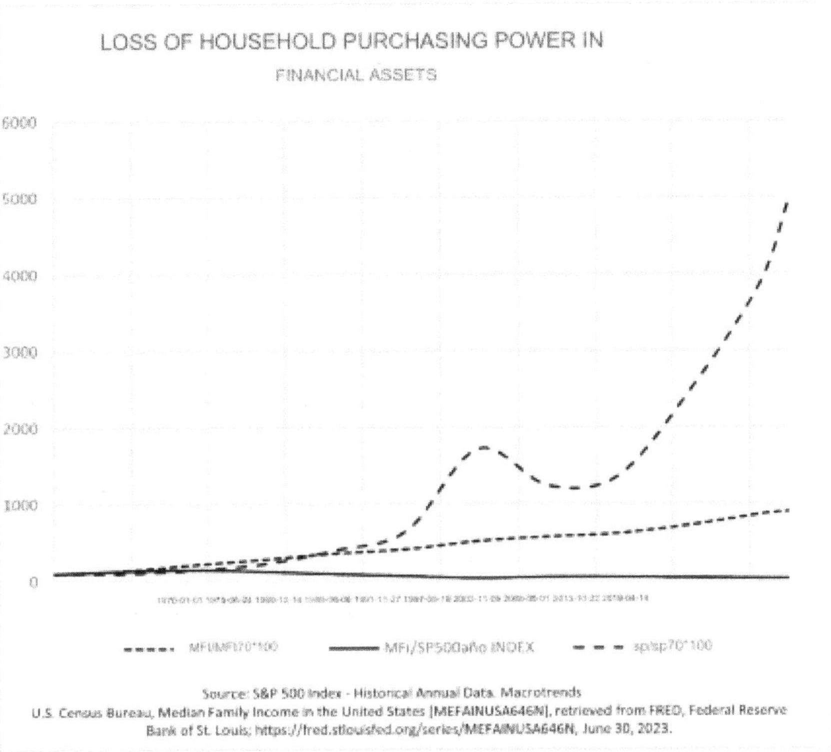

Source: S&P 500 Index - Historical Annual Data. Macrotrends
U.S. Census Bureau, Median Family Income in the United States [MEFAINUSA646N], retrieved from FRED, Federal Reserve Bank of St. Louis; https://fred.stlouisfed.org/series/MEFAINUSA646N, June 30, 2023.

Fig. 1: Comparison chart between 3 indicators indexed to 1970, the evolution of the SP 500, the average household income, and an index constructed from the average household income divided by the value of the SP 500. The speed with which the SP 500 has increased its share price represents the increase in the nominal value of the financial assets. As you can see from the second indicator, the average household income grew at a much slower rate than financial assets. It can be understood how these have become outdated, compared to the value of the stock market. Finally, to measure the loss of purchasing power of families and their consequent impoverishment, we use the third indicator which is constructed by dividing the average income of families by the value of the SP 500. Thanks to this operation, it is evident how, although the 3 indicators have started from 1970 indexed at 100, the real purchasing power of families is continuously and steadily reduced. This demonstrates a loss of purchasing power, the gradual but continuous destruction of the middle class, and its inability to invest and build a stable economic future. Today's society, thanks to access to easy and fast consumer credit, becomes de facto a system where professionals work to pay the quotes of the easy credits they obtain at usurious rates.

As I mentioned earlier at the beginning of this chapter, there is a whole legion of economists that I define as catastrophists. These economists announce on a timely basis the possible fall of stock prices in biblical proportions. The doomsayers have recognized the risks associated with central bank actions, but they are confusing current valuations as an expression of the real value of financial assets. They fail to understand that the cost evolution of these assets represents only an indicator of nominal increase. The values we examine of financial and non-financial assets reflect a continuous growth in their nominal value, but of a lower intrinsic value. Money is gradually losing its essential role as a representation and store of value to become mere pieces of paper.

When we compare the evolution of the SP500 stock indexes (Fig. 2) with the creation of a monetary base, we observe a correlation between these two indicators and the actions of central banks. This analysis can also be applied to many of the European indices which will give us similar results; however, the reality of things is that these two indices represent a very significant percentage of the world's market capitalization, the New York Stock Exchange being in terms of market capitalization and as a financial center, the center of the world of money. This further explains the significance of the U.S. dollar compared to the other currencies of the world.

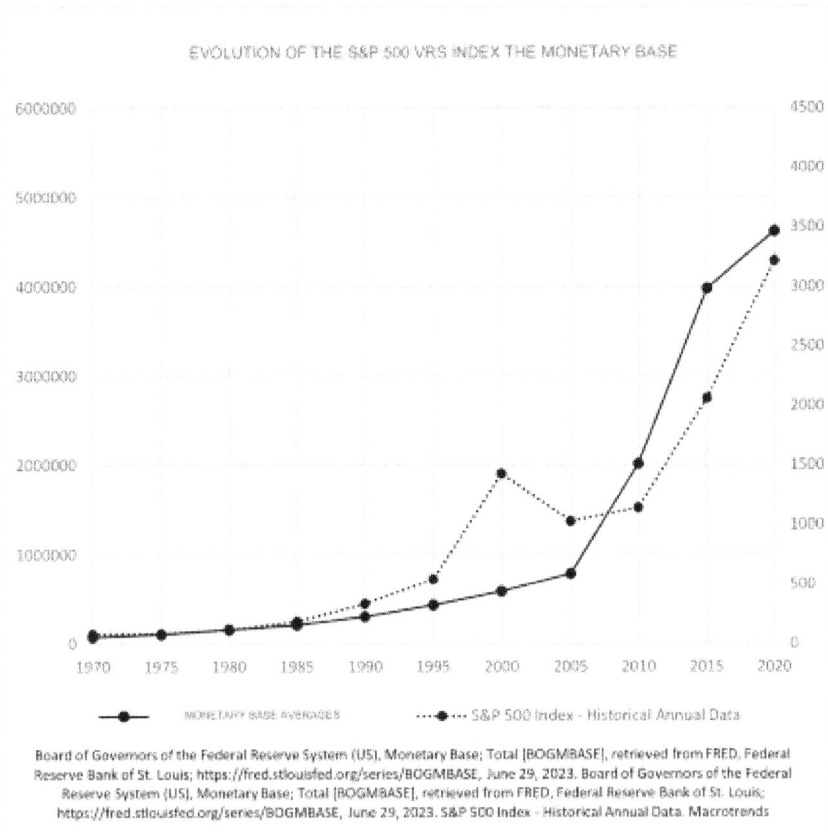

Board of Governors of the Federal Reserve System (US), Monetary Base; Total [BOGMBASE], retrieved from FRED, Federal Reserve Bank of St. Louis; https://fred.stlouisfed.org/series/BOGMBASE, June 29, 2023. Board of Governors of the Federal Reserve System (US), Monetary Base; Total [BOGMBASE], retrieved from FRED, Federal Reserve Bank of St. Louis; https://fred.stlouisfed.org/series/BOGMBASE, June 29, 2023. S&P 500 Index - Historical Annual Data. Macrotrends

Fig. 2: Representative graph in a two-dimensional scale of the evolution of the SP 500 index and the expansion of the US monetary base for the period 1970-2020. You can see how these two indicators proceed over time in a synchronous manner, as the monetary base increases, normally followed by an increase in stock prices. These are to a large extent a reflection of the oversupply of money in the system. Instead of being invested in the real economy, money finds its use at the financial level and becomes an inflationary factor in the assets of that sector of the economy.

10.5 Yield crisis

When we examine financial assets and their soaring share prices, we can also refer in our analysis to some global companies that play an essential economic role within most of the countries of the planet. Take Apple as an example, with a market capitalization of around 3 trillion dollars[74]. What stands out about this company is undoubtedly the ability of the management team to produce unique strategies and products that are highly demanded by its customers.

Apple is indeed a remarkable company when it comes to generating value. Upon analyzing its market capitalization, we note that it has undoubtedly been one of the most lucrative investments over the past twenty years. However, I would like to reflect on two aspects of this company that generate some doubt in my mind. The first aspect I consider refers to the dividends that this company distributes annually to its investors. At the time of writing this book, the dividend that Apple distributed to its shareholders was less than 0.6% (0.52%), when the price per share was 193 USD. In practical terms, this dividend is less than 1 USD per share. If we think about it, consider the risk of owning a company, even one as successful as Apple. Is it worth considering the dividend paid on the investment of 0.6 dollars per share? If we think about the ratio of risking 193 USD for less than a dollar of dividend per year, shows once again how little value the legal currencies represent.

The analysis regarding Apple has to go further. Many of you will think that Apple went from being worth very little to 193 USD per share in 20 years, which represents an exceptional market capitalization. You are right, it is. However, if we analyze how the market capitalization of Apple and many, many other financial and non-financial assets have evolved over the years from the other perspective, which is the ability of currencies and the dollar to represent intrinsic value by themselves, we find a somewhat bleak reality. Please understand that I speak of currencies in the plural, as they are interconnected. The abilities of currencies to contain and represent intrinsic value are very limited, "FIAT" currencies have lost intrinsic value inversely proportional to their increase in units in circulation. In conclusion, the substantial increases in stock market values of stocks like Apple, which often pay minimal or no dividends, is once again an expression of the inflation that has hit the financial assets of planet Earth.

10.6 What happens when a good is not scarce?

If we analyze the interest rates of fixed income investments over the past four decades, we encounter a disconcerting reality. Financial assets yield less and less and this is a trend that has been with us for decades.

When we compare the trend of interest rates at which the resources of those who lend money to the public sector are remunerated, with the introduction of an increase of monetary base in the system, we observe an inverse relationship between these two phenomena. The more money supply in the system, the less interest paid on the debt. This point has been touched between 2020-2021 with interest rates on 10-year bonds at virtually zero. In other words, what I have just written means that, if you had invested your money in 10-year U.S. treasury bonds at that time, what you would have collected in interest would have been zero, committing your savings for 10 years (Fig. 3). Not bad, right?

We saw that the only instrument used by central banks in such a situation is the injection of money into the economy, through the purchase of securities in the market; in other words, the creation of money out of nothing. But I want to reflect on another concept, if you look at how the monetary base increases over time and interest rates fall over time, what we observe is something very simple, here we have in an easily understandable way the definition of the value of a good. The scarcity of a good is what determines its value. In the case of money, its scarcity determines its value and, therefore, its ability to maintain its value over time. Through borrowing money, we pay rent on it, which is an interest. If we look at it from the other side, the one who takes our money pays us in interest rate; it is as simple as that. When a good loses its characteristic of scarcity, the outcome can be alarming because it loses its value. This relationship is well explained by the evolution of interest rates over the years about the creation of electronic money.

Don't be fooled by rising rates due to central banks' actions to control inflation. What could follow is that, at the first signs of recession, there will be a change of course to once again have an open bar at the party of creating money out of thin air.

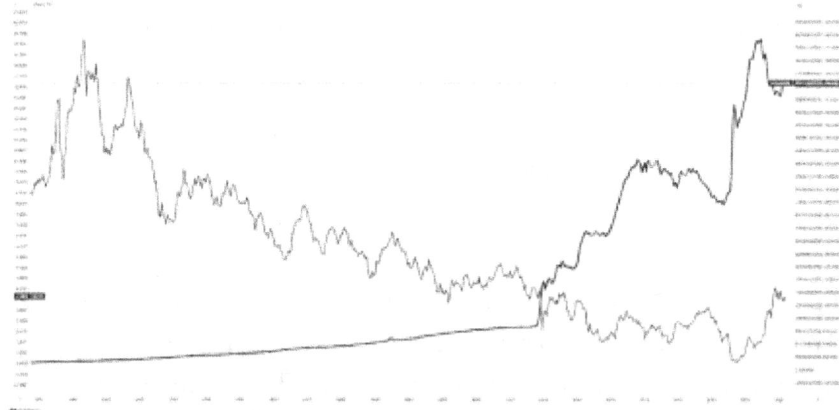

Fig. 3 Comparative chart of the evolution of the monetary base and the interest on 10-year bonds (Chart prepared with the Tradingview charting program): Comparison on a two-dimensional scale of the evolution of the monetary base and the interest on 10-year US government bonds. There is a perfectly inverse relationship between the two indicators: as the money supply increases, the yields on these bonds decrease. Since the beginning of the 1980s with four decades, U.S. Treasury bonds have decreased their yields during the same period that the financial system was flooded with an oversupply of money, which is the main cause of the increase in the nominal cost of financial and non-financial assets and at the same time the loss of value of the dollar.

10.7 Bitcoin

When discussing cryptocurrencies, it is important to differentiate Bitcoin and a selection of a few others versus a universe of thousands of these electronic currencies. The vast majority of them represent only a mere speculative attempt and will probably be worthless in the future. Cryptocurrencies are digital currencies that are linked to a cryptographic code. I apologize for the extreme synthesis that I used to describe them, if there are any experts they will have quite fertile ground for criticism, but the following story is not to explain what they are but to explain what happened to their market prices.

I believe that Bitcoin, along with Ethereum perhaps, are currencies with the potential to maintain their value over time and are not simply an expression of a momentary fad, but represent the evolution of what could be a new concept of money. On the contrary, I believe that there are, as I explained at the beginning, many thousands of other currencies that were only speculative expressions, some of which ended up losing THOUSANDS of millions of dollars. There have been many scandals where unsuspecting investors lost everything.

When discussing Bitcoin, which is one of the oldest and most recognized crypto, we can analyze it from three perspectives. The first perspective is held by those who believe in Bitcoin as a form of digital property, offering various advantages over physical property.

The second perspective is from those who do not understand how a complex cryptographic code can be an expression of so much value.

Finally, we have a third perspective, which in my opinion is likely to be the most accurate. This perspective assumes that governments do not want competition with any other type of money than the one issued by themselves. Many governments will probably introduce their own digital currency and the same these nations may not be willing to accept what could be defined as a competitor (other currencies) with no controls on their creation to share the pie. Finally, a sane egoism could be part of the true nature of the public sector.

Once again, we encounter a financial asset, Bitcoin, whose value is not fully understood. Bitcoin has reached a price close to 70000 USD per unit. However, this asset has an interesting feature that describes and proves once again our theory, the maximum limited number of pieces that can exist of it which are 21000000 and not one more piece. This characteristic of Bitcoin explains everything to us. On the one hand, we have the traditional type coins that have no limit in their creation, and with a simple computer click increase the amount of them in circulation exponentially. On the other hand, we have Bitcoin, a complex abstract cryptographic code that exists in a finite and predetermined number of units. From this perspective, it becomes easier to comprehend why Bitcoin can attain such high value.

10.8 The house

When we talk about the house, we are referring to what the majority of families worldwide consider their primary major investment. The house is what in the collective imagination represents an investment. If we analyze the costs of houses over the last decades, we see how they have increased significantly. When talking about the house we also have another reflection on the mechanisms by which inflation is calculated. Since the 80's it was one of the first goods to be eliminated from the inflation calculation to be substituted with some form of alternative income that underestimates the evolution of its real value.

The statistical institutes will explain to us that the value of the house is eliminated since it partially represents an investment. Therefore, the current way of calculating its contribution to inflation refers to the part that is equivalent to rent and this would be according to their version more correct. Under this same line of explanation, we have the confirmation that the criticisms sustained in this work on the conceptualization of inflation and how it is calculated are correct. It raises the crucial question of why the calculation of inflation is restricted solely to consumer goods and does not include a percentage of investment goods.

Answering this question is as simple as asking it. If the statistical institutes had calculated inflation including investment goods, it would have provided a very clear picture of the loss of value of money over time. Limiting the calculation of inflation to consumer goods, considering the competition between companies around the globe has resulted in an explanation of inflation that is lower than it is. We believe that this is not the correct description of inflation but rather a way of hiding the problem, so as not to address it at its root. In the next chapter, we will explore how inflation has been devastating and destructive for the middle- and lower-income classes in different countries (Fig. 4).

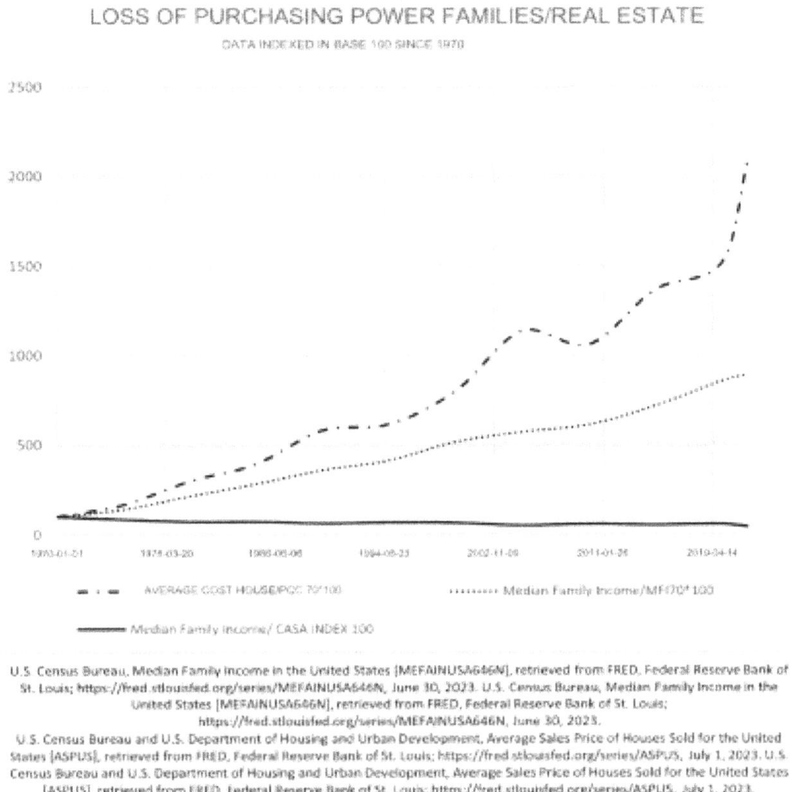

U.S. Census Bureau, Median Family Income in the United States [MEFAINUSA646N], retrieved from FRED, Federal Reserve Bank of St. Louis; https://fred.stlouisfed.org/series/MEFAINUSA646N, June 30, 2023. U.S. Census Bureau, Median Family Income in the United States [MEFAINUSA646N], retrieved from FRED, Federal Reserve Bank of St. Louis; https://fred.stlouisfed.org/series/MEFAINUSA646N, June 30, 2023.
U.S. Census Bureau and U.S. Department of Housing and Urban Development, Average Sales Price of Houses Sold for the United States [ASPUS], retrieved from FRED, Federal Reserve Bank of St. Louis; https://fred.stlouisfed.org/series/ASPUS, July 1, 2023. U.S. Census Bureau and U.S. Department of Housing and Urban Development, Average Sales Price of Houses Sold for the United States [ASPUS], retrieved from FRED, Federal Reserve Bank of St. Louis; https://fred.stlouisfed.org/series/ASPUS, July 1, 2023.

Fig. 4: Representative graph of the purchasing power of families over real estate indexed on a base 100 to 1970. It shows the comparative data of the evolution of house prices, the average household income, and the index obtained from the average household income divided by the cost of houses. These 3 indicators show us how the monetary euphoria that was unleashed since the unfortunate decision of Richard Nixon's government to abandon the relationship between the US dollar and gold, putting an end to the Bretton Woods agreements, has impoverished American families.

Freeing the production of dollars from the constraints of a fixed convertibility rate with gold is the element that allowed politicians and monetary authorities in the United States and in the major Western economies to use the monetary instruments as they pleased in order to influence the economy.

The results of this decision have been the constant and continuous impoverishment of the middle class in the last 5 decades. The uncontrolled increase in the cost of financial and non-financial assets has made these assets unattainable investments for the majority of the population, who today have seen their salaries fall behind in comparison to these assets.

10.9 Art

Art, I must confess, is one of my weaknesses. Throughout my professional career, I have to travel for business reasons, and as a tourist, this allowed me to visit many countries. One of the things that gives me the most pleasure is to visit museums, some of which, due to their level of importance, I have visited dozens of times, each one of them I have been learning something different. Over many subsequent visits I have discovered details that had escaped me previously. Having made this premise, I am fundamentally convinced that art is priceless, and the numbers I am going to present below will prove it.

The SALVADOR MUNDI is a painting attributed to Leonardo da Vinci. I use the term ''attributed'' because not all experts agree that it was painted by Leonardo himself, which raises strong doubts about its authenticity [75]. This is not the case with the Mona Lisa, exhibited at the LOUVRE. This unique painting was auctioned by Christie's[76] for four hundred and fifty million dollars a few years ago.

Over the years there have been dozens of works that have been valued in the hundreds of millions of dollars, from Leonardo[77] to Willem de Kooning[78], through the Renaissance to modern art and all styles, and we could say tastes. Artists like Pablo Picasso, Claude Monet, and Vincent Van Gogh go hand in hand with Jackson Pollock and Banksy, all quoted in exorbitant sums of money.

These works that are traded for hundreds of millions of dollars bear the signature and unique artistic expression of renowned artists who have left an indelible mark on history. They undoubtedly have and represent a very high value that will remain for centuries to come; but we are not talking about the most iconic works of humanity, works such as Leonardo's Mona Lisa, Vermeer's Girl with a Pearl Earring, Michelangelo's David. I wonder, if second-rate works can fetch hundreds of millions of dollars, what value could they represent? For those who, like me, have a deep love for art, the answer is clear: these artworks are unique pieces of inestimable value, which represent an abstract visualization of money. For others who perhaps do not love art as much as I do and are probably a bit more practical and pragmatic, perhaps they are not worth those amounts of money. Perhaps the same quantity of money could be used for charitable or very important works for the good of society.

However, the point to end these reflections is not about art but money, and the question is: How much money is it worth? The answer at this stage of the story is quite obvious.

10.10 Extreme luxury goods

When discussing extreme luxury goods, we do not refer to highly collectible items. To illustrate, let's make an example of the Rolex "Daytona[79]", owned by Paul Newman and sold at auction for nearly $ 18 million[80], which is understandable based on the unique characteristics of the piece and its former owner.

When we talk about extreme luxury goods, we are referring to the world of watches, or other goods that can be priced at exorbitant prices. For example, in the case of watches we have the Rolex "Daytona" series or other brands, whether they are made of gold, steel, or other materials that are quoted at a much higher price than the normal list price in the secondary market[81], where supposed expert investors are willing to pay several multiples of their retail values because of their scarcity. Collectibles, on the contrary, whether watches or other items, have a uniqueness that sets them apart from all others, whereas a serial product remains a serial product and has no implied investment value.

Buying a serial product and paying significantly more than its list value is a way of throwing money away, since due to its characteristics this same product is one of many thousands produced, with no characteristics of uniqueness or particularities beyond a supposed difficulty in finding it in the market generated largely by speculators.

Among these watch brands are Rolex, Audemars Piguet[82] , Patek Philippe,[83] and Richard Mille[84]. Some of their models are occasionally sold and resold at prices much higher than the original boutique value. In theory, there are thousands of potential customers with a wallet full of bills, willing to pay more than what they are worth, justifying to themselves and others what they consider an investment. With this reflection I am not saying that for those who can afford it, considering that it's always a good idea to spend the money as you think best. What strikes me is an expression of the abundance of monetary resources in the system to the point of raising pieces of a list value of about 5000 USD, to requests for sale above the 30000 USD, as happens to a Rolex Oyster Perpetual[85] with Tiffany blue dial[86].

A few years ago, Patek Philippe introduced a steel Nautilus model[87] , with the same Tiffany blue dial that was sold for around the 6,000,000 dollars at an auction. It is important to consider the dials of other colors like blue, or white that have been quoted at a minimum of four times their list value to probably sometimes eight times their value, i.e., the watch that is worth according to the manufacturer around 30,000 USD sold between 100,000 USD and 200,000 USD.

The amount of money in circulation in the economy raises excessively the prices of watches and many other items. For example, one Hermès[88] women's bag that is equally scarce in stores as the Nautilus in a Patek Philippe store. I am referring to the Birkin, which as in the case of watches, is not easy to find. It can only be obtained in the secondary resale market, as their purchase is virtually impossible in the stores of the same brand. Indeed, some bags can be worth hundreds of thousands of dollars, accessible to a lucky few who can afford them, when you can find in popular markets some similar bags for only a few tens of dollars. As in the case of watches, we do not make this reflection talking about unique pieces, which due to their uniqueness in the collectibles market have a defined price; we simply refer to the bags that this exclusive luxury brand usually produces.

The distortion between the concept of using money to invest in resources and spend money on a mass-produced good, even if it is considered a luxury, does not justify, under any reasoning, considering it an object of investment. This simply explains the explosion of the monetary base in today's economic systems. For some there are so many resources, that they can pay several times the value of a good that does not meet any of the characteristics to be considered an investment good, due to its serial production. I believe that it is important to live well, and it is fair for those who can afford it to spend their money on the luxuries they consider right, but it is sad to walk the streets of the big cities of certain countries seeing so many people who do not have a roof over their heads, food, and access to basic medical care. The responsibility for these social inequalities lies in the misuse of public resources and not in who spends their money as they see fit. Considering these reflections, please reread chapter 6, where we have the statistics institute explaining that, if a brand of cheese increases in price, the consumer will probably buy the cheapest and therefore the inflation formula must be corrected so that it reflects reality more accurately. In my opinion, this explanation is obviously incorrect. This fact explains very well the extra-valuation of goods that are supposedly luxury items; but the only difference that sets them apart from other similar products is speculative scarcity, since it is only one more reference of standard catalog lines. A truly exclusive good is for example Leonardo's painting because there is only one of it.

10.11 Like a river in full

To conclude, we should visualize a full river that breaks the banks and overflows in all directions. This is the appropriate way to conceptualize the creation of the current monetary base. The result of the first wave of unlimited money printing was during the subprime mortgage crisis, at the end of the first decade of the 2000s. During the pandemic period, there has been a second wave of money creation out of thin air. The damage has already been done and it is consolidated; repairing it, if it is still possible, will require years and years of sacrifices.

Keeping inflation relatively under control in consumer products is achieved thanks to the intense global competition among companies, as a result of the globalization phenomenon. Where this flood of money has done the most damage is in investment goods, which have increased their market prices in an uncontrolled manner. For the fortunate beneficiaries, this abundance of money made it possible to buy and raise the prices of any investment asset. The amount of money available to investors has been so substantial that it has led to the revaluation of luxury goods and turned them into investment assets in the collective imagination.

Finally, we must analyze how this unequal abundance of monetary resources affects the middle class and the sectors of society with less purchasing power.

10.12 How inflation destroys the middle class

Thanks to changes in the methodology for calculating inflation, governments can present lower levels of nominal inflation concerning their true values in real terms. However, as I discussed in previous chapters, to arrive at a more consistent measure of inflation, we have to take into account the influence of the value of the goods that are the object of investment. The construction of an investment patrimony by consumers is a process of using money, earned through normal and necessary work in a modern consumerist and capitalist society. This patrimony will serve for the most varied uses, from guaranteeing a better retirement at the time of retirement to helping one's children. In the end, it does not matter the use, because it depends on the free will of each person.

The first non-financial asset that families acquire is a house. Within the economic development of households, the house is considered for most middle-class individuals the first investment; this process begins when savings allow paying a premium and continues over many years through the acquisition of mortgage debt. If we analyze how house prices have varied over the last 50 years in relation to the average citizen's salary, we see that acquiring this prime asset has become increasingly difficult to achieve.

Financial assets represent another form of investment and use of money earned monthly by individuals and families, and the concept of having savings to be able to face the difficult moments of life when they come is well understood in all latitudes. Similar to the previous exercise, if we compare how the monthly disposable income of families and the value of financial assets have varied, we can see how the ability to build a future for oneself through one's work has been gradually destroyed.

Another important element of comparison to consider is education. Undoubtedly education represents a form of personal improvement by excellence. Thanks to education, individuals and their families progress in life; they achieve better jobs and build their companies, becoming independent and thus progress economically. The cost of universities has increased constantly over the years, making access impossible for a large part of the population.

10.13 An inverse redistribution of wealth like the flood of bills benefits only a fortunate few

If we compare how average incomes by quintiles and the top 5% earners of the population have evolved from the late 1960s to the present day in the United States, it becomes evident that the middle class has been left with a stagnant income over the studied decades.

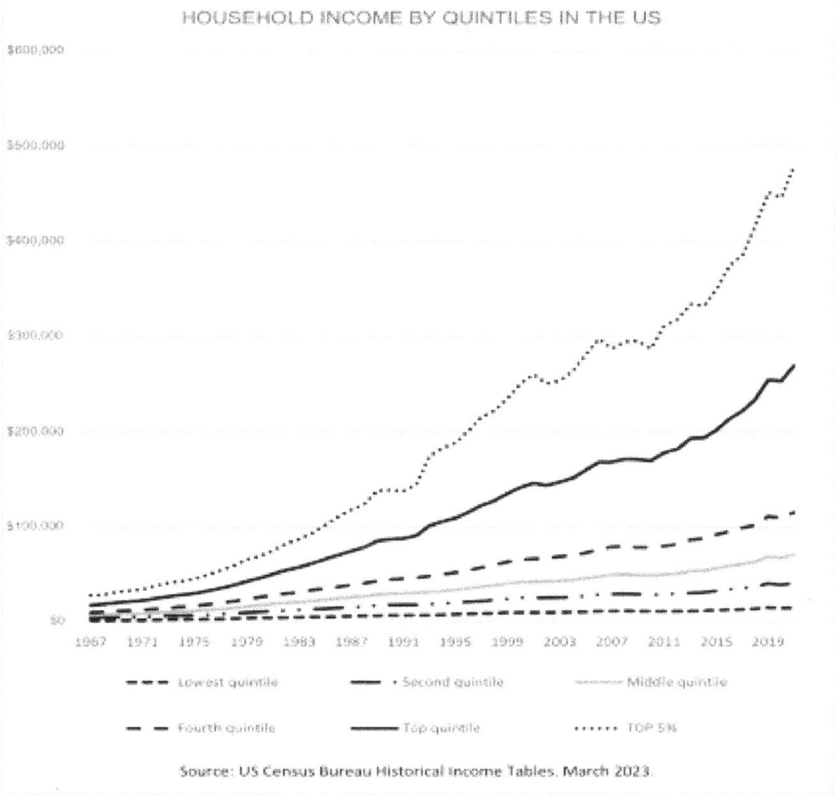

(Fig. 5). Graph representing the redistribution of wealth over time. This graph clearly shows how, over the last 55 years, two transcendental social and economic phenomena have occurred. The first phenomenon shows a redistribution of wealth from the lowest income socioeconomic

classes to the 5% of the population with the highest income level and to the fifth quintile, which we have defined as an inverse redistribution of wealth. The other aspect shows how the incomes of the first four quintiles are stagnant and lagging behind the redistribution of the country's economic wealth. If we integrate these indicators with the other comparisons of average incomes that have been made in the book, we can appreciate how an impoverishment of society has occurred over the last decades, and how this phenomenon evolves constantly and continuously.

This first indicator gives us a very real picture of a frightening phenomenon, which is the opposite of that sought by the policy of income redistribution and represents an inverse redistribution of resources. The poorest transfer their resources to the richest, it is as simple as that. It can be seen how the 5% of the lucky ones end up with most of the resources. Meanwhile, the only quintile that shows a significant improvement in its income is the fifth quintile. In other words, 20% of the wealthiest people are becoming richer. If we compare this quintile with 5% of the population with the highest income, we also notice another important divergence.

For the plotters, I would like to reassure them that the outcome of this redistribution is not the result of a sinister plan implemented by the Illuminati, or related to the reptilians, nothing of the sort. What must be very clear is that these inequalities are the result of the system. It is not in anyone's interest to see such significant segments of the population lose their patrimony; so many differences are not in anyone's interest. In history, these differences sooner or later end up in undesirable readjustments. What we do see, and finally have to recognize is that the same system, due to the irrationality of public spending, which is the main cause of real inflation, has built this new reality. The only way is to become clearly aware of this new reality and its danger for society. We must choose to correct these inequalities.

At the same time, I would like to point out to those who believe that it is possible to solve these problems through income redistributive actions, to consider once and for all that the ineffectiveness of the traditional income redistribution strategies are some of the causes that provoke more inequalities.

10.14 The steady and continuous decline in the quality of investment products: a problem not only

of the mass consumer products

In the mass consumer goods sector, quality is constantly decreasing for the goods purchased by the middle-class, contrary to the conceptualization used by statistical institutes, which consider quality changes in terms only of improvements. If we reflect on it, the excessive competition generated by globalization pushes companies to the continuous search for reduction and optimization of production costs. Therefore, the intrinsic quality of most of the products present in the market decreases. Companies at the same time try to make up for this decrease in quality with new aesthetics, plus some extra functionalities that take advantage of technological advances possible with a few cents of investment.

For those who still have doubts that quality has declined across the board in almost every category of consumer products, think about the calls you make to get information on some service you have purchased, it may be a financial service, a quick mail location, or some after-sales service for a durable product. The intensive use of intelligent telephone exchanges has probably left us stuck on the line for many minutes without any real operator answering. Most of the time those who call to have some quick service end up hanging up the phone without any answer at all. Many years ago, it was not like that, because the available services were of much better quality.

To analyze this aspect, we will focus on real estate, education, the profitability of financial assets, and finally on products that are not investments but are considered by many as such, such as luxury goods from a middle-class buyer's perspective.

When discussing the quality of real estate, we have to contextualize it with the increase of its nominal value and the fact that for many people the possibility of purchase and investment by the family has gone away. Students who have to move from one city to another to go to university or young people with their first jobs do not have the money to buy or rent an apartment by themselves, and must live with somebody else in the same situation. The level of salaries no longer enables a professional university graduate in Europe to rent an apartment and live independently. I am not referring to uneducated workers; I am referring to university graduates who do not have enough money to be able to rent an apartment on their own, much less to buy one. Any of us who know the rental situation in the big cities of Europe like Paris, Madrid, or Milan, know that with your college degree in your pocket, if you move to one of these cities you are going to have to share an apartment. Those who live in these conditions know that in case of an emergency to go to the bathroom, a line should be respected because there might be one of the roommates who had the same emergency standing before.

Financial products: The profitability of financial products has been decreasing over the years. It is possible to observe a small rebound in 2022 due to the actions on interest rates taken by central banks. However, this will likely be a momentary effect and not a long-term one. The decline in yields of financial products shows us how their quality has declined but most of its risk has not changed.

If we compare the average level of per capita income in 1970 and the cost of tuition at Harvard, we see that this prestigious American university was within reach of the middle class. However, if we perform the same analysis today, the annual cost is significantly higher, making Harvard available only for the extra-rich (Fig. 6). For those who are middle class and want their child to study, you can probably afford a public university in the neighborhood or around the corner of where you live, which, like the other, will educate your offspring. But with all due respect to the university near the neighborhood, I consider Harvard to be of a higher standard. In this case, we also observe an important decrease in quality for the citizens.

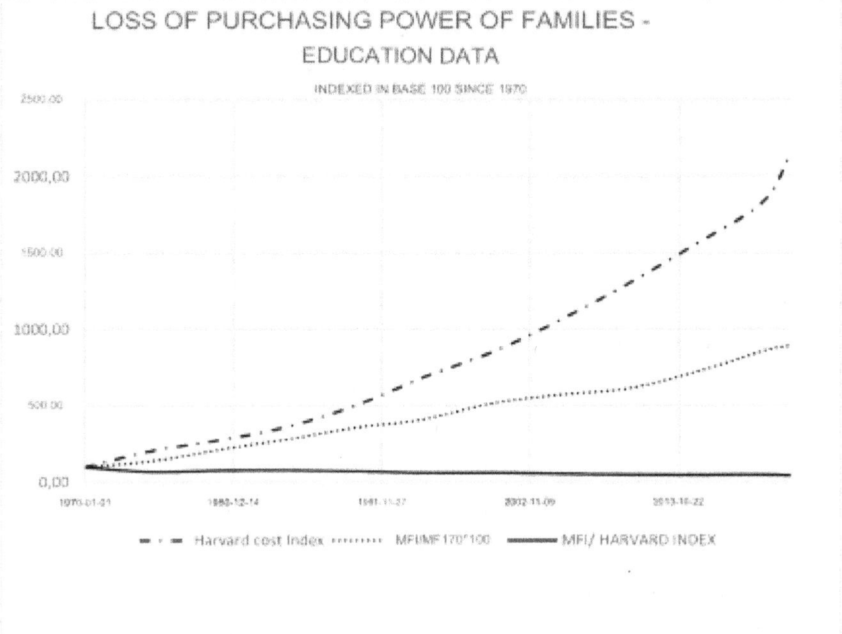

Fig. 6: Graph of the loss of purchasing power of families over time; indexed in base 100 from 1970 Harvard University tuition costs, median family income, and an index composed of median family income divided by Harvard tuition cost. The data provided by this study are emblematic. In 1970, middle-class families had the possibility of having their children study at one of the best universities in the United States and the world; today, due to the continuous and constant impoverishment of the middle class, this is impossible, and this university campus remains only for the super-rich or for those students who assume debts for the rest of their lives.

Another important fact of this study is how the quality of products for the middle class is declining. If today a middle-class family wants their children to study, the only option available without going into debt for the next century is to send them to more economic universities or free universities. We believe that the quality of study and the image that comes with obtaining a degree from Harvard may be superior to the same degree from a free university.

Lastly, if we refer to luxury products, for example, to ROLEX, a brand of watches that we all know, for someone of the middle class to buy one of these watches means using a large part of the year's salary, when a few decades ago they were perfectly accessible to all. The solution is to buy a less known watch, of a more modest brand and perhaps not so good, which implies a drop in quality.

To conclude, the point concerning quality is extremely important and, in my opinion, it has been misinterpreted by statistical institutes. As a fact of the matter, the qualitative aspect of the goods and services purchased demonstrates the destruction of the middle class from an economic point of view. Because to live they have to choose lower quality products since they can no longer afford the quality products they used to consume anymore. This substitution, so often used on a theoretical level by the statistics institute, is in fact a further demonstration of the harmful effects of inflation. Globalization and the excessive competition offer us more products, which deceive us with a theoretical abundance; but in fact, we are in front of the opposite: instead of abundance, impoverishment of quality. This situation was analyzed by statistical institutes on the quality associated with the concept of substitution where consumers, faced with an increase in the cost of some products, decide to substitute them. This substitution could be paradoxically extrapolated to its maximum expression by identifying homeless individuals, living on handouts and social charity, as people who have opted for the concept of substitutions. At the end of the day, we have in the largest cities of the planet someone that does not deny these people meals or a roof over their heads.

It would be highly beneficial for governments to correctly analyze the socioeconomic situation of the middle class, to help them not with empty ideological proclamations of past eras and centuries, but with concrete actions to improve their living situation, their finances, and their patrimony.

11 White holes and black holes - the day after

11.1 The lord of the apocalypse and his brave warriors

Unfortunately, the apocalypse's "capo" did not arrive accompanied by his brave warriors, to rescue the sleeping beauty from her captors. Nor did he offer one of his mighty horsemen as a husband, with everyone living happily ever after as in a Disney movie. Similarly, he did not come to free people oppressed by tyranny and thus reestablish international justice. History teaches us how oppressed peoples end up, and how entire cultures have disappeared leaving only an archaeological memory.

Although in the world of movies and Hollywood studios, it is common to see endings where justice triumphs, reality is a little different. The Sleeping Beauty[89] did not wake up to a gentle kiss from a prince madly in love with her, nor did she end up married in an ostentatious wedding with all the drunken guests dancing and telling jokes. Talia (the sleeping beauty's name) was simply raped by a nobleman, who happened to be hunting near the palace where she slept. As a result of the rape, she had two children, Sol and Luna, who survived with the help of the fairies of the forest. She finally woke up when one of the twins sucked her finger and pulled out the poisoned splinter. In the end, the nobleman's wife, aware of her husband's forest adventures, made an unsuccessful attempt to have Talia killed and her husband eat the children he had from his relationship with her. The plot against the harmless Talia and her children was organized with the complicity of the Kitchener, who would have them cooked for dinner. Once she informed her husband about the nature of the dishes that he had at dinner, he exploded in anger. For the story's sake, the Kitchener did not dare to execute that brutality. The plan failed and the nobleman ordered a harsh punishment for his wife[90]. Eventually, Talia ended up living with the man who had raped her in his palace. By the way, the Kitchener took an important administrative position in the Castle. History teaches us that usually whoever is stronger wins. Just as economic and hegemonic balances also most of the time change in favor of the stronger oppressor, destroying cultures and civilizations.

This tale of Sleeping Beauty was probably born as a tale of oral tradition. Its first version was written by Giambattista Basile around 1600. What is interesting and worthy of reflection is how these stories are changed and manipulated over the centuries by different writers, and perhaps the most famous are the Brothers Grimm. The story has reached us in the famous version of the Walt Disney film (1959), which differs from its previous versions, changing a hard story that dealt with very strong themes such as rape, cannibalism, and the bonfire to the idyllic tale of a handsome prince marrying a beautiful princess and where everyone ends up living happily. By analyzing how the tale evolved from its first version to the following versions, we can observe that it was presented more sweetly until it reached the Disney movie. It was manipulated many times so as not to disturb the public's spirits and conscience. If we bring this example of how the story can change the reality of specific concrete facts into an improved reality, and try to understand the technological evolution of our days with the world of the metaverse, we have a very alarming picture of reality. The metaverse represents the pursuit of an idyllic, imaginary reality that has the power to take us away from the sadness of life to empower us in a virtual environment without dangers, diseases, and real deaths, where if we want, we can be conquerors, as well as multimillionaires and the heroes of the story. The collective consciousness seeks solace in fiction, distancing itself from reality and constructing alternative stories, sweetened with pills of ephemeral happiness. Human beings shy away from the harshness of reality, and take refuge in its modified version, in its stories. A similar phenomenon occurs when we elect our representatives: we believe their stories, we do not call them to account, and we continue to support them despite their failure to fulfill their commitments. We are drawn to pretty stories with a happy ending rather than the harsh reality.

Should we question whether what we have been told about inflation is anything more than an ephemeral tale where everything ends well, and things will sort themselves out? How can these major changes occurring at the planetary level evolve and what scenarios we will have to confront in the future?

11.2 Black holes and white holes

If we examine the current situation of the overvaluation of financial and non-financial assets, accompanied by the expansion of the monetary base from a physical science perspective, we could compare it to the final phase of the life of a star. In essence, the life of the stars can end with a great implosion that generates a black hole. The shape of this black hole could be that of a funnel whose interior holds the remains of that great implosion.

Finally, we have to recognize that in the universe there are millions of black holes, therefore the common sense of things that nothing lasts forever has its foundation of truth. Time horizons may vary and today there are many new theories about what happens and how black holes end up evolving. I find it interesting to think that they finally evolve into possible white holes, which could potentially expel the remains of the imploded star and create new conditions for the development of planets.

These statements can indeed be subject to criticism, mainly because of the time horizon, since humanity and its economic-financial contextualization do not seem to have enough time between the origin of a black hole and its evolution towards a white hole. But there is an underlying element that must be recognized as correct in the analysis, which is the visualization of the great nominal financial overvaluation of the assets under investment and its possible economic-monetary consequences for mankind.

When considering possible scenarios for the current situation, we can undoubtedly give more probabilities of a possible implosion, since the continuous deterioration of the intrinsic value of the currency will destroy its basic primary function, which is that of an instrument whose essential function is being a container and expression of value in itself, a function that is being lost little by little, but in a sustained manner. In this logic of thought, the problem would cause the evolution of the black hole into a white hole, which would release all the debris that the black hole had absorbed in the implosion.

This perspective is a bit frightening, but accurately describes the inflationary phenomenon. Regardless of the efforts made to contain inflation, it eventually returns because the monetary nature of the financial economic system in which we live and its interrelationships with policies and interest groups are endemically inflationary. Monetary economic implosion would lead us into a black hole, into uncharted territory, but after a while, we would return through the white hole to an eventual inflationary system. This is because the nature of political administration is to evolve toward irrational expenditures of public money, that in the long run drive inflation out of control. We have seen over the last millennium how this story has been repeated in a recurring manner even before the Keynesian economists were telling their fairy tales.

11.3 Where economic models go wrong in the calculation of inflation

The various economic models that study inflation often make several mistakes. Firstly, in the conceptualization and magnitude of the phenomenon. Secondly, when calculating the phenomenon, they omit essential elements such as the evolution of prices of financial and non-financial assets.

It is overly simplistic to view consumers as beings whose only concern is the purchase of milk, meat, cheddar cheese, gasoline, and housing rent adorned by an outfit and a pair of shoes. The description I just provided, which neglects to consider the totality of the elements on which the "CPI" calculations are based,[91] is a representation of how inflation has been conceptualized by the statistical institutes.

The primary mistake made by these institutes is not to include in the calculation of inflation the increase of nominal value of financial and non-financial assets. I am especially referring to real estate, as well as stock market indexes. By omitting the inclusion of these two categories of assets, we are presented with a completely erroneous visualization of inflation. The result of repeatedly miscalculating a phenomenon leads us over time away from understanding it. Visually, it is like repeating a lie over the years over and over again, until we are convinced that it is true. When we lack understanding of something, it becomes challenging to correct it. As time goes by, this reality, studied and conceptualized erroneously, becomes something different from what it is. Thus, we have heard over and over again the same story about inflation, but each time we hear it, we move away from the possible understanding of the same phenomenon and from the necessary recipe to correct it at its root.

11.4 Slow and gradual loss of currency value

A slow and gradual devaluation of the currencies of different "FIAT" type countries awaits us in the most probable future scenario. The basis of analysis on which this scenario is built relies on the consideration that to address inflation, we, as individuals, affected by it and the consequent political systems, must first recognize it accurately and second be willing to face a period of sacrifices that will restore order to the numbers.

Under this scenario, when nominal inflation is at its peak, governments introduce some palliative measures, but they do not cure the phenomenon. They achieve some apparent results, and at the first sign of economic crisis, as if they were addicted to injections of money, they resume the party as if nothing had happened before.

Under the logic of this modus operandi, there is no real understanding of the inflationary phenomenon. It is limited to a few products and a calculation methodology that is adjusted to show us better results, which significantly deviates from a real and complete understanding of the phenomenon itself. The reality of things in the last one hundred and twenty years has proven to be quite different[92] (Fig. 1).

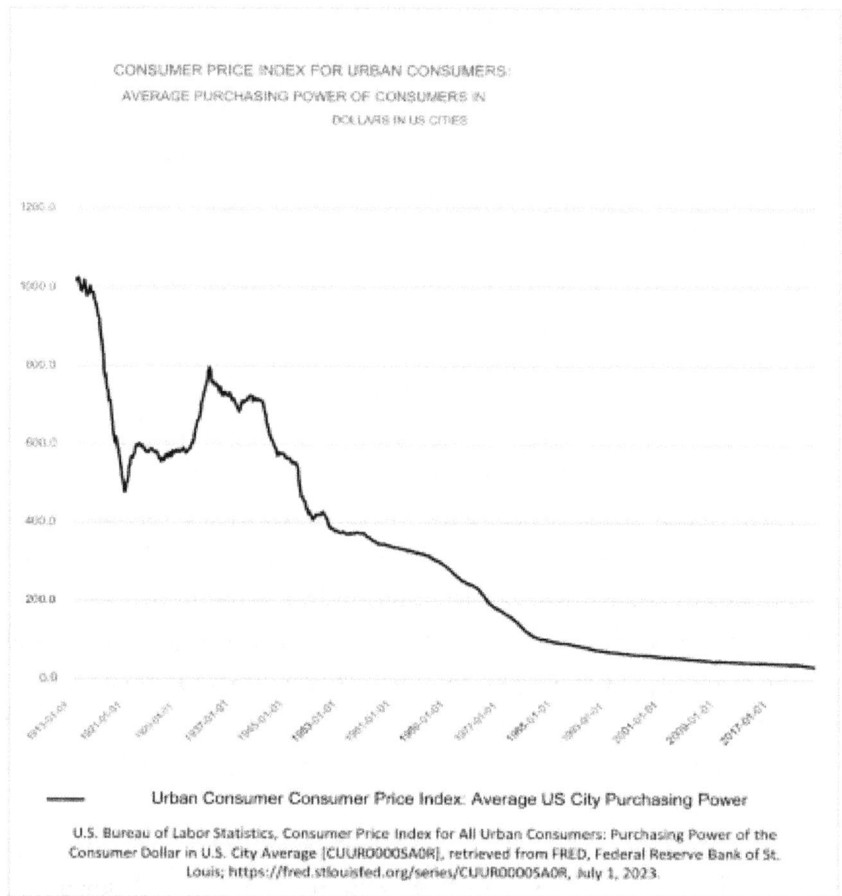

U.S. Bureau of Labor Statistics, Consumer Price Index for All Urban Consumers: Purchasing Power of the Consumer Dollar in U.S. City Average [CUUR0000SA0R], retrieved from FRED, Federal Reserve Bank of St. Louis; https://fred.stlouisfed.org/series/CUUR0000SA0R, July 1, 2023.

Fig. 1: This is the Graph of the study of how the dollar in the last 120 years has seen most of its value destroyed by inflation. Be aware that this graph considers the purchasing power of the U.S. urban consumer by means of the consumer price index, but does not consider the evolution of the cost of financial assets. Estimating the impact of these assets would show an even greater and faster loss in the value of the dollar.

In this scenario, the loss of value over the next few decades will continue at the same rate as in the past. In practical terms, a house worth a few hundred thousand dollars today will be worth a few million dollars, just as a pair of shoes will be worth a few thousand dollars, and a cup of coffee will probably be worth a hundred dollars.

The seriousness of this reality is that it represents a lost war where no prisoners are taken. The victims of this war are the middle class and the poorest classes. If the trend continues, they will become poorer and poorer and work will not become a source of personal fulfillment, that allows them to grow economically and build a portfolio of financial and non-financial assets, providing them with life stability. Work will end up merely a means to buy the newspaper and nothing more.

11.5 New currency as a substitute for the dollar

This other scenario has some possibilities, like the ones described in the previous paragraphs. I am referring to the potential abandonment of the dollar as the global currency of exchanges that could occur in future decades. It is based on the assumption that empires are not eternal and in the current hyper-technological era, characterized by a worrying demographic decline. The succession in the leadership of the world becomes faster than it would have happened in the past. If the Roman Empire, in its various declinations, lasted more than 1000 years, the North American empire, under this logic will have a much shorter lifespan. The devaluation of the currency could be, as in the time of Diocletian, a harbinger of what the future has in store for us.

The dramatic nature of the current situation is partly the result of the demographic decline, which has been imposing itself on the economy, forcing governments to take outlandish monetary actions to govern the economy. I am referring to the unjustified injection of money into the system. These monetary actions have had economic results opposite to what the authorities expected, gradually destroying the middle class as we know it.

Finally, the use of the dollar as a weapon or military instrument is creating the conditions for opposition to the dollar hegemony by a group of nations led by China. These countries do not face any demographic problems, and have strong growing economies and many natural resources, and may decide to take a path towards their own monetary independence. Under such a scenario we could witness a more rapid decline of the dollar as the currency used in world exchanges and the emergence of a new alternative currency in competition with the greenbacks. This would be the expression of the emergence of a new young empire antagonistic to the old one we know.

11.6 The great reset

It is important to understand what we are talking about when we discuss this trend. Today the World Economic Forum, in which a few millionaires participate, has become aware of the many inequalities in the world. It is easy for them to recognize these inequalities from their own private planes and rest in high-luxury hotels, with their bank accounts that have several zeros more than those of ordinary citizens. In this perspective I imagine these gentlemen having caviar and champagne for breakfast, around ten o'clock in the morning, reading the news of the new Greta Thunberg protest[93] about the dangers of climate change. You can understand very well that this is a completely different perspective from that of the people who mid-morning, after several hours of factory work, have a coffee with some dry cookies. From the table with caviar and champagne, we have the vision of those who baptized the need for a planetary change called the "Great Reset"[94]. I wonder if this small group of fortunate people in their luxurious lives can understand the needs of a peasant in Vietnam or a cattle farmer in Argentina. Undoubtedly, many of them already consume synthetic or vegetarian meat. Have any of them woken up several times a year to pick tomatoes before the sun rises, or have any of them found themselves a few times in their lives in a supermarket counting the money in their pockets to see what they could buy? There is a famous saying, I hope you will forgive my choice of words, according to which it is very easy to prostitute the private parts of others and not one's own. I think when we study what these influential thinkers are planning, this saying adheres perfectly to the reality of things.

Many conspiracy theories have been born around this phenomenon, which base their idea on the fact that the power of the Earth wants to migrate to a new financial economic system where we would all be controlled in a large matrix. Part of this theory believes that the great economies of the planet would migrate to digital currency, and by means of digital currency it will be possible to achieve a much stricter control over its citizens, and those who do not speak the language that the powerful would like to hear with a simple click of a computer would be silenced into oblivion. Simultaneously, this theory proposes a society where property does not exist, and everything can be rented or shared. In this context, I wonder, would the large shareholders of global companies be willing to give up their shares to the community?

For those who are experts in this theory, I apologize if I have synthesized the phenomenon too simplistically, but it is another of the possibilities before us.

11.7 The catastrophists

We continue to explore the possibilities of extreme events. Among these are the catastrophists, a group of economists that have understood very well the problems caused by unlimited monetary expansion. According to their theory, we would be on the verge of a vertical fall in the value of financial assets. This is a result of the valuations of the same financial assets and non-financial assets reaching exorbitant values, which would represent a bubble. Every bubble sooner or later bursts, leading to a reset of values to more rational levels.

The stock market has experienced significant corrections in its history and therefore, these theorists are partly correct. However, some of them have been for years and years warning of this event that ultimately never happens. The list of economists chanting the same story that we are on the verge of a crash that will occur in the next quarter or month is getting longer and longer. This stock market correction is not coming punctually.

What these economists do not understand is the amount of money printed and how it changes the nominal values of financial assets; a stock that is worth 100 USD today would probably have been worth 10 USD in 2005. The bubble is nothing more than a nominal representation of a fictitious reality.

Despite these considerations, corrections may come, but the recovery time to the so-called "high values" to which we are accustomed would be very fast. Therefore, I consider the predictions of these catastrophists very improbable, even if they have a basis in affirming that monetary expansion is the cause of strong imbalances and mismatches.

11.8 War

This is a scenario that demands a great deal of respect, because throughout history wars have been the protagonists of great readjustments in the economy, in politics, and in the administration of states. Fortunately, in the past, weapons were not as lethal as they are today. The reality is frightening, there are nuclear powers that with a fraction of their weapons can destroy the planet.

We have conflicts that could escalate into atomic conflicts, which would have the potential to destroy life as we know it. If one of these unfortunate events were to occur, it would be catastrophic for humanity and inflation would likely be the least of our concerns. In such an event, the anecdote that a metallic coin or precious metal is far more valuable than a paper bill would no doubt be very apt.

We hope that the leaders of the world will have the wisdom to keep that scenario at bay, although logically it must be considered because it is a possibility, but hopefully an extremely remote one.

In this regard, there is a famous quote attributed to Albert Einstein, who said that he does not know how the Third World War will be fought, but he was sure that the fourth would be with sticks and stones. I have listened to much debate on the current war in Eastern Europe and I am surprised at the ease with which so many analysts speak and describe techniques, tactics, and armaments, who seem to have understood absolutely nothing of the danger of nuclear weapons, talking about them as if they were describing traditional cartridges.

11.9 Reptilians arrive for real, the hunt for easy proteins

The universe is so vast that it is difficult to truly comprehend its vastness, to be the only living form inhabiting it is a bit limiting and at the same time selfish. This is one of the rare cases where a conspiracy theory finally demonstrates some basis of sound reasoning. For years, there have been groups of people who claim to have seen unidentified flying objects. These groups of people have been very critical of the information that government agencies have given us. Eventually, the Pentagon, as well as other countries, acknowledged the possibility that we are not alone in the universe[95], recognizing the danger that this represents for humans.

If we start from the fact of what can happen when a more advanced civilization discovers another, history is not favorable in this case. Most of the time the less advanced civilization ends up in conditions of slavery or destroyed by the other. If a civilization has therefore the technology to be able to travel to Earth, we could affirm that it would be far more advanced than the hominids and artificial intelligence that live and pollute this beautiful planet daily.

If we consider the ideas from movies that imagined the arrival of extraterrestrials, we can think that for the little green Martians, the Earth could represent an almost inexhaustible source of protein, where potentially bipedal hominids could become an exclusive delicacy rich in these nutrients. We do not know what may happen in the future. We may visualize this situation as a joke, a humorous report, but there is an incontrovertible fact: the future brings surprises that are impossible to visualize. How many of those who lived through the Great Depression would have imagined that a metaverse would come to exist in which virtual properties have value? How many in Richard Nixon's time would have visualized the arrival of Bitcoins?

In short, scientific advances and the surprises that the future holds for us go far beyond what we can see, even beyond our imagination.

12 The light at the end of the tunnel, economic and monetary policy strategies to stabilize the system

12.1 Conspiracy theorists

Beyond the concrete risk of some extraterrestrial invasion of Earth, by delving into various conspiracy theories, we should dedicate many days to their study to have an idea of what they are about. These theories range from the Illuminati[96], to the reptilians[97], which would have an already stable presence on our planet, and who are those that control the destiny of humanity, without of course mentioning several obscure powers that emanate very little luminosity and are difficult to see clearly, making them equally difficult to understand. There are thousands and thousands of videos and writings, which can even be considered entertaining and amusing in moments of boredom. Despite the fact that Eratosthenes was able to understand the shape of the Earth and measure its circumference more than 2200 years ago, there are still an abundance of supporters of the flat earthers theories[98] that are convinced of the exact opposite. Many of these theories can be summarized as an occult power that through the manipulation of power imposes its nefarious plan to a defenseless humanity.

I am not entirely sure humanity itself is so helpless, but it is certainly quite naïve in the sense that many times the members of this hominid species easily believe in any story, particularly conspiratorial ones. The irrationality of public spending and the consequences of inflation are the theories that clearly explain the loss of value of the middle class' wealth. I do not want to disappoint you in this respect, but I consider that there is no kind of plot behind this.

No corporation, let alone any government, would benefit from the decline of the middle class as a result of its strong impoverishment. Any country, as well as any private for-profit or non-profit organization, would rather have around itself and as constituents of its society and its environment prosperous families and individuals with high purchasing power than beggars living on handouts.

The system that leads to the irrationality of public spending is, as explained in the theory I enunciated a few chapters ago, responsible for such distortions which do not occur consciously as a result of a precise strategy but are the offspring of an imperfect and polluted system that causes them. Politicians, public administrators, as well as the different forces representing opposing and divergent interests are players who are unaware of this imperfect and highly polluted system, which is mainly responsible for inflation and the economic destruction of the middle class. This middle class is the numerical majority in terms of voters, but lacks enough power to influence governmental decisions.

To correct this situation and embark on a new path that gradually restores the middle class and its value in society requires great sacrifices from all parties involved, as well as an understanding of the gravity of the principles I describe throughout these pages. We cannot expect to rectify a problem if we are not perfectly clear of what the problem is, what its causes are, and therefore what kind of solutions are needed to solve it once and for all.

12.2 Let's start with a new formula for inflation determination

We conclude that the methodology used to calculate inflation and the changes made by the statistical institutes, in particular, "BLS"[99] , do not represent the phenomenon correctly and underestimate it. The changes in the calculation implemented since the early 1980s have the sole merit of making inflation appear lower than it is, but they describe the phenomenon incorrectly and underestimate it. In 1983 "BLS" removed the value of houses from the calculation formula by eliminating the most important asset of families. This modification in the formula represents a serious conceptual error because it also eliminates the concept of investment goods from inflation.

Ideally, we should have two values of inflation: the first relating to consumer goods, and the second, more importantly, also includes goods that are the object of investment. The second value of inflation will be more broadly crucial than the first one. Among investment goods, we must consider real estate, because it is the main asset of households, and financial goods, which represent a country's stock market performance. Financial and non-financial investment assets should then represent about 30%-35% of the index value and no less.

The "SHELTER" component, which represents about 33% of the calculation of consumer Price indexes, is the part that most needs to be reformulated. The reformulation should leave a part of it as representative of rental and hotel costs and expand with another segment to represent housing costs and the real estate sector itself.

Finally, the remaining 67% of the index should be reformulated, to leave room for the financial asset components, which in any case should not be less than 10%.

Changing the different weights of the components contained in the index to include investments would lead to a profound conceptual modification of its calculation. The other area of modification of how inflation is calculated today, is to return to a "COGI" type concept[100] as an alternative to the new calculation philosophy based on the "COLI" system[101]. I consider the use of standard of living maintenance a way of manipulating the index, because it involves changing the goods based on the Price evolution. Therefore, the previous system, which referred to a basket of fixed products, although not perfect, is surely more consistent.

Measuring quality is not an easy task and normally this parameter has been used by the statistics institute "BLS" in order to reduce the value of the products, trying to isolate the component of their cost that represented the qualitative improvements. Quality improvements, driven by globalization, have lost sight of the fact that they make up the vast majority of the supposed improvements. Many of the technological or aesthetic changes are mere makeovers to products that have been substantially losing quality, which makes it particularly difficult to estimate qualitative-positive or negative changes. I consider it more convenient to eliminate them from the basis of analysis because including them would make us incur in potentially greater errors.

Regarding the use of geometric measures to better "rearrange" spending, beyond the exotic formulas widely explained by the Institute of Statistics, it introduces further interference that compromises the purity of the numbers; therefore, I recommend eliminating them.

Accurately measuring inflation allows us to intervene in the phenomenon on time and in the right way. At the same time, controlling inflation preserves the patrimonial position of the middle class in the long term. It is not just any number that is given to us and should be deemed correct just because it has been elaborated by an institution. In this respect, beyond outlandish conspiracy theories, it is necessary to have a good level of criticality to be able to evaluate the data provided to us.

12.3 From Bretton Woods to the permanent party

We are confronted with a significant dilemma of major proportions, to which it is not easy to find a concrete solution that would allow us to conceptualize money as a currency comprehensively and correctly. The system of anchoring to the price of gold, before the end of the Bretton Woods agreements, was not the solution either, or probably in the long term would potentially have meant a kind of brake for the economy. Alternatively, the solution of evolving towards "fiat currencies"[102] has opened the way to the monetary disorder in which we are living, a disorder that has destroyed the basic function of money, which is to represent intrinsic value. Its uniqueness is unfortunately trivialized by countries that freely print electronic money without any kind of limit or backing.

The ideal evolution would be to have a monetary system represented by currencies that have some kind of anchor, with real assets that would represent the intrinsic value of the money itself. Belonging to a gold standard undoubtedly benefits the gold-producing countries and puts non-producing countries at a disadvantage. It is important for currencies to have some kind of anchor that is not limiting, but at the same time guarantees the owners of the money an intrinsic value. Although the concept may seem a bit abstract, in practice it would guarantee its value for the users and at the same time its uniqueness due to the limitation in its creation. As a practical example, we could think that for a gold-producing country, it would be logical and consistent to anchor the value of its currency to this metal. For other countries that are not lucky enough to be direct producers of the yellow metal, they could think of a container of value to back up the currencies.

Finally, the possibility of relating the value of the currency to something concrete and realistic, beyond a promise of its ideal value, allows the system greater stability and adherence to economic reality between its currency and the value of its economy.

12.4 The role of banks from the paleolithic[103] to the present day

In this monetary economic system, banks have evolved a lot from the traditional idea we might have of them. This basic idea of banks would be institutions where we deposit our savings and that do their job of financial intermediation, lending money to those who need it and helping the economy to develop over time. However, not that many years later, this is a paleolithic view of banks, as these institutions have evolved far beyond what we would consider their basic functions.

While banks serve as an essential instrument of monetary policy, their function is much more complex, where the critical points of complexity refer to their role in the acquisition of government securities, and their profitability objectives are just like those of any other company. The essential difference between banks and any other company is that these institutions, although in many cases are considered private, de facto have a very strong state interference of guidance and control. Within banks, there exists a dualism between the concept of an institution that participates in monetary policies and companies in search of a healthy return, like any other private company on the planet. This dualism is not at all easy to manage in a way that must please the King and the Pope, who sometimes have divergent objectives. At this point in the reading, you may be wondering, what about the customers? Did I forget about them, perhaps? No doubt it is a good question that I will answer in the best way that my vision of the situation allows me at the moment: I believe that customers are important for banks, but within this scheme I do not perceive how important they can be. In other words, for banks, customers and the image you have of them are an accessory concept and no longer the essential and fundamental reason for their own existence. If you think about it, this statement is a bit strong and should incite another question: If customers are something accessory for banks, what is really the focus of the business as such? If the answer is formulated by any banker, it is very likely to assure you that the main objective would be the customers.

During the pandemic period in the United States, the reserve requirement was reduced close to zero[104]. This reduction could be perceived as allowing banks to increase money creation without limits, although there is always some kind of limit, after all. But in order to understand the essence of banking dualism, we have to visualize on the one hand the need for the State to place its securities. Ultimately, the economy for the citizens and the yields on the securities do not make these instruments profitable enough to make them palatable, unless they are seen in a logic of strong leverage, in which case they can produce interesting results. On the other hand, we have the explosion of the derivatives markets. The financial crisis of 2007-2010 has taught us nothing and the derivatives market has continued to grow steadily to unimaginable levels[105]. Derivatives are highly speculative instruments. In the case of large banks, which we define as "Market Makers"[106], these are the ones that issue in many cases this type of instruments and allow them to be liquid. The derivatives market is one of the instruments used by banks in order to improve their profitability. The underlying problem in the use of these instruments is that they are extremely dangerous and could lead to a banking crisis of this type.

Due to the conflicting interests at play, large banks are forgetting what their core business should be, which is to serve the credit needs of their customers. As a result, entrepreneurs, small investors, the middle class, and savers do not serve as a priority, but as an accessory business. Granting credit to help generate businesses may no longer be so attractive or convenient. This causes access to financing for those who have good ideas to be a complicated process that slows down the real economy to the advantage of a financial economy that does not produce goods and services, but rather electronic money as a means to finance irrational government spending.

Over the past two decades, there has been an economic evolution from a real economy to an economy of finance. The logic and the great financial moments have prevailed over the concept of getting one's hands dirty to create products and therefore create wealth. Ultimately, these are open questions that serve to understand the state of the situation and how it can evolve from a monetary and economic point of view. It is clear to understand the answer to the question posed a few paragraphs ago, regarding what clients represent for large financial institutions. The answer is quite clear: customers have become one of the many business priorities, but not the first one.

12.5 Following the logic implies strong readjustments

This system needs some corrections, but carrying out this process requires a strong commitment from the different parties involved in it, a commitment that I see as not only difficult to achieve but also utopian, to put it better. The moment the different players or actors are not willing to assume the sacrifices involved in making a change, it becomes unattainable.

Instead of embracing change, it is more common to control the system through the use of palliatives; within the palliative mechanisms, the losers, as we have seen, are the middle class and the socioeconomic classes that are less fortunate in terms of their income levels. They cannot be in the big boys' game because they do not control the capital.

The famous saying that "there is no evil lasts 100 years or a body that can withstand it" holds true in many instances. The current economic and monetary dissonances that are causing the reverse redistribution of wealth, impoverishing the middle class and the less wealthy sectors of society, are also the main cause of the current strong social imbalance in which we live. This imbalance will be so profound that it will mark the origin of a radical restructuring of the economy and society, just like the famous saying. No one has a crystal ball to foresee the future exactly; however, the current situation of constant loss of value of money will reach a limit and eventually, market forces will be forced to require a major structural readjustment. For many of us it is not easy to understand the nature of these adjustments, because they sometimes take several decades, but seen from a historical perspective they are easier to understand and to logically schematize.

12.6 For investors

The biggest issue with the loss of value of money has its effects on investors and those who can save, since, due to inflation, the value of their savings is gradually destroyed. I am not referring to the large financial groups that have structures to deal with this problem, I am referring to small investors, small businessmen, independent workers, and employees with various levels of responsibilities. These groups find themselves in a situation where the resources that represent money and savings are very unprofitable in terms of the associated investment risks.

We have seen how when a good becomes less scarce, its value decreases. This phenomenon happens with money, because it is less and less scarce and what it can produce is less profitability. By observing the yield curve of US treasury bonds, the trivialization of money is quite clear, because it is no longer a scarce resource and therefore of little value. It is important to understand this aspect well when I say of little value: from a marginal point of view, money can become worthless, as in the well-known cases of Venezuela or Zimbabwe.

Investors must grasp this paradigm very well to implement strategies that will allow them to face this economic reality. Not being prepared means condemning your own savings to disappear into nothingness. It is just a matter of time, and patience and the real inflation levels that we have seen are much higher than the nominal inflation declared by the statistical institutes.

Large investors and financial groups do indeed possess crucial advantages over small players in the investment market, starting with easier access to credit. For small investors, any business they want to set up will be strongly limited by the ability to access credit, whether it is a new business activity or simply investing in the stock market. The large groups have easier access and the necessary knowledge to manage the credit instrument that the small ones do not have.

Another important differentiating element: at the level of analysis and access to market information, large groups have the advantage of having more sources of information to elaborate better decisions in less time. When small investors have access to information and make their decisions, it is often too late compared to those who do it as a job and with more experience.

Another noteworthy advantage of specialized investors and large banks is that they work with a concept of detachment from money. In the case of small investors, the situation is completely different because money costs them a lot, so there is an attachment to saving it instead of using the resources in the investment process. This becomes a counterproductive factor that influences buying and selling decisions in the wrong way.

12.7 Protecting savings and building a wealth portfolio in times of financial turmoil

Facing this reality of things is possible thanks to the awareness of the situation; without knowing clearly what can happen to one's life savings, they are doomed to lose their value.

Indeed, a very significant portion of the population shows a lack of interest in financial matters, including their own finances. This lack of interest is reflected in three key elements that describe the situation. The spending pattern of individuals is undoubtedly one of the factors that keep individuals and families from being able to build an investment portfolio and thus reach financial prosperity. Spending money on useless goods, that are mistakenly considered investment pieces, as well as getting to spend more than one actually can, overcharging credit cards, is the most damaging pattern of individuals. It often takes many years of work in order to chase debt repayment, and every time debt is reduced, there is a new excuse to acquire a new one and go back to the beginning or to a worse situation. Life floating in a debt bubble is the illusion that many professionals have, but it is a completely wrong illusion. Yes, they are debt bubbles, but instead of floating they pull down drowning and limiting the possibilities of growth.

The second pattern that commonly influences the way professionals invest is to delegate investment decisions to someone else. Making the right decisions implies a process of study and analysis, and in a way it can be liberating to delegate that responsibility to an external "expert". The essential point to understand about this second flawed pattern is that the external expert is not often truly qualified. Other times the interests of this third party diverge from the objectives and interests of the direct interested party, and people could end up trusting someone who has neither the skills nor the qualifications to be able to advise. This last category includes improvised financial sanctimonious people who are nothing more than false prophets.

The extremely low profitability of financial assets is combined in a nefarious cocktail with one of the most negative human emotions: greed, a third pattern that influences investment decisions. Human beings, whether we want to admit it or not, are to some extent greedy. If it is controlled and if it is not predominant in our way of living, greed is a negative feeling that does not make us grow but, I repeat, if it is controlled it does not cause major problems. The bottom line is when greed becomes the guiding feeling of our actions. When this happens and when this is mixed with a very low profitability of financial assets, we are in trouble. If we examine closely, many of the catastrophic financial events of the early 2020s, such as the crash of many cryptocurrencies, are in that nefarious scheme. Greed, coupled with a very low financial culture, makes many individuals fall into the traps of those who promise exceptional returns that are not based on any concrete element of profitability and from time to time end up in sad news of bankruptcies of companies and consequent loss of money by their customers. Now, usually, the ones who get hit the hardest by these financial pirates end up being the small investors and, finally, the middle class we are talking so much about.

12.8 How to start

We cannot expect to successfully climb Mount Everest without adequate training to prepare us for such an adventure. The first step for those who want to take control of their own financial destiny is to study. We cannot pretend to know everything if we do not first study, understand, and internalize knowledge.

Studying becomes essential in today's financial complexity, and it should be an interesting and stimulating process. However, it is seen by many as a slow and boring process. These people are deeply mistaken. Let's consider how leisure time is normally spent: watching television, overeating, and overdrinking without considering how these patterns can damage our physique and our brains. The mind also needs a dose of training to stay awake, lucid, and proactive.

The markets and how they work must be studied very well. Within this study, we must understand the mechanisms and risks associated with investments. Risks must be well delimited in their nature, and we must understand how they can affect the financial decisions we make. Every decision is accompanied by some level of risk; however, when we are perfectly clear and aware, we will be able to manage and protect ourselves from them.

Typical educational institutions do not teach these things, sometimes the same professors who should teach finance are not sufficiently prepared for the current reality to be able to transmit knowledge. For this reason, investment processes are usually delegated by most individuals to third-party professionals.

Being educated and well-prepared on the subject allows us to interact with experts on an equal footing. This is a particularly important aspect of the study, if we do not know the subject, anything they tell us can be true. However, if we have studied the problem very well, we can interact with the experts of the institutions in which we are investing correctly. Understanding what professionals are telling us, and asking the right questions help to finally make better decisions. This process is accurately described by an English word: "challenging"[107]. And thanks to a good management of this concept, our results will be much better; the decisions will be conscious and not imposed. Only through study can we know where we are going in order to tread a safer and firmer path.

12.9 A good strategic plan

If we intend to visit a foreign country, it would be a bit complicated to arrive at the airport without a ticket, without knowing where to go, without a passport or the financial means to make the trip. To organize a trip, you have to plan. The secret to make this trip enriching, interesting, and add value to our life is a good planning. Improvising during a trip often leads to poor results. There are many people who, out of insecurity, prefer to go on an organized trip, which implies being limited in hours, spending a lot of time on a bus or a boat, waiting for the rest of the group to arrive and be ready to finally eat in mediocre restaurants with poor quality food.

To organize an enriching trip abroad, you have to plan it very well, starting with the basic things such as the documents you need, the wardrobe according to the time of the year chosen, booking tickets, planes, and cars, everything to make things go well. The work does not end with these basic elements of decision, adding variables should be considered. For example, consider a plan B if things do not go as planned, or even a plan C, if things do not go as desired again. I will tell you an anecdote of a friend who went to the Kola Peninsula for a salmon fly fishing adventure, finally had terrible weather, and spent eight days in the tent without being able to take out the fly-fishing rods. In order to get things the way we want them to go, we have to work for them in the right way and this involves planning.

When we talk about patrimonial investments, we are discussing our future, how to invest in the rewards of our work. When we are successful at work, it will bear us good fruits; if we are less successful, we will have regular or mediocre fruits, but the big difference towards a path that will take us to the end of the tunnel and that will show us a light for the future is how these fruits are used. Only thanks to a very detailed planning, accompanied by a correct implementation strategy, will we have a successful path in the extremely complex reality that I have described in this book.

The first step in the study is followed by strategic planning, and finally the review and correction of things to further adjust the objectives we have set for ourselves. This will allow us to go on the path to the light and finally be able to face the financial turmoil in which the world is.

12.10 Tidying up the house

In order to explain this concept, within the process of heritage construction, I would like to summarize some ideas of Carl Gustav Jung. I apologize in advance for summarizing in a few concepts the complex ideas developed by this great thinker, which, like no other, have marked a new way of looking at man in contemporary society. A powerful idea developed by Jung is that, to liberate human potential, it is necessary to have our own inner knowledge to analyze and overcome the dark sides of the personality and ultimately release the positive energy towards a perspective of growth and light. This introspective process can be achieved through therapy. If we apply this vision of the human being to his economic reality and personal fulfillment, we have the answer to many of the questions that we can find in our path of personal growth.

The way out of the tunnel towards the construction of a patrimonial portfolio requires making the first important and transcendental decision: to change one's ways of living. We can translate this concept by means of a metaphor that is easy to understand, which is to put the house in order. If you live in a very cluttered environment, it is difficult to concentrate because that clutter distracts you and does not allow you to focus on the essentials. This concept of putting the house in order is very important and, like all important things, requires some degree or level of sacrifice. This concept of the house is representative not only of a situation of physical disorder, but also of the emotional work that we have to do in ourselves to reach that order, to shape that order in our life, and prevent it from remaining only in a cold purpose of intent. It needs to be internalized by us. Being able to work on ourselves from the point of view of the motivations that lead us to a state of disorder allows us to internally heal ourselves and finally be able to cure in practical terms many of the deficiencies we have in the management of our lives, as well as our finances.

Putting our house in order involves analyzing the motivations that have kept us in a state of imbalance and disorder. This process begins by putting our house in order from a financial point of view, which implies initially the elimination of unhealthy debts that are dragging on for a long time, and that are the main responsibility for not being able to build a patrimonial investment portfolio that can face the threats of inflation. Credit cards give an erroneous idea of power, causing many individuals to carry an endless amount of debt throughout their professional careers, working to pay the minimum card fees and exorbitant interest rates. The goal of such work is to become free of these unhealthy debts as a first step.

The importance and transcendence of this work is seen in the understanding, not only of simply eliminating the debts that do not allow us to develop, but also of working on the futile motivations that have led us to incur in these obligations.

A second important step is to eliminate debts that are associated with assets that are not investment objects. This category includes things that we have bought for our ego, but that do not give us in the long term any economic benefit and that we use very little throughout the year. An example could be a sports car that is stored in the garage, or a yacht that involves heavy maintenance costs and is used only a few days a year.

Engaging an important inner work that corrects in its origin the behaviors that lead us to unnecessary expenses and reduce our capacity to build a patrimonial investment portfolio, is a way to heal and open the way to a personal patrimonial and financial development that guarantees us a better life. It means healing the cause and eliminating the symptoms of the disease.

The third step, perhaps the most challenging to take in the logic of reordering our life, is to cut toxic relationships that absorb our resources and do not allow us to develop our full potential. These relationships include friends, relatives, and other similar connections who, instead of supporting our path to success, are attached to us and drain us of resources and energy. This is usually a difficult process because it involves feelings, and it has to be carried out very well in a way that allows us to perhaps not completely break the relationship and move on to another plane. It is easy to write and very difficult to implement, but we must be wise and choose the right words that enable us to heal unhealthy situations. Finally, what cannot be healed and cured through dialogue and understanding must be cut with a scalpel. When it comes to debts, studying and self-analysis will allow us to heal and correct this aspect of unhealthy relationships.

After putting our house in order, we are prepared to face the financial turbulence that accompanies us throughout our professional career. Realistically, it is very difficult for governments to have the capacity to fix the problem of inflation as such, therefore, it is up to us to make the right decisions so that this problem does not suck us in or drown us. The difficulty of organizing our homes as a symbolic visualization of ourselves goes far beyond a behavioral and cognitivist analysis of ourselves as human beings. It requires a deep introspection and understanding of the problems and their causes as a first step to undo the shell that does not allow us to develop and thus be able to embark on the right path.

12.11 Types of assets

Finally, we have our investment plan, which must precisely describe what type of asset we want to invest in and how we are going to do it. The basic problem we face is the low profitability of financial and non-financial assets, with high levels of risk. Not easy if we think about it.

There is a common belief that fixed-income assets are safer investment instruments than equities or stocks; but nothing could be further from the truth. To confuse the obligation that someone takes to pay a fixed interest on an amount of money borrowed and then pay back the principal is a big mistake. The commitment to these payments does not guarantee that it will be fulfilled without considering the destruction of the value of the money.

The stock market, as we have seen, has very high prices. This is an expression of inflation and a loss in the value of money. The profitability in terms of dividends distributed is minimal, considering the implicit risk in these assets. Moreover, the market prices of companies can be quite irrational. Some companies might see their prices penalized by simple news or small events, while others are sought after by the market without a logical explanation. Finally, in a few days, the market can correct the value of a stock significantly.

When structuring an equity investment portfolio, real estate must certainly be considered. In this regard, it is necessary to carefully consider our home, and whether it is representative of an investment property or simply part of our assets, which does not fall into the category of investment property. As with all categories of assets, there is also an overvaluation of real estate, which makes the practical selection of investments more difficult. Another element that characterizes real estate is the impact on our way of living, from the processes of purchasing goods to the offices where we go to work. Commercial real estate has been significantly affected by this socioeconomic change. What was a good investment a few years ago, such as having an office center or a store for rent, today may have run out of tenants and may no longer be a good investment. There is a major paradigm shift in society driven by technology that needs to be well understood to make your portfolio profitable.

Understanding precious metals and their inclusion in an equity investment portfolio as a hedge against inflation is another alternative to study in times of high inflation. On the one hand, gold represents intrinsic value - everyone agrees with this - but owning gold does not produce cash flow. In fact, some large investors choose not to invest in it because they consider it an unproductive asset.

Now we come to a range of complex financial instruments: derivatives and the importance of understanding these instruments of protection and eventual generation of profitability. The most sophisticated investors use these instruments to improve their numbers and be more profitable. Here again, the task is not easy because these instruments are difficult to understand, difficult to structure and, if misused, can lead to significant losses.

The universe of investments is much broader than what we can frame within fixed categories. The art world and collections, for instance, can be very illiquid instruments, but they protect their value over time. There are companies specialized in art that make this market accessible to smaller investors; they are new investments and as such are not framed within the logic of security so clearly.

As you have observed, the world of possible investments is very wide and has many possibilities. At the same time, most of the possible instruments and investment objects have important valuations due to the abundance of money and the effects of inflation.

12.12 What decisions to make?

The society in which we live creates an illusion of abundance and easy pleasure, which has been taking shape in everyday life. From the unrealistic images of modeling contests with models who can barely walk, so thin that any nutritionist should be concerned about their health, to the entertainment industry that presents a fictitious reality for the few with their private jets and abundance. All this noise around us does nothing but create more confusion in our minds; it projects false models of life that in the reality of each one of us are quite unattainable.

Human beings want and desire everything at once, without understanding the importance of sacrifice and the implications it holds for having a full and successful life. One of the confusing factors is the environment of abundance that is painted in the movie reality. The entertainment industry modifies the stories according to the fashions that design happy endings in order to make us feel happier.

In the end, all this is noise around us, which takes us away from the construction of a full life and the possibility of building a wealth portfolio that lasts over the years. Finally, if I may take a poetic license, it is an inflationary reality.

The answer to the initial question is that there is no one-size-fits-all recipe for asset types, investment strategies, and wealth management to protect yourself from inflation. To achieve these objectives you have to study, develop a life plan and an investment strategy that goes along with that life plan. There is no universal recipe, but every recipe has to be based on the individual's needs and has to be the result of the work that you as professionals, and investors have to start to reach a path of real success.

One of the most common mistakes is believing that the road will be easy, which in turn takes them further away from their goal. The ease of achieving things is the element that causes them to make wrong decisions, and wrong expenses, and incur in inappropriate debt.

12.13 Conclusion

Due to the irrationality of public spending, correcting the inflationary phenomenon becomes very complex for rich societies in a phase of strong aging of the demographic structure of the population. I am referring to Europe and the large developed Western countries that have potentially declining economies as a result of the demographic evolution of their society.

Structural adjustments in public spending will be more difficult for countries undergoing major demographic changes, but it is an imperative for these governments, which should, as their main social objective, improve their capacity to care for their elderly population. Spending requirements vary greatly based on individuals' birth dates.

The middle class and the lower-income social classes of the population are the most affected by the disconnect between the irrationality of public spending -the main cause of inflation- and the reverse redistribution of resources, which reduces their real purchasing power, as well as their savings and assets. For citizens, there is little hope for change in the management of public spending and the fiscal policy of their governments, since the political-administrative structure of each country is extremely complex, and it is almost impossible to influence the modification and orientation of their administrative activity. For citizens, cultural growth is the only viable option, leading to a better understanding of the economic and inflationary mechanisms within their country. The disinterest in politics at the same time demonstrates the awareness of those who vote, because their vote has no impact, since no matter which party reaches the government, it will give continuity to the existing situation and demonstrate the inability of politics to bring real changes that benefit their constituents.

By following a line of rational thought, we should conclude that one of the first actions that should be taken by those who come to power is the reduction of inflation, to maintain the welfare of its population; however, it is amply demonstrated by the theory of the irrationality of public spending and the consequent irrationality of administrative actions that this is not possible. Realistically, and looking at the perspective of a broader temporal arc, history tells us that in the development of governments, changes come, but not when they could have an impact on improving the lives of citizens. These changes usually come at the wrong time. Analyzing the evolution of the great absolute monarchies and their end, as well as the history of the great empires, shows us that when situations of imbalance become so widespread that the system can no longer sustain the bureaucratic and administrative structure, it does come to be corrected by means of sometimes abrupt and rapid changes.

For citizens, the situation is more difficult to handle, since inflation is the expression of an incurable, asymptomatic, and degenerative disease. If we use this metaphor, we can understand, in essence, the dangers for the average person in our society. The reality of many countries is a reality of an aging population, which in the future will need more resources that governments will probably not be able to redirect to those most in need. Let us remember that government spending is driven by a totally irrational logic, which does not allocate resources where they are truly needed and allocates far more resources than it should to spending that is perfectly useless and destroys the value and wealth of its middle-class citizens.

Citizens who come to understand this dystopia will have the opportunity to take action, defending themselves from the reality of the facts and understanding the difficulty -if not impossibility- of bringing about changes that will have an impact on this reality. Ultimately, it is necessary to think that disinterest in politics works against the collective interest, even if there is an inability of the individual to have an impact. The moving away from the ballot box makes the situation even worse.

The glimmer of hope that individuals possess within their society lies in their ability to empower themselves by studying, improving their spending decisions, not taking on unproductive debts, and finally investing to move towards a more prosperous path that protects their patrimony and guarantees long-term quality of life. It is only through this empowerment that we can catch a glimpse of the light at the end of the tunnel. This light is represented by the resurgence of the middle class and the individual in a robotically cold reality of a virtual world that does nothing but lead us to collective irrelevance as human beings.

The lord of the economic and financial apocalypse

The dark reality of inflation and its true causes

Inflation is a degenerative, asymptomatic and endemic disease of our society. It represents the greatest economic calamity, affecting the middle class and workers. Like a sneak thief, it steals moments of life, silently but inexorably destroys the value of savings and household assets.

The real causes are kept hidden and their explanation is incomplete and partial. Monetary authorities and statistical institutes limit themselves to recording nominal values using inadequate analysis methodologies and data observations, which distort reality.

This book analyzes what are the true causes and who are responsible for inflation, as well as how it destroys the savings and wealth of families.

A new theory of inflation and public employment, in order to correctly understand and gain a new perspective on this economic reality.

About the author

Giuseppe Ruffini

He has developed his professional and academic career in Europe and America, in various areas such as business management, project development and culture, and is a passionate researcher of the social, historical and economic phenomena that affect societies.

A great reader, tireless traveler and art lover, this book summarizes many of the observations made over the last few years on current economic phenomena, with a realistic, sometimes irreverent approach and simple language that will allow readers to better understand socioeconomic events and the impact they have on their lives.

[1]

[2] Refers to economists and economic theory that follow the philosophical school of thought of British economist John Maynard Keynes.

[3] Refers to economists and economic theory that follow the philosophical school of thought of the American economist Milton Friedman.

[4] Milton Friedman was a renowned American economist and Nobel laureate in the same discipline.

[5] John Maynard Keynes, British economist and Nobel laureate, founder of Keynesian economic philosophy.

[6] Pivoting: Refers to when the Federal Reserve will change monetary policy from tight to neutral or from neutral to expansionary.

[7] "To pivot or not to pivot—this is the dilemma": This dilemma was one of the main topics of discussion in economic forums throughout 2022- 2023.

[8] Quantitative Tightening also known by its English acronym "QT": this term refers to a restrictive monetary policy where the central bank sells securities to the market to restrict its liquidity and control inflation.

[9] Bear Market: This refers to a stock market where the price of securities traded tends to fall, losing value over a certain period of time. To be considered in this state of "Bear", the accumulated losses in the indexes must reach 20%.

[10] Classification according to the author.

[11] Cash Settled: Monetary arrangement for its terminology in English.

[12] Physical delivery: Physical delivery of the goods that are the object of the future contract.

[13] Trader: Person actively involved in buying and selling securities in the stock or in the futures markets for a profit.

[14] It refers to the number of newborns from a female population of 1000 aged between 15 and 49.

[15] Reference study: Dr Joshua Smith - - Research Scientist, MBBS, BMedSci, PGCertMedEd, 30 December 2022, why do Gen Z and millennial men have lower testosterone levels? Odds are your grandad had higher testosterone levels than you - but why?

[16] David Stanway and Tony Munroe, Three-child policy: China lifts cap on births in major policy shift. Reuters, June 1, 2021

[17] United Nations, Department of Economic and Social Affairs, Population Division. World Population Prospects: The 2015 Revision (Medium variant).

United Nations, Department of Economic and Social Affairs, Population Division. World Population Prospects: The 2019 Revision (Medium variant).

United Nations, Department of Economic and Social Affairs, Population Division. World Population Prospects: The 2022 Revision (Medium variant).

United Nations, Department of Economic and Social Affairs (2013). Trends in International Migrant Stock: Migrants by Destination and Origin (United Nations database, POP/DB/MIG/Stock/Rev.2013).

Boden, T.A., G. Marland, and R.J. Andres. 2016. Global, Regional, and National Fossil-Fuel CO_2 Emissions. Carbon Dioxide Information Analysis Center, Oak Ridge National Laboratory, U.S. Department of Energy, Oak Ridge, Tenn., U.S.A. doi 10.3334/CDIAC/00001_V2016.

1959-2013 estimates for fossil fuels are from the Carbon Dioxide Information Analysis Center (CDIAC) at Oak Ridge National Laboratory. http://cdiac.ornl.gov/trends/emis/meth_reg.html.

◇ 2014 and 2015 estimates are preliminary and are based on energy statistics published by BP (data in red). https://www.bp.com/content/dam/bp/pdf/energy-economics/statistical-review-2016/bp-statistical-review-of-world-energy-2016-full-report.pdf

[18] Birth rate is the total number of newborns in a year over 1000 people.

[19] Zombie companies: Companies that are unable to generate a healthy cash flow and minimum return on their investments and live on bank loans over bank loans.

[20] Liquidity Trap: Refers to the central bank's inability to operate the monetary policy instrument of interest rate intervention when the level of interest rates is close to zero.

[21] Quantitative easing (QE): Refers to the monetary policy action of central banks that acquire securities injecting liquidity into the economy, thus increasing the monetary base of the system.

[22] Author's note: corresponds to the monetary entity addicted to the creation of euros or dollars.

[23] Reference: https://www.federalreserve.gov/monetarypolicy/reservereq.htm.
Board of governors of the Federal Reserve System, Policy tools, Reserve requirements, number 106:
Effective for the reserve maintenance period beginning March 26, 2020, the 10 percent required reserve ratio against net transaction deposits above the low reserve tranche level was reduced to 0 percent, the 3 percent required reserve ratio against net transaction deposits in the low reserve tranche was reduced to 0 percent. The action reduced required reserves by an estimated $200 billion.

[24] This formula is originally attributed to Jean Bodin; however, it could have seen its origin in the thought and work of the Salamanca school in Martin De Azpilicueta.

[25] Through the Bretton Woods conference, important agreements were reached that led among many things to the establishment of the International Monetary Fund and at the same time formed the basis for monetary and trade exchanges that helped Western economies in the economic recovery that followed the devastation caused by World War II.

[26] Kraken: Sea monster from Norse mythology.

[27] Vietnam War Facts, Costs, and Timeline, How the Vietnam War Affects You Today, By **Kimberly Amadeo** , Updated on March 29, 2022,

[28] NATO: North Atlantic Treaty Organization.

[29] Repo or repurchase agreement: It is an operation between a commercial bank and the central bank, where the former delivers a sum of money to the latter in exchange for financial securities that in the short term will be returned to the Central Bank in exchange for an interest that is defined as the REPO rate. These are operations that, in addition to the purpose of producing an interest rate, have the objective of monetary control. The Federal Reserve operates with more than two trillion dollars that are used in the very short term in these operations.

Repo and reverse repo transactions can also occur between commercial banks and their clients.

[30] Reverse repo: is the opposite operation of REPO.

[31] Mortgage-backed Backed Securities (MBS) are financial instruments backed by mortgages.

[32] Subprime mortgages are bank loans secured by mortgages, which have a high probability of not being repaid. Extreme credit facilities were the cause of this phenomenon at the end of the first decade of the 2000s in the United States, which led to the global financial crisis of 2007-2010.

[33] Prêt à porter: French term used in the fashion world to describe a collection of practical dresses ready to be worn in the most varied conditions.

[34] FIAT type coins: It is a Latin word that means be done or so be it, it refers to fiduciary money where it represents value by decree or by law of the governmental authority. They are currencies that have no value by themselves or by being backed by some other good but acquire this status and validity by law.

[35] CPI, or Consumer Price Index, is a measure of the price indexes of consumers.

[36] Note that the deflator does not coincide exactly with the consumer price index data as this is the expression of all products produced in an economy and not that of a more limited basket of goods and services as used by the "CPIs".

[37] CPI-U: Consumer Price Index of Urban Workers

[38] CPI-W for its acronym in English: consumer price index of office employee-type consumers known as clerical workers.

[39] PPI, Producer Price Index: This is the producer price index.

[40] Harmonized Consumer Price Index, which refers to the evolution of consumer price indexes for the European Union.

[41] OECD: Organization for Economic Cooperation and Development

[42] COLA or "Cost of Living Adjustments": Means the increase in benefits received by citizens as a result of inflation in order to maintain their standard of living. These adjustments do not necessarily coincide exactly with the evolution of inflation.

[43] Shelter costs: A term that defines the costs for the consumer's home.

[44] Rent Of Primary Residence: This is the index referring to the rent of the primary residence.

[45] Owners' Equivalent Rent of Residence: The index that represents the equivalent rental value for homeowners.

[46] Lodging Away from Home: Costs related to renting while traveling.

[47] BLS: U.S. Bureau of Labor and Statistics.

[48] Refers to the most important change in the methodology used to calculate inflation.

[49] COGI or Cost Of Goods Index. It refers to the methodology that considers two baskets of products and services that remain unchanged over time for the calculation of the "CPI".

[50] COLI or Cost Of Living Index. It refers to the methodology of two baskets of products that vary according to the logic that consumers substitute expensive products for cheaper products in order to calculate the "CPI".

[51] No. 515-PUBLIC COMMENT ON INFLATION MEASUREMENT AND THE CHAINED-CPI (C-CPI)

April 8th, 2013, http://www.shadowstats.com/article/no-438-public-comment-on-inflation-measurement

[52] U.S: Bureau of Labor Statistics, Consumer Price Index, Frequently Asked Questions about Hedonic Quality Adjustment in the CPI, https://www.bls.gov/cpi/quality-adjustment/questions-and-answers.htm#:~:text=Hedonic%20quality%20ad

[53] U.S: Bureau of Labor Statistics, Consumer Price Index, Quality Adjustment in the CPI; https://www.bls.gov/cpi/quality-adjustment/home.htm

[54] U.S: Bureau of Labor Statistics, Consumer Price Index, Common Misconceptions about the Consumer Price Index: Questions and Answers,

https://www.bls.gov/cpi/factsheets/ common-misconceptions-about-cpi.htm.

[55] U.S: Bureau of Labor Statistics, Consumer Price Index, Research Issues Related to the Geometric Mean Formula for Elementary Indexes; https://www.bls.gov/news.release/ cpi.br121996.geors.htm

[56] See: Shadow Government Statistics

[57] Price Index Concepts and Measurement: Introduction: What are the Issues? Erwin Diewert, John Greenlees and Charles Hulten1 VERSION. March 12, 2008.

[58] Author's Note: The Roman Empire is considered the longest-lived empire, taking into consideration its duration: 1,476 years (27 B.C. - 1,453 A.D.).

[59] Weaponization: This term refers to the use of the US dollar as a weapon for the resolution of conflicts between nations. The dollar becomes a weapon through economic and monetary sanctions that are applied to some of the warring parties or as an instrument of political pressure.

[60] Letter of intent written by Warren Buffet on June 26, 2006, in which one of the conditions for donations to the Bill and Melinda Gate Foundation was that at least one of them was to be committed to managing the donated funds. https://www.berkshirehathaway.com/donate/bmgfltr.pdf

[61] Warren Buffet's gifts to Bill Gates' foundation are worth..., Money Control news, July 18,2022

[62] How taxing the rich paradoxically resulted in more inequality for all AUGUST 24, 2017 FREE MARKETS AND CAPITALISM

[63] Jackson Pollock: famous American painter representing the artistic vein of abstract expressionism.

[64] SVB: Silicon Valey Bank, for its acronym in English

[65] What did the FED do after Silicon Valley bank and signature Bank failed, JamesLee, David Wessel, March 22, 2023. Brookings education.

[66] Switzerland's second largest bank.

[67] Credit Suisse erases more than $50 billion from Swiss National Bank after share crash 30%, By Mark Thompson and Anna Cooban, CNN, Wed March 15, 2023

[68] Quantitative Tightening.

[69] This term is used because inflation represents the waste that this hypothetical body produces.

[70] Article 316 of the Costa Rican penal code qualifies threats to public officials with sentences ranging from one month to two years imprisonment, stating the following: Whoever threatens a public official because of his functions, addressing him personally or publicly, or by means of written, telegraphic or telephonic communication or through hierarchical channels, shall be punished with imprisonment from one month to two years. Although this article of the penal code typifies threats to public officials, if we read it carefully we notice that such threats are mainly referred to the work of these public workers since it encompasses this concept when referring to the bosses of these same employees. In other words, the citizen who claims justly for a service (to which he was entitled) that is provided inadequately and insufficiently, can be sent to jail, being the claim of possible interpretation as a threat and therefore an illegal act.

[71] Gross national income

[72] SP500: Stock index of the 500 largest companies listed on the New York Stock Exchange.

[73] Reviewing Recent Evidence of the Effect of Taxes on Economic Growth, May 21, 2021, Alex Durante

[74] Apple's market capitalization at the close of trading on 6/30/2023, 3,051 billion, source Yahoo Finance.

[75] Doubts about the authorship of 'Salvator Mundi', the most expensive painting in history, **MIGUEL LORENCI**
BREAKING NEWS UPDATED 26/12/2022 AT 05:00, Heraldo Leisure & culture.

[76] High-value auction house.

[77] Leonardo da Vinci: multifaceted polymath representative of the culture and sciences of the Italian Renaissance.

[78] Artist representative of American abstract expressionism.

[79] Famous Rolex branded chronograph

[80] Paul Newman's 'Paul Newman' Rolex Daytona Sells For $17.8 Million, A Record For A Wristwatch At Auction

Hyla Ames Bauer Former Contributor
https://www.forbes.com/sites/hylabauer/2017/10/26/paul-newmans-paul-newman-daytona-sells-for-15-5-million-a-record-for-a-wristwatch-at-auction/?sh=9372bd05313f

[81] It refers to sales made between third parties after the product has been acquired from someone as a trading object to an authorized dealer.

[82] Famous Swiss watch brand

[83] Famous Swiss watch brand

[84] Famous Swiss watch brand

[85] Rolex brand model

[86] Tiffany Jewelry Shade of Blue

[87] Model of the watch brand Patek Philippe

[88] Luxury brand

[89] The terrifying story behind the tale of 'Sleeping Beauty', Milenio digital, Mexico City 10/04/2021 https://www.milenio.com/cultura/la-bella-durmiente-la-verdadera-historia-detras-del-cuento.

[90] That actually ended up burning alive.

[91] CPI: Consumer price index (Consumer price index)

[92] https://fred.stlouisfed.org/series/CUUR0000SA0R.

[93] Greta Thunberg: Young Swedish environmentalist who became famous for her protests and for crossing the Atlantic on a fossil fuel-free sailboat owned by a billionaire who took her to give a lecture at the United Nations.

[94] Great Reset: This is an initiative of the World Economic Forum to achieve a planetary change. However, we are left with the question of whether the members of this forum will leave their private jets and their luxurious lives to reduce their carbon emissions and thus help the planet, or whether this initiative is only oriented to the less economically fortunate classes, reserving for the oligarchic elites all the benefits they already have. What do you think?

[95] WATCH: Pentagon holds briefing on UFO reports, fighting in eastern Ukraine, Jan 12, 2023, by associated press

https://www.pbs.org/newshour/politics/watch-live-pentagon-holds-briefing-following-russias-release-of-u-s-veteran-who-crossed-border

[96] Name of a secret society.

[97] Reptilian: lizard men who play a prominent role in fantasy or science fiction literature, ufology and contemporary conspiracy theories.

[98] This term refers to those who consider the Earth to be flat.

[99] BLS: Bureau of Labor Statistics, the U.S. Bureau of Labor Statistics, is the U.S. statistical office responsible for calculating consumer price indexes.

[100] COGI: Cost of goods index, refers to the inflation calculation methodology that compares 2 equal baskets of products and services.

[101] COLI: Cost of living index, refers to the inflation calculation methodology that instead of comparing two equal baskets of products and services takes into account the possibility that consumers substitute some products or services for cheaper and therefore more accessible ones due to an increase in their cost.

[102] Fiat Currencies: Refers to fiat currencies where the value is established by law by the State. These currencies differ from other currencies in that their value was backed by some good or commodity; in the most common case, this was gold.

[103] Paleolithic as a visual expression of ancient, does not refer to the Paleolithic era as such.

[104] https://www.federalreserve.gov/monetarypolicy/reservereq.htm, Board of directors of the federal reserve system reserve requirements, Reserve requirements

[105] https://www.world-exchanges.org/storage/app/media/2021%20Annual%20Derivatives%20Report.pdf

[106] Market Maker, by its English description, refers to large banks that allow the market to be liquid by buying and selling securities directly and profiting from the price differences between purchases and sales. These large banks or institutions are also very active in the derivatives market, which even allows the liquidity of these instruments.

[107] This term refers to the fact of challenging the knowledge of the advisors who advise us on these financial investments, whose main objective is to improve our investment decisions.

About the Author

He has developed his professional and academic career in Europe and America, in various areas such as business management, project development and culture, and he is a passionate researcher of the social, historical economic phenomena that affect societies.

A great reader, tireless traveler and art lover, this book summarizes many of the observations made over the last few years on current economic phenomena, with a realistic, sometimes irreverent approach, and simple language that will allow readers to better understand socioeconomic events and the impact they have on their lives.

Read more at https://omniavalue.com/.